BLACKS IN THE UNITED STATES:
A GEOGRAPHIC PERSPECTIVE

Blacks in the United States: A Geographic Perspective

George A. Davis
Ohio State University

O. Fred Donaldson
California School of Professional Psychology

HOUGHTON MIFFLIN COMPANY   BOSTON
Atlanta   Dallas   Geneva, Illinois
Hopewell, New Jersey   Palo Alto   London

To our mothers
Emma E. Copher
Winnifred D. Donaldson

Contents

Preface

The geography of Blacks in the United States begins with the forced migration of slaves from Africa in pre-revolutionary times to the problems facing Blacks in today's ghettoes. Our study focuses not only on the spatial distribution of Blacks, but on the many different forces that have influenced the movement of Blacks from one area to another.

This, then, is the story of the black peoples' search for home. It is the first book in a new and growing field, and it will doubtless provoke controversy. It is our hope that at the very least it will fill a gap in the field of geography as well as in black studies. The book can be used in a variety of courses, including black geography, black studies, introductory human or cultural geography, U.S. and social geography, and special problems courses.

We wish to express our appreciation to our editors at Houghton Mifflin and to Professors Mark Lowry II, Robert C. Ziegenfus, Joseph T. Darden, and Robert B. McNee, who reviewed the original manuscript and offered many suggestions for its improvement. We are grateful for the assistance of Judy Strain, our typist, and Dana Bateman and Mark Cokes, our student research assistants at Ohio State University. Finally, our deepest thanks go to our families, and to Catherine Stansel, Dick Morrill, Dean Louder, Barbara Williams, Paul Villeneuve, Ann and Joe, Roselle, and Anthony and Etienne. Their patience, encouragement, and faith in the value of our work have sustained us throughout.

George A. Davis

O. Fred Donaldson

BLACKS IN THE UNITED STATES:
A GEOGRAPHIC PERSPECTIVE

Margaret Bourke-White, Time-Life Picture Agency.

1 Introduction: Blacks in the United States

The sociospatial patterning of America has order and meaning, much of which is racial in origin and design. When one studies the geography of the United States, he is, in essence, examining the locations, separations, connections, and movements of its people and their institutions. What has been ignored is that these movements, connections, separations, and locations have been influenced and determined by race relations. This is reflected in the presence of geographic terminology in the rhetoric of race relations: integration, segregation, colony, community control, separation, ghetto, inner-city, apartheid, busing, "keeping their distance," "knowing their place." Distance and place are spatial as well as social terms.

Another of the geographic results of this dual society has been the identification of American regions with place names, both specific and generic, that have become synonymous with black people. The Black Belt, Coontown, Buttermilk Bottom, Black Bottom, Harlem, Watts, Cotton Curtain, ghetto, and inner-city are such examples.

In a purely academic sense the geographic examination of black America is no more nor no less important than that of China or the Basque region of Spain. Regions or peoples, however, are rarely studied from a purely academic point of view. Russian and Chinese studies in the 1950s and 1960s and black studies in the late 1960s have served, for example, both the need for knowledge and the need for the establishment of social and political policy. In Russian and Chinese studies, however, geographers became involved with both the academic and social-political policy aspects of these areas of study. They have not become so involved in black studies. Morrill has pointed out that geography is a conservative field in the sense that geographers have preferred not to question either the rightness or the responsibility of sociospatial problems. Problems such as housing, integration, segregation, school busing, and the location of jobs and services as they relate to the needs of black Americans have been largely ignored by geographers. We feel that there is a need for both academic and social-political policy involvement by geographers in black studies; this book is an attempt to help meet these needs. We attempt not only to present the general sociospatial processes affecting black Americans but to bring the reader closer to some of the human beings who know the fear, experience the hope, and live the confusion that these processes can bring.

1

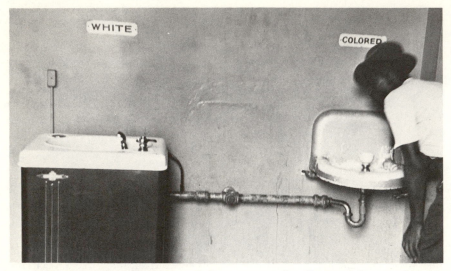

A graphic illustration of the statement that "separate but equal is inherently unequal."

Elliott Erwitt, Magnum Photos.

There are four important points to keep in mind while reading this book that should be made explicit, because they have characterized the geography of race relations in America from the outset. First, Blacks have rebelled against the statuses and roles accorded them by Whites, and consequently the most savage white oppression occurred when black rebellion was feared or experienced. Second, in the long span of time, there has been some degree of ambiguity in white attitudes and actions with respect to Blacks which caused differences in the patterns of control over time and space. Third, despite the ambiguity, Blacks have been consistently regarded as inferior to Whites; the ambiguity is not primarily in whether or not Blacks are inferior but in what means the inferiority is to be maintained. Finally, location, relative numbers, and movement of Blacks with respect to those of Whites have, to a large degree, determined the nature of race relations in America.

This examination of black America emphasizes the spatial processes of migration and segregation. Chapters 2, 3, and 4 deal with the relation between racism and black migration. Chapters 5 and 6 examine the sociospatial process of segregation. Chapter 7 discusses the sociospatial relationship between contemporary black and white Americas and alternatives to the present relationship. Chapter 8 examines the problems and processes presented earlier in the book from the perspective of black literature, poetry, and music. The Appendixes present a number of exercises that may be undertaken by students to simulate some of the issues we have presented and discussed in the text.

The most significant phase of black migration began in the second decade of the nineteenth century. From then on the major black population movements occurred about every 20 to 30 years—at the time of the Fugitive Slave Law in 1850, after the Civil War around 1870, at the time of the Chicago World's Fair in 1893, and around World War I in 1915 and World War II in 1945.

Most of the movement since 1890 has been concentrated in the states east of the Mississippi, and has been from south to north across the Ohio River and the Mason-Dixon line. Prior to 1890, migration of Blacks was not great and seems to have been local, from state to state, and only to a slight extent out of the South. But after 1890 the northward direction of movement has been steadfastly maintained.

At first the spatial pattern of migration was from north to south. Prior to the Civil War there were two streams of black population movement. One was a northward march led by people such as Harriet Tubman; the counterstream was in the opposite direction, led by slave owners. With the close of the Civil War, the opening of the West, and the development of the railroad, an additional spatial dimension was added to black migration—an east-to-west movement. The couriers of this new movement included Pullman porters.

The next three large movements were again south to north, but also rural to urban. The great gains through migration have been in the industrial cities of the North, such as Chicago, Detroit, Cleveland, and Philadelphia; and the chief losses have been sustained by four southern states: Mississippi, Alabama, Georgia, and South Carolina.

It is a cruel irony that the black search for a sanctuary from racism has resulted not in the finding of one, but in the nationalization of racism.

Migration is one of the equilibrium-producing mechanisms in society. This, of course, could help explain the pervasiveness of the white mechanisms of control over the location and movement of Blacks. Justice Harlan in a dissenting opinion in *Plessy v. Ferguson* (1896) defined personal liberty in spatial terms as "the power of locomotion of changing situation, or removing one's person to whatsoever places one's own inclination may direct, without imprisonment or restraint, unless by due process of law" (McEntire, 1960). This freedom of sociospatial movement has been consistently and systematically denied to Blacks. In fact, it was the possibility of greater geographic mobility as a consequence of the abolition of slavery, along with the urbanization and industrialization of the United States, that undermined the old mechanisms of social caste distance and brought about their replacement by racial segregation.

The control of the movements of black people has always been one of the factors by which they are contained. During slavery, for example, Blacks were often moved much as one moved one's livestock. In the South, even after slavery, the "right of way" remained the "racial right of way." Baron has likened black movement in modern American society to a fly in a spider's web, "they can wiggle but they cannot move very far" (Baron, 1969).

Segregation and separatism have been a part of the pattern of American geography for a long time. Both the social and the spatial orders in America have served to maintain the superior-inferior positioning of Whites over Blacks. To most Whites, segregation has not been a departure from democratic principles, but simply the spatial expression of the "natural" order relegating the black person to an inferior position. The early Protestants in America, for example, conceived of the maintenance of "place" and "distance" orders between types of people as part of the Divine Order.

There seem to have been three major residential patterns for Blacks, depending on their relative numbers and status and the economic roles which they played. The plantation with its rigid social and spatial structure is one type. Commonly, on the plantation the Blacks outnumbered the Whites and were used as agricultural laborers. Another type is the mixed population pattern more common in the rural and smaller urban areas of the North and South. In this case, the number of Blacks was relatively small as compared to the number of Whites. Whites and Blacks were used as household servants and workers in small businesses. Finally, in some rural areas and in urban areas, Blacks have been greatly segregated. Again the number of Blacks tended to be large relative to the number of Whites, but in this case their economic roles were more diverse.

If the Civil War did anything to alter the geographic patterns of Blacks in America, it nationalized the process of segregation. With the diffusion of the black population after the Civil War, many more small towns, cities, and rural areas had to deal with the issue of race. The process of segregation now became one of nationwide development. In urban areas the result has been the growth of the black ghetto. In the rural areas the name of slave was changed to sharecropper or tenant, but the sociospatial relationship between Blacks and Whites remains virtually unaltered.

Even though in most cases black America is not a formally established political region but an informal social region, it is evident that the presence of two Americas and the boundaries between them have been important components in the behavior of Americans. As an example, the fundamental problem of housing for Blacks has not only been one of the quantity or quality of dwellings, important as these may be, but also one of whether Blacks should be concentrated in separate areas or be free to seek their housing in the general market.

The urban ghetto, for example, performs many of the same functions, both social and spatial, as the plantation. Both the plantation and the ghetto are adaptations in space and time to the racism of the society in which they exist. Until the larger society's definition of the inmate groups changes, social institutions will be developed to confine them. Thus, with the destruction of one such institution, the plantation, by external forces, the inmates are transferred to another form of restrictive institution, the ghetto. The restrictive forces of the ghetto may be more diffuse than those of the plantation; but they share the same spatial function, to exercise custody over the different and unequal. In both cases control of the basic institutions of society is owned and operated by Whites. Also, in both cases racial differences are used as criteria, which become legal and moral standards, for the decision about who can live outside and who should be forced to live within the confined area. "Even though the physical boundaries are often less static in the ghetto than the plantation, they are always made salient in the minds of the populace" (Bryce-Laporte, 1971). The fact that Blacks and Whites have not been separated by extensive mileage and political boundaries is not sufficient for producing cohesion; it is the pattern of interaction that defines social communities, not just spatial contiguity. The location of these boundaries is seen and felt in residence patterns; in the geography of urban services like hospitals, garbage collection areas, and police stations, and in actions of pedestrians.

Inferior or nonexistent services for Blacks are a common means of per-
petuating racism, as the above "White only" New Orleans laundromat
shows. From racism, segregation: below is a typical scene of street life
in the black ghetto.

*Top: Leonard Freed, Magnum Photos; bottom: Children's Bureau Photograph by Esther
Bubley.*

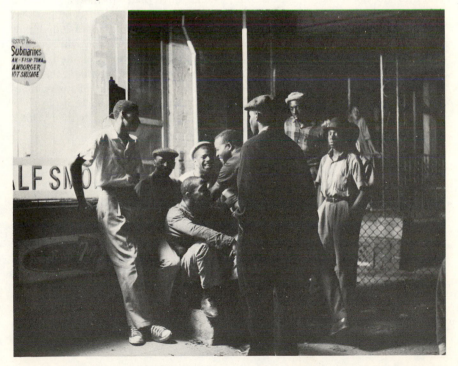

Although the stress in the first half of the book will be on the spatial processes of segregation and migration, the remainder of the text will treat the geography of black America from a different sociospatial perspective.

Chapter 8 will concentrate on the black perception, or image, of America through the use of black music, poetry, novels, and folktales. These narrative forms provide valuable information and feelings that are often ignored or not understood by social scientists. They demonstrate, in a perhaps more dramatic way, what we are trying to do throughout the book, that is, to present the geography of black America as perceived and lived by Blacks.

We are interested in the conceptions that black people have of their world. These images or conceptions may or may not be an "accurate" reflection of the "objective" real world. But, either way, they are the basis upon which much individual and group action and social policy have been developed. If we, as geographers, are looking for explanations of human behavior in terms of an environment, then our main interest is in the subjective rather than in the objective. Once it is recognized that the subjectively conceived environmental image is as important as the "objective reality," then cultural background and socioeconomic position become important elements in the study of the determinants of man's spatial behavior. Black and white conceptions often are at odds.

Powdermaker points out that there is no isolated black community; this may be true in the sense that Blacks have always had to function in an environment in which Whites were in power. But this does not mean that two communities do not exist; it means that Blacks have had to function in two communities. A separate world for the Blacks has been established by law and custom in the United States, and the dimensions and the conduct of individuals in this black world have been determined by those living in the white world.

Not only are the number of places that he may go severely limited by the white man's conception of propriety, but in an unfamiliar environment the black individual must be prepared for the uncertainty of the bounds of his confinement. Despite agreement among Whites that Blacks should be kept "in their place," the complexity of racial codes in time and space indicates that Whites are not in agreement as to just what that place should be.

SELECTED BIBLIOGRAPHY

1. Ambrose, Peter: Analytical Human Geography, American Elsevier, New York, 1969.
2. Baron, Harold M.: The Web of Urban Racism in Louis L. Knowles and Kenneth Prewitt, "Institutional Racism in America," Prentice-Hall, New York, 1969, p. 144.
3. Bryce-Laporte, R. Simon: The Slave Plantation: Background to Present Conditions of Urban Blacks, in Peter Orleans and William Russell, Jr., (eds.), "Race, Changes and Urban Society," Urban Affairs Annual Reviews, vol. 5, Sage Publishing, Beverly Hills, Cal., 1971, p. 277.

4. Johnson, Charles S.: "Patterns of Negro Segregation," Harper and Brothers, New York, 1943.
5. McEntire, Davis: "Residence and Race: Report to the Commission on Race and Housing," University of California Press, Berkeley, Cal., 1960.
6. Morrill, Richard: "The Spatial Organization of Society," Wadsworth Publishing Co., Belmont, Cal., 1970.
7. Powdermaker, Hortense: "After Freedom," Atheneum, New York, 1968, p. xiv.
8. Sundiata, Phonan Goldman: The White Reaction to the Black Assertion, *The Black Scholar*, vol. 1 (March, 1970), Prentice-Hall, Englewood Cliffs, N.J., 1969.
9. Woodson, Carter G.: "A Century of Negro Migration," Association for the Study of Negro Life & History, Washington, D.C., 1918, p. 17.

100 DOLLARS
REWARD!

Ranaway from the subscriber on the 27th of July, my Black Woman, named

EMILY,

Seventeen years of age, well grown, black color, has a whining voice. She took with her one dark calico and one blue and white dress, a red corded gingham bonnet; a white striped shawl and slippers. I will pay the above reward if taken near the Ohio river on the Kentucky side, or **THREE HUNDRED DOLLARS**, if taken in the State of Ohio, and delivered to me near Lewisburg, Mason County, Ky.   **THO'S. H. WILLIAMS.**

August 4, 1853.

2 Pre-Civil War Black Migration

SOME DEFINITIONS AND PRINCIPLES

Before beginning the analysis of migration patterns of black Americans, it is desirable to establish some basic definitions of and present a few principles of migration. Migration may be defined broadly as a permanent or semipermanent change of residence. No restriction is placed upon the distance of the move or upon the voluntary or involuntary nature of the act, and no distinction is made between external and internal migration. Thus, a move across the hall from one apartment to another is counted as just as much an act of migration as a move from Bombay, India, to Cedar Rapids, Iowa; though, of course, the initiation and consequences of such moves are vastly different. However, not all kinds of spatial mobility are included in this definition. Excluded, for example, are the continual movements of nomads and migratory workers, for whom there is no long-term residence, and temporary movements like those to the mountains for the summer.

No matter how short or how long, how easy or how difficult, every act of migration involves an origin, a destination, an intervening set of obstacles, and personal factors.

Although migration may result from a combination of factors at origin and destination, a simple adding of pluses and minuses does not decide nor describe the act of migration. The decision to move must be strong enough to overcome the natural inertia which always exists. Moreover, between each two points there is a set of intervening obstacles which range from manageable in some cases to insurmountable in others. The most studied of these obstacles is distance, which, while omnipresent, is by no means as important as personal factors. Physical isolation, inertia, prejudice, and ignorance are some other factors which inhibit the freedom of population movement.

Another common principle of migration is that it takes place in well-defined streams. Major migration flows produce counterflows. Basically, the reason for this is that opportunities are not geographically uniform, but are localized. Also, knowledge is not spread uniformly but in uneven flows. In their study of migration from southern Appalachia, for example, Hillery *et al.* found that migration systems were comprised of points of origin, points of destination, and flows. They further found that southern Appalachia does not constitute a single

9

region in the minds of its out-migrants. Rather the region is thought of as the "backyards" of the non-Appalachian areas to which the migrants move. Although these systems are not completely independent, migrants from one area go to different places than do those from a neighboring area. This general type of migration system is also typical of the black rural to urban migration from 1915 to 1960.

It is not so much the actual factors at origin and destination as the perception of these factors which leads ultimately to migration. Particularly in the case of the black American, there has been an acute awareness of conditions at the place of origin, but because of poor communications there has been only a limited perception of conditions at point of destination. Total frustration with the conditions at the place of origin, together with a frantic hope for a better life, is a simplistic explanation for migration.

Usually the individual has less knowledge of conditions at the destination than he does of those at the origin. When considering reasons for moving, the migrant tends to overevaluate the positive elements at the destination and underestimate the negative elements. This evaluative process tends to be reversed for the place of origin. Letters from migrants act as feedback mechanisms. But even then, their information is likely to be more positive than negative, as the migrant is not likely to want his family and friends back home to know that he made a mistake, if such is the case.

When the migrant is accepted by and strongly values his point of origin but the opposite conditions exist at the point of destination, he will probably isolate himself from his new community and the migration is likely to be temporary. Conversely, when the point of origin is less desired than the point of destination, the degree of integration is considerably greater, acculturation is easier and faster, and the migration is expected to be permanent.

For black Americans this has been a complex process, for while the forces pushing them out of the rural South have been extremely strong, many still feel that the South is "home." And, because the black migrant has been subjected to much hostility in the North, there has been black migration back to the South. Some writers put the decision to isolate oneself in a new place on the migrant; for Blacks, of course, this has not been the case, but rather it is the host society that isolates them. The decision to migrate, therefore, is seldom completely rational, and for some persons the rational component is much less than the irrational.

Migration is a complex process in which social and personal as well as economic pressures are filtered through the particular norms and values of the societal and social groups to which the migrant belongs. His own attitudes also provide a screen through which the decision to move must be sifted. Black migration is thus a reflection of the interworkings of the sociocultural norms operating in America at a given time and place and also the reaction of a given individual to these various sets of values and norms.

Migration has been throughout history a human attempt to improve one's social and economic position. Morrill (1965) has called migration one of the primary equilibrium-producing mechanisms in society. Much of this migration has been from rural agricultural areas to industrial cities. "Unless he migrates to a city, a man of humble origin in the country has almost ceased to have any chance to climb" (Sorokin, 1959).

Toffler makes the point that the "overthrow of the tyranny of geography has opened new freedom to millions." In addition, "freedom from fixed social position is linked so closely with freedom from fixed geographical position, that when superindustrial man feels socially constricted his first impulse is to relocate" (Toffler, 1970). But migration has not made the black American a superindustrial man; his social position has remained fixed regardless of his geographic position. Socioeconomic tyranny for the black man has not felt the "demise of geography."

THE INTERNAL SLAVE TRADE

Europeans and Africans traveled great distances as explorers and traders, but extensive migrations were not a way of life. On the other hand, as early as 1440, under the command of Prince Henry the Navigator, Portugal participated in the forced migration of Blacks from Africa to Europe. Spain followed Portugal's lead, and by the beginning of the sixteenth century, Blacks were brought to the New World in significant numbers. Aptheker discussed a colony in Pedee, South Carolina, as early as 1526, which contained about 100 Blacks.

The period of slavery opening in the 1660s began an era of enormous importation of Africans to supply badly needed labor for an agrarian economy. The first significant clusters of Blacks developed in the important tidewater agricultural regions of Virginia, Maryland, and North Carolina. Until the end of the seventeenth century, tobacco was the primary crop, grown in large quantities chiefly for export to England.

With the introduction of rice as a staple crop in the 1690s the first major internal shift in the black population occurred, as South Carolina rice fields became the home of more and more black persons from the tidewater region as well as directly from Africa. Rice was successfully grown in the South Carolina lowlands and soon became the chief produce exported through Charleston. The growing of rice required marshy, swampy land which was found in abundance in South Carolina.

Georgia was similar in climate and type of land; therefore, as it was open to slavery, the cultivation of indigo and rice increased markedly and set in motion the forced southward migration of thousands of Blacks into that colony. Rice and indigo were grown mainly in the low-lying coastal regions and the hot, humid islands off the coast. So important was black labor that the largest plantations in North America were located in the colonies of South Carolina and Georgia. In fact, in many counties in these two colonies, Blacks outnumbered Whites, although only in South Carolina were slaves in a consistent majority.

North of Chesapeake Bay the growing season was so short and fishing and shipping were so important that agriculture never became the major commercial venture. This made slave labor economically so unprofitable that slavery never gained a firm foothold in the middle and New England colonies. As a consequence, the black population outside of the colonial South remained relatively small.

There is evidence of slavery in each of the four New England colonies—Massachusetts, Connecticut, Rhode Island, and New Hampshire—by the middle of the sixteenth century. But by 1700 Blacks numbered only about 1,000 in a total population of 90,000. At no time would Blacks constitute as much as 5 percent of the people within any of the New England colonies, except in Rhode Island where Blacks were recorded in 1755 as being 14 percent of the population.

Generally Blacks were located in cities such as Newport, Rhode Island, where they constituted 25 percent of the population. In addition to the usual skilled trades (such as barbering, fishing, and cooperage), Rhode Island employed a large number of Blacks on many dairy farms.

Slavery was common in both New Jersey and New York, but on a small scale, during the period of Dutch settlement. The Dutch India Company, a major slave-trading organization, and the Dutch government hoped to stimulate agriculture by encouraging the importation of slaves to the New Netherlands. Their efforts bore little fruit. Blacks formed about 12 percent of the population in New York and New Jersey during the eighteenth century. They worked in a wide variety of occupations, including domestic servitude, mining, carpentering, cooperage, tanning, and shoemaking.

By 1750 there were at least 236,000 slaves in the American colonies (including French Louisiana). Slavery still predominated in Virginia, Maryland, and the Carolinas, as depicted in Table 2.1. Although settlement moved slowly westward from the coast, slavery did not become dominant in the Piedmont or mountain areas, owing mainly to the small size of farms. The plantation system was slowly spreading from the upper South, Virginia and Maryland, to the lower South, the Carolinas and Georgia.

Between 1750 and 1800 some 500,000 to 1 million slaves were brought to this country. New England shippers began to share in the fortunes to be made from the slave trade; but with the exception of Rhode Island and Providence plantations, slave labor in agriculture was rare in the North, although slaves as domestic servants in the home and shop were fairly common.

With time exploitative agriculture in the more accessible, but marginal, lands near the Virginia coast wore out the land. The new slave shipments were now destined for the Carolinas and Georgia. Around 1780 a new and valuable crop, cotton, was introduced—greatly increasing the demand both for land, especially in more southerly, warmer areas, and for slaves to clear the land and to farm it. At first, because of its high humidity requirements, cotton was grown mainly along the coast, from Virginia to Georgia; but plant disease, land erosion, demand for more cotton varieties, and the invention of the cotton gin in 1793 led to a fairly rapid shift south and west after 1800. Meanwhile, the American market for slaves, as well as the points of import, was shifting south

STATE	TOTAL NUMBER OF FAMILIES		SLAVEHOLDING FAMILIES		NUMBER OF SLAVES	AVERAGE NUMBER OF SLAVES PER FAMILY
	Black	White	Black	White		
Maine	37	16,572	0	0	0	0
New Hampshire	83	23,962	0	125	157	1.3
Vermont	23	17,969	0	0	0	0
Massachusetts	630	65,149	0	0	0	0
Rhode Island	442	10,354	0	461	958	2.1
Connecticut	419	40,462	6	557	2,648	1.7
New York	693	54,783	9	787	21,193	2.7
Pennsylvania	552	73,322	7	851	3,707	2.0
Maryland	282	32,012	84	12,142	193,036	7.5
N. Carolina	680	48,021	28	14,945	100,783	6.7
S. Carolina	320	25,552	61	8,798	107,094	2.1
New Jersey	not known		4,760 (est.)		11,423	2.4
Delaware	"		1,856 (est.)		3,887	4.3
Virginia	"		34,026 (est.)		292,627	8.5
Georgia	"		2,419 (est.)		29,264	12.1
Kentucky	"		1,855 (est.)		12,430	6.7
Tennessee	"		510 (est.)		3,417	6.7

Table 2.1:   Slaveholding Families, 1790.

Source: Negro Population 1790–1915, Department of Commerce, Bureau of the Census, Washington, D.C., Government Printing Office, 1918 (from tables on p. 6).

and west to Alabama and Mobile, and to the Mississippi delta through New Orleans.

In the older, settled areas, especially in Virginia, the black population had grown rather in excess of local needs, simply through years of natural increase. Instead of being feared, the "surplus" was desired, for slaveowners in declining farming areas found it most profitable to specialize in the breeding and raising of slaves for sale and shipment to the expanding plantation areas of the Southwest. The local slave markets, like Alexandria, blatantly advertised the fecundity of female slaves, and owners gave privileges to women who bore many children. Slaves were thought of as capital investment, earning between 5 and 15 percent per year.

From 1810 to 1865 a large and profitable internal trade in slaves occurred from the "old" to the "new" South (see Figure 2.1). In the early part of the century, before 1830, Blacks went mainly from Virginia and Maryland to Kentucky, Tennessee, Georgia, and Alabama; after 1830, the Carolinas, and even Georgia and Kentucky, began to "export" slaves to Mississippi, Arkansas, Louisiana, and Texas. Table 2.2 summarizes the relationship between the shift-

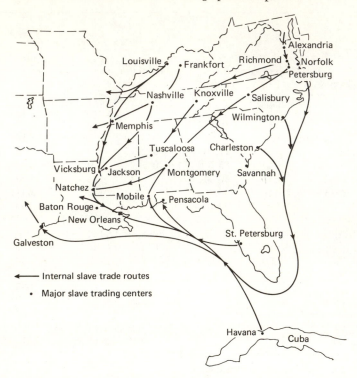

Figure 2.1   The Internal Slave Trade, 1810 to 1860.

ing black population and the expansion of cotton. The trade routes ran along the coast, down the Piedmont, along the Appalachian corridor, and down the Ohio-Mississippi river system.

As a consequence of the relative decline of agriculture on the coastal plain and its rapid expansion in the Southwest, the distribution of slaves changed radically between 1790 and 1880 (see Figure 2.2). Although Virginia remained the leading slave state, its slave population had increased rather slowly; Maryland dropped from second to tenth in number of slaves. From 1790 to 1850, the majority (51 percent) of the population in Tennessee, Alabama, Mississippi, and Louisiana were slaves. By 1850 the center of the black population had shifted from Virginia to South Carolina and, by 1865, west into Georgia.

Slaves were exported along the internal slave-trade routes from Delaware, Maryland, Virginia, North Carolina, Kentucky, Tennessee, Missouri, and the District of Columbia into South Carolina, Georgia, Alabama, Mississippi, Louisiana, Arkansas, and Florida. North Carolina, Tennessee, and Missouri were importing as well as exporting states.

There were three principal modes of movement southward. One was by

REGION	SHIFT IN COTTON PRODUCTION (%)			SHIFT IN SLAVE POPULATION (in 10³)		
	1815	1825	1850	1790	1820	1850
Virginia Maryland	25	10	5	396	532	570
North Carolina South Carolina	45	35	15	208	463	674
Georgia Florida	20	30	25	30	150	420
Texas Alabama Louisiana Mississippi Arkansas Oklahoma	10*	30*	55*	1†	143†	1,000†

Table 2.2: Shifts in Cotton Production and Slave Population, 1790 to 1850.

 * Oklahoma not included in region.
 † Louisiana not included in region.
Source: *U.S. Censuses of Population and Agriculture Statistics, various years.*

boat along the East Coast through the Gulf of Mexico to New Orleans and intervening ports. East Coast ports such as Norfolk, Richmond, Petersburg, Baltimore, Alexandria, Georgetown, and Washington City had vessels that were constantly used in this trade. An ad from the *National Intelligencer*, a Washington, D.C., paper (probably in the late 1820s), called for slaves as follows:

> Alexandria and New Orleans packets . . . Will sail as above, on the first of January . . . on the fifteenth of January . . . on the first of February. They will continue to leave this port on the first and fifteenth of each month throughout the shipping season. Servants that are intended to be shipped, will at any time be received for safe keeping at twenty-five cents a day.

A second way of moving slaves to the South was by steamers and floats down the Ohio, Mississippi, and other rivers tributary to New Orleans. The third way was by forced marches overland usually along the most public and frequented highways, leading through the chief cities and towns.

In 1836, the *Virginia Times* estimated that during the preceding twelve months Virginia exported 40,000 slaves with an aggregate value of $24 million. According to the *Natchez Courier* (Mississippi) the states of Louisiana, Mississippi, Alabama, and Arkansas imported 250,000 slaves from more northern or eastern states during 1836.

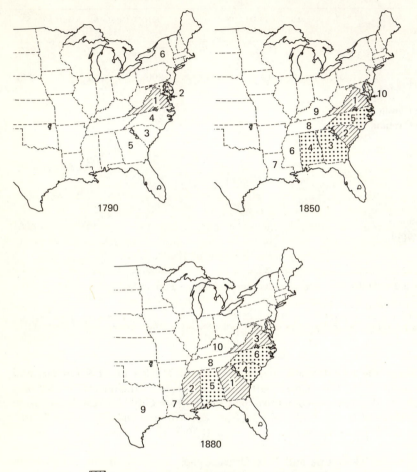

1790

1850

1880

▨ States with a greater than 25 percent black population
▦ States with a black population of 50 percent
1 2 Rank of states: the smaller the integer the larger the
       black population in each state

Figure 2.2 Changing Concentration of the Black Population.

In 1829 the *Baltimore Register* said that slave dealing had become a large
business. In 1831 Virginia was called a "Negro-raising state for other states."
And in 1832 Thomas Jefferson Randolph declared that Virginia had been
converted into "one grand menagerie where men are reared for the market like
oxen for the shambles." "Allowing for Virginia one-half of the whole exporta-
tion during the period in question (1836) and we have the appalling sum total
of eighty thousand slaves exported in a single year from the breeding states."

(Anonymous, 1969). It should be noted, however, that much of the evidence as to the numbers of slaves moved on the internal slave trade is indefinite.

EARLY CONTROLS ON BLACK MOBILITY AND MIGRATION

Free and Black was a contradiction in terms as far as Whites were concerned. Slave codes were sociospatial regulations designed to control an alien population. Along with numbers, freedom of movement for Blacks was greatly feared by Whites; this apprehension was institutionalized in slave codes. "All the Colonies were anxious to pass laws to restrain slaves from running away" (Zilversmit, 1967).

There were variations in the black codes from colony to colony and then from state to state, but the general point of view was identical in this legislation. This was that the codes should protect Whites from the dangers arising from the presence of large numbers of Blacks, from their uncontrolled movement, and simply from the relative location of Blacks.

Most of the important provisions of the slave codes, for example, were the same throughout the states. Specific examples of the codes that relate to the control of the black person as a geographic being are given.

Louisiana: "Requires the patrol to visit all places suspected of unlawful assemblages of slaves . . . any slave found at such assembly, or strolling about without a pass, shall receive any number of lashes, at the discretion of the patrol, not exceeding twenty" (Gara, 1967).

Virginia: "Any slave, for rambling in the night, or riding horses by day without leave, or running away may be punished by whipping, cropping, or branding in the cheek, or otherwise, not rendering him unfit for labor" (Gara, 1967).

Delaware: "More than six men slaves, meeting together, not belonging to one master, unless on lawful business of their owners, may be whipped to the extent of twenty-one lashes each" (Gara, 1967).

District of Columbia—1827: "Any free colored person coming there to reside, should give the mayor satisfactory evidence of his freedom, and enter bond with two freehold sureties, in the sum of five hundred dollars, for his good conduct, to be renewed each year for three years; or failing to do so, must leave the city, or be committed to the workhouse, for not more than one year, and if he still refuses to go, may be again committed for the same period, and so on" (Gara, 1967).

There was also federal legislation to aid in the recovery of runaway slaves. The U.S. Constitution, for example, required "the giving up of any runaway slaves to their masters." And the Federal Act of 1793 provided "that any master or his agent may seize any person whom he claims as a 'fugitive from service,' and take him before a judge of the U.S. Court, or magistrate of the city or county where he is taken, and the magistrate, on proof, in support of the claim, to his satisfaction, must give the claimant a certificate authorizing the removal of such fugitive to the state he fled from" (Gara, 1967).

Interstate migration of Blacks was severely restricted if not completely prohibited by the 1830s. In no southern state could the black person move about as he wished, and in northern areas it was dangerous to try.

By 1835 most of the southern and several northern states had restricted or prohibited immigration of free Blacks. In Georgia, for example, free Blacks could not return to the state after they had left for any length of time. Fear on the part of Whites prompted restrictive measures in other states, such as Indiana, Illinois, Ohio, Massachusetts, and Pennsylvania, and in the Oregon Territory. In the case of Indiana, Illinois, and Oregon, antiblack immigration clauses were incorporated into their respective constitutions.

In the Atlantic seaboard states, as well as in Alabama, Mississippi, and Louisiana, free black sailors were imprisoned on their ships while in port.

Southern Controls

Slaves in the South were not permitted to leave the plantation without their master's permission. In North Carolina free Blacks were not to go beyond the county adjoining the one in which they resided. The comprehensive measures set forth in the South Carolina "Act for the better ordering and governing of Negroes and Slaves" in 1712 served as a model for the rest of the southern slave codes during the colonial and national periods. The act had at least two sections that dealt specifically with the restriction of black movement off the plantation. Section VIII of the South Carolina Slave Code of 1712 reads as follows:

> And be it further enacted by the authority aforesaid, That no owner or head of any family shall give a ticket to any slave to go to Charleston, or from plantation to plantation, on Sunday, excepting it be for and about such particular business as cannot be reasonably delayed to another time, under the forfeiture of ten shillings; and in every ticket in that case given, shall be mentioned the particular business that slave is sent about, or that slave shall be dealt with as if he had no ticket (Berry, 1971).

As indicated in Section VIII slaves were not allowed to leave their plantation without a "ticket" or note from their master explaining their travels. Georgia's early slave code, for example, required that no more than seven slaves could be allowed to be out together unless accompanied by a white person.

The patrol was one of the devices used to enforce the black codes. These patrols were restricted in membership to free white men, who served for a stated period of time. Counties were usually divided into "beats" or areas of patrol. The patrols were to apprehend Blacks found "out of place" and return them to their masters or commit them to jail. They were also to visit assemblies of Blacks where disorder might develop or where conspiracy might be planned.

Northern Controls

Whites in the northern states bordering the South feared that immigration of Blacks might so increase their numbers as to make them numerically important parts of the white community. The result was the proliferation of laws limiting and prohibiting black migration and settlement in these states. Illinois and Indiana, for example, forbade black immigration.

In many states the legal codes designed to exclude the Black from participation in white society were far more severe than the black codes drafted by the Confederate states immediately after the Civil War. The truth is that Blacks were not generally welcomed in the North. Some northern states attempted to discourage black settlers by requiring them to register their certificates of freedom at a county clerk's office and to present bonds of $500 or $1,000 guaranteeing that they would not disturb the peace or become public charges.

Stringent black codes were found in what was sometimes known as the "Valley of Democracy." In Illinois it was a misdemeanor for a Black to enter the state to set up permanent residence. The 1851 state constitution of Indiana barred Blacks from the state. Ohio also took steps to ward off black migrants.

> The first of these (Black Laws) passed in 1804, provided that no Negro could reside in Ohio without a court certificate declaring him to be a freeman and not an escaped slave. Negroes who entered a county had to register with the county clerk. In 1807 a more stringent set of regulations required all Negroes who entered the state to post a five-hundred-dollar bond to pay for their support in case of want (Peskin, 1966).

Most northern versions of the more publicized southern black codes served to harass Blacks residing in the states, but they did not prohibit immigration. Nevertheless, even though they were not universally nor consistently enforced, the very presence of these laws on the books served as a silent threat and, at times, much more than that. For example, almost 8,000 Blacks were driven out of Portsmouth, New Hampshire, in 1830 for failure to register and post bond; in the preceding year over 1,000 Blacks were forced to leave Cincinnati for Canada.

In 1705 the New York Colonial Assembly enacted a law which provided that any slaves caught traveling 40 miles north of Albany would be executed, if they had been seen by credible witnesses. And in New York City in 1710 Blacks were forbidden to appear in the streets after nightfall without a lantern with a candle in it. Throughout the province of New York there were stringent restrictions on the assembly and movement of slaves in the eighteenth century.

The same kind of restrictions were found in the other northern colonies. Any black person found outside of the town limits in Connecticut in 1690 was to be caught and returned to his owner; a 1703 Rhode Island law prohibited Blacks from being on the streets at night. Blacks found more than 5 miles from home in New Jersey were to be whipped according to its 1714 slave code. According to the slave code of Pennsylvania in 1726, Blacks were not to be out after nine o'clock, were not to meet in groups of more than four, and were not to go more than 10 miles from their masters without a pass. A Delaware law of 1721 also forbade meetings among slaves.

The myth of the "lazy" Black, and its use as justification for enslavement, had early beginnings. The slave codes of Pennsylvania, New York, and New Jersey, for example, claimed that free Blacks were idle people and very often a charge on the place in which they resided. The New York Slave Code of 1712 and the New Jersey Slave Code of 1714 barred any black man from holding property or houses. The importance of this line of thought is that it demonstrates the circle of oppression in which free Blacks were not allowed land ownership, freedom of movement, or employment; then according to Whites, if Blacks were not employed or land owners, they must by definition be lazy and a charge on the community; thus they should be enslaved so that they can be useful.

Since it was more than black movement itself that white society feared, it could not very well allow other forms of spatial interaction that might incite insurrection. To allow Blacks to carry mail, for example, would be contrary to the intention of the slave codes to restrict their knowledge about other people and places. As Postmaster General Gidion Granger warned in 1802, "Everything which tends to increase their [blacks'] knowledge of natural rights of men and things, or that affords them an opportunity of associating, acquiring and communicating sentiments and of establishing a chain or line of intelligence might excite alarm" (Litwack, 1961). Thus from 1810 to 1862 Blacks were excluded from carrying mail.

Whether or not these sociospatial codes were consistently enforced, they served as a constant reminder to Blacks and as a reassurance to Whites that the former were in an inferior, unstable position. The codes also provided legal sanction and excuse for white violence.

PATTERNS OF ESCAPE—FROM STATION TO STATION

The Underground Railroad

The primary impetus for the black movement to the North was the search for freedom. This was the pattern characterized by the Underground Railroad, the

LIBERTY LINE.
NEW ARRÁNGEMENT---NIGHT AND DAY.

The improved and splendid Locomotives, Clarkson and Lundy, with their trains fitted up in the best style of accommodation for passengers, will run their regular trips during the present season, between the borders of the Patriarchal Dominion and Libertyville, Upper Canada. Gentlemen and Ladies, who may wish to improve their health or circumstances, by a northern tour; are respectfully invited to give us their patronage.

SEATS FREE, *irrespective of color.*

Necessary Clothing furnished gratuitously to such as have "*fallen among thieves.*"

"Hide the outcasts—let the oppressed go free."—*Bible.*

☞For seats apply at any of the trap doors, or to the conductor of the train.

J. CROSS, *Proprietor.*

N. B. For the special benefit of Pro-Slavery Police Officers, an extra heavy wagon for Texas, will be furnished, whenever it may be necessary, in which they will be forwarded as dead freight, to the "Valley of Rascals," always at the risk of the owners.

☞Extra Overcoats provided for such of them as are afflicted with protracted *chilly-phobia.*

The Underground Railroad consisted of a network of mostly Northern abolitionists who secretly helped as many as 100,000 escaped slaves reach safety in the North and in Canada. Although neither underground nor a railroad, railroad terminology was used as a code, as the above advertisement from an 1844 newspaper indicates.

Harriet Tubman (c. 1820–1913), herself an escaped slave, was a prime force in the Underground Railroad. Described as "the Moses of her people", she made 19 trips into the South to bring out slaves, helping more than 300 slaves to freedom.

Top: Historical Pictures Service, Chicago; bottom: Culver Pictures, Inc.

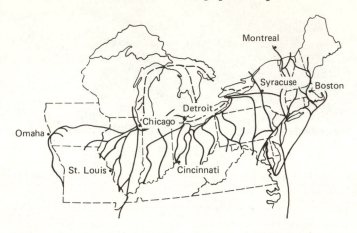

Figure 2.3   Part of the Underground Railroad System.

(From Siebert, Wilbur, "The Underground Railroad from Slavery to Freedom," Russell & Russell, New York, 1898; and Breyfogle, William, "Make Free: The Story of the Underground Railroad," J. B. Lippincott, Philadelphia, 1958.)

abolitionists, and the southern slave "patterolls."

Depending on time and place, the black slave had a number of options in terms of places to which he could escape. These options included Mexico, Canada, free states, southern cities, maroon colonies, or Indian tribes in the southeast such as the Creeks, Cherokees, and Seminoles. In the early nineteenth century a movement developed among white abolitionists and some Blacks for emigration of Blacks to colonies in Africa. The Liberian colony was established in 1821, but only about 15,000 emigrated over a 50-year period.

Escape of the individual slave to "freedom" in the North was a more practical alternative than armed rebellion in the South, but the chances of success were not high, considering the great distances to be traveled, the visibility of the black fugitive, and his ignorance of geography beyond his immediate area. Nevertheless hundreds of thousands of attempts resulted in some many thousand successful escapes. Many, perhaps most, slaves had no help from anyone in making their escapes. The Underground Railroad was the clandestine network of antislavery individuals, including many escaped slaves, and the byways linking them, by which an escaped slave could be guided into a haven in the North or in Canada. So perilous was the journey within the South that little is known about the routes or the mechanisms; within the North the "railway" was more organized (see Figure 2.3) but still secret, since the National Anti-Slave Laws of 1850 required northern states to return escaped slaves and permitted owners' representatives to go north and capture them. There is still controversy over the nature of the Underground Railroad. Some argue that it was not a systemized network but rather a restricted number of Blacks and Whites organized to move slaves in certain localities.

Others have suggested that an extensive network of organized aid existed among Quakers in eastern Pennsylvania around 1786. Blacks were aided by the Quakers. By the mid-eighteenth century, the Quaker Society took the position that all members of the Society should free their slaves. Unlike other groups, Quakers were concerned not only with freedom for Blacks per se, but also with their welfare. There was, however, a general reaction against this stand by most of the white community. Thus the problem was to find a relatively non-hostile environment in which the freed Blacks could settle. Pennsylvania was logical because of its geographic location and because it was the home of many Quakers. But the primary factor that had made Pennsylvania a haven for escaped slaves, its location, was also to make it a liability. Pennsylvania was too close to the slave states, and southern agents found it easy to recapture escaped Blacks residing in the state.

By 1840 there appear to have been at least fourteen states around the Great Lakes traversed by numerous and irregular lines of the Underground Railroad. The natural routes of the Mississippi and Ohio Rivers and their tributaries, and the valleys of the Appalachian range, were probable paths to freedom. Siebert divides the underground system into three parts: Pennsylvania, New York, and New Jersey; New England; and the five states of the Northwest Territory. In this system Phoenixville, Pennsylvania is regarded as the central point of the total system.

Escapes before the Civil War (about 90,000 went North on the Underground Railroad) and movement northward during and just after the Civil War added up to a sizable migration of Blacks.

At different times certain border cities were seen by Blacks as entry points or gateways to freedom. During the 1700s Pittsburgh was an *entrepôt* to freedom for slaves escaping to the Northwest Territory. By the turn of the century, Cleveland also served this function; it was touted as the "Negro's Paradise" (Peskin, 1966). Before 1850 most movement was to Baltimore, Philadelphia, Cincinnati, and other cities close to the South. Others went to the relative security of the small, free black communities of northern cities, such as New York City, Chicago, Rochester, and Boston, where many joined the growing abolitionist forces in the North.

After the Anti-Fugitive Slave Law of 1850 was enacted, migrants had to reach Canada to be safe.

> These kind friends gave me something to eat, and started me on my way to Canada, with a recommendation to a friend on my way. This was the commencement of what was called the under ground rail to Canada. I walked with bold courage, trusting in the arm of Omnipotence; guided by the unchangeable North Star by night, and inspired by an elevated thought that I was fleeing from a land of slavery and oppression, bidding farewell to handcuffs, whips, thumbscrews and chains (Osofsky, 1969).

Indian Groups of the Southeast

Besides the Underground Railroad routes to the North, there were other options available to the escaped slave. These included maroon colonies and Indian groups such as the Creeks, Cherokees, and Seminoles.

Escape by Blacks to Florida and specifically to the areas of the Creeks and Seminoles seems to have been relatively common during the latter part of the eighteenth and the beginning of the nineteenth centuries. The Spanish were tolerant of the presence of Blacks in Florida, and the Spanish crown refused to extradite the runaways. Spain's apparent friendliness was self-serving, however, not altruistic. It wanted Florida to serve as a buffer betweeen its colonies to the south and the British areas on the continent, and by not offending the Indians it was able to keep the British-Americans at arm's length for a while.

Blacks arrived among the Creeks and Seminoles in a variety of ways: some were purchased; some were given by British agents in return for help during the War; some were captured; some joined the British and their Indian allies for the promise of asylum; and some escaped.

By 1812 there were black towns with populations of several thousand among the Seminoles, causing much consternation in the white population of Georgia. The interaction between Georgia and the federal government with respect to the "disposal" of Blacks and Indians was a prelude to much of the later conflict over the place of Blacks in the country, namely the matter of "states rights." In fact, the first exercise of the treaty-making power under the Constitution made on August 1, 1790, "was put forth for the benefit of the slave interests of Georgia" (Giddings, 1969).

According to the Treaty of Galphinton, "the Indians shall restore all the negroes, horses and other property, that are or may hereafter be among them, belonging to the citizens of this state, or to any other person whatever, to such person as the governor shall appoint" (Giddings, 1969). This treaty was illegal on both sides. First, according to the Articles of Confederation, Georgia, as a state, could not make treaties. Secondly, the treaty was signed by only two of the 100 Creek towns, yet it was felt by Georgians to be ratified by all the Creeks as well as by the Seminoles of Florida. This treaty was put into effect by the federal government in 1790.

The language in the third article of the treaty as it was made between the United States and the Creek chiefs was as follows:

> The Creek nation shall deliver, as soon as practicable . . . all citizens of the United States, white inhabitants or negroes, who are now prisoners in any part of the said nation (Giddings, 1969).

The stipulation for the return of prisoners would seem to leave those Blacks residing among the Creeks and especially among the Seminoles, as they were not parties to the treaty, untouched, as they were definitely not prisoners of the Indians. But such was not the interpretation by Whites; all Blacks were to be returned. In fact, it was the Whites who had held them as prisoners and would, upon their return, hold them as prisoners again.

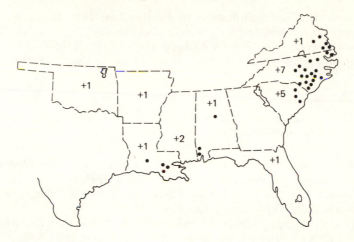

Figure 2.4 Location of Maroon Colonies in the United States, 1672 to 1864.

Blacks continued to escape to Florida and Georgia while slaveholders continued their agitation for federal action to back the Fugitive Slave clause of the Constitution. Finally, the federal government decided that the best solution would be to forcibly move the Indians out of Florida, opening the state for settlement by slaveholders. "There was no niche or corner of safety for the free Black in a slave society. If even one little enclave of Indians and Blacks remained unmolested, it posed a threat to the institution of slavery" (Berry, 1971).

Those Blacks who moved to the lands "provided" the Creeks and Seminoles west of the Mississippi did not yet arrive in the land of freedom. Blacks who were fugitive slaves did not belong in Indian Territory and could be forcibly removed to the custody of the slaveholders. Thus, as the Blacks who migrated north had to do, those who moved westward had to flee to another country, Mexico.

Maroon Colonies

Figure 2.4 shows the location of many of the maroon colonies throughout the southern states prior to the Civil War. Most of these colonies were in isolated mountains or swampy areas. The most noted was on the North Carolina–Virginia border. It was called Dismal Swamp, home for about 2,000 black fugitives. There is evidence of at least fifty-nine such communities in various places and at various times from 1672 to 1864.

Whites seemed to take alarm at these isolated groups of Blacks only when they were accidently uncovered or when their actions became so dangerous as to cause alarm and their destruction was therefore felt to be necessary. As an item from Wilmington, North Carolina, dated January 7, 1831, read, "There has been much shooting of Negroes in this neighborhood recently, in consequence of symptoms of liberty having been discovered among them" (Aptheker, 1939).

SELECTED BIBLIOGRAPHY

1. Anonymous: "Slavery and Internal Slave Trade in the U.S. of North America," Detroit, Negro History Press, 1969.
2. Aptheker, Herbert: "American Negro Slave Revolts," New York, International Publishers, 1963.
3. ————: Maroons within the Present Limits of the United States, *Journal of Negro History*, vol. 24, pp. 167–184, April, 1939.
4. Bennett, Lerone: "Before the Mayflower: A History of the Negro in America, 1619–1964," Baltimore, Md., Penguin Books, 1962.
5. Berry, Mary Frances: "Black Resistance–White Law," New York, Appleton-Century Crofts, 1971.
6. Fishel, Leslie H. and Benjamin Quarles: "The Black American: A Documentary History," rev. ed., New York, Morrow, 1967.
7. Franklin, John Hope: "From Slavery to Freedom," New York, Alfred A. Knopf, 1967.
8. Gara, Larry: "The Liberty Line," Lexington, University of Kentucky Press, 1967.
9. Giddings, Joshua R.: "Exiles of Florida," New York, Arno Press, 1969.
10. Hillery, George A., Jr., James S. Brown, and Gordon F. DeJeng: Migration Systems of the Southern Appalachians: Some Demographic Observations, *Rural Sociology*, vol. 30, pp. 33–48, 1965.
11. Lee, Everett S., A Theory of Migration, "Population Geography: A Reader" edited by George J. Demko, Harold M. Rose, and George A. Schnell, New York, McGraw-Hill, Inc., 1970.
12. Litwack, Leon F.: "North of Slavery, The Negro in the Free States, 1790–1860," Chicago, University of Chicago Press, 1961.
13. McManus, Edgar J.: "History of Negro Slavery in New York," Syracuse, Syracuse University Press, 1966.
14. Meier, August and Elliott Rudwick: "From Plantation to Ghetto," New York, Hill and Wang, 1966.
15. Morrill, Richard: "The Spatial Organization of Society," Wadsworth Publishing Co., Belmont, Calif., 1965.
16. Osofsky, Gilbert (ed.): "Puttin' On Ole Massa," New York, Harper Torch Books, 1969, p. 85.
17. Peskin, Allan (ed.) and John Malvin: "North into Freedom: The Autobiography of John Malvin, Free Negro, 1879–1880," Cleveland, Western Reserve University, 1966.

18. Siebert, Wilbur H.: "The Underground Railroad from Slavery to Freedom," New York, Russell & Russell, 1898.
19. Sorokin, P. A.: "Social and Cultural Mobility," New York, Free Press, 1959.
20. Toffler, Alvin: "Future Shock," New York, Random House, 1970, pp. 77.
21. Zilversmit, Arthur: "The First Emancipation: The Abolition of Slavery in the North," Chicago, University of Chicago Press, 1967.

Courtesy of the New York Historical Society, New York City.

3 Post-Civil War Black Migration: Part One

Inasmuch as the "field-to-factory" migration patterns were taking place some five decades before the conclusion of the Civil War, it seems appropriate to begin our discussion with a limited summary of some of the reasons for and results of these ante-bellum migrations. The demand by northern and British textile interests after the War of 1812 had stimulated the expansion of cotton cultivation into the Piedmont region and into the Black Belt. In the 1820s and 1830s the cotton crop almost quadrupled; from 1840 to 1860 it more than doubled, reaching the unprecedented total of 4.9 million bales by the opening of the Civil War. The increased demand for cotton was accompanied by the increased production of hemp for rope and cotton bagging. At the same time that the craving for tobacco was growing, the need for rice, wheat, corn, and livestock was increasing dramatically.

Along with increased production of raw materials came greater needs for finished products and services. These functions were performed primarily in urban areas. Urban slaves, like most other city workers—free and slave, native and immigrant—engaged in commercial occupations or in domestic service. Urban slaves were typically artisans and craftsmen, stevedores and draymen, barbers and common laborers, and house and hotel servants. The earliest significant growth in urban slaves was observed in seaboard cities such as Charleston, while their numbers in river towns such as Louisville grew rapidly after 1840. Slaves formed substantial portions of urban populations, amounting to as much as 50 percent in Charleston by 1850. Altogether, 70,000 slaves lived in the eight major cities of this time, and in Mobile, Savannah, and especially in Richmond (as well as in some interior towns, such as Montgomery), the slave population was expanding with considerable vitality.

In the 1850s the slave states' industrial production almost doubled, so that by 1860, the South contained about 15 percent of national industrial capacity. The value of southern manufactured goods alone increased from $34 million in 1840 to nearly $100 million in 1860. The *Charleston Mercury* in February, 1855, stated that the DeKalb Textile Mills in Camden, South Carolina, were so successful that there was an average 13 percent profit in the year of 1855 on initial investments.

By 1865, the economic apparatus which led to the postwar migration was in motion. There was a confused and complex migration process taking place in the South during the 40 years after the Civil War. This should be no surprise as there was also a great change in socioeconomic conditions, not only in the South but nationwide.

One of the results of the new "freedom" following slavery was the wandering about of many Blacks. In part, this was an attempt to test their spatial freedom. Some became migrant workers; others were to remain homeless. For the majority of Blacks, migration was more defined. They moved from the fields to the more productive agricultural lands of Louisiana, Texas, and Oklahoma in the late 1860s and early 1870s and later to the plains of Kansas and to Indian Territory in 1879. Some moved from the fields to the mining camps in the Appalachians in the late 1880s and 1890s. But the vast majority were members of the trek to the factories of the industrial North. There was also a small counterstream of black migration to the South, which has continued.

The migration of large numbers of Blacks during this period was, on the one hand, to escape racism in its many forms and, on the other, to increase one's socioeconomic position. During the period of 1880 to 1960 opportunities for Blacks have always ranked at the bottom-most level throughout the country. For Blacks, classical economists notwithstanding, differences in opportunities are not erased by moving, whether it is done every decade or every generation; despite population shifts the opportunities for Blacks are persistently low.

Since the Civil War the largest black migrations have taken place during periods of acute economic crises—toward the close of the depression of the 1870s, at the height of the Populist-agrarian agitation around 1890, and again during the depression that hit the country before World War I.

FROM FIELD TO FACTORY: RURAL-URBAN MIGRATION PATTERNS

The greatest change in black population has not been in numbers but in location, away from the South and the farms and into the cities of the North. These have been the predominant characteristics of the shift in black population since the Civil War. At the end of the Civil War just over 90 percent of the total black population remained in the South, much as it had since 1790. This proportion dropped slowly at first and decreased dramatically later. Until 1920 the South still contained virtually nine out of ten of the black people in the country.

Most of the early out-migration went to the cities of the Northeast; but as Figure 3.1 indicates, the Northcentral and, later, the Western states gradually increased their share of the black migrants. The decline in out-migration from the South from 1930 to 1940 is also evident in Figure 3.1. The Depression halted much of the northward black movement until late in the period when black labor was again needed in the defense programs in 1938 and 1939.

During the years 1860 to 1940 the Northeast and the Northcentral regions received 90 percent of the black out-migration from the South. But in the years after 1940 the migration of Blacks to the West increased, making up more than 20 percent of the total out-migration of southern Blacks (see Figure 3.2).

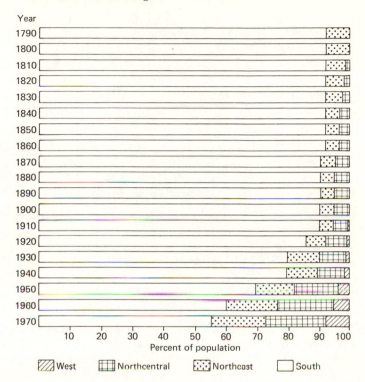

Figure 3.1 Black Population Distribution by Region, 1790 to 1970.
(From various Bureau of the Census Reports.)

Although the North has remained the major destination of Blacks migrating from the South, the proportion of the migrants who head westward has increased. In 1970 the West was the destination of 22 percent of the Blacks migrating from the South.

Migration flows during this long period from 1860 to 1970 were not uniform. The small, steady out-migrations prior to 1910 were followed by the dramatic "great migration" of 1915. It was this great migration that marked a significant change in the distribution of Blacks in the United States. Most, if not all, of this increase in the northern, urban black population originated in the rural areas of the South.

The out-migration of Blacks from the South to the North and West has continued to be the primary reason for the declining proportion of the black population in the South. The proportion of the black population living in the South declined from 68 percent in 1950 to 53 percent in 1970. Migration to the North has often depopulated small black hamlets in the South. Such has been the case in Mayflower, North Carolina. In three decades the town's population has dropped from 100 to twenty-eight families. By the summer of 1969, the community ceased to exist except "in the minds of its few remaining citizens."

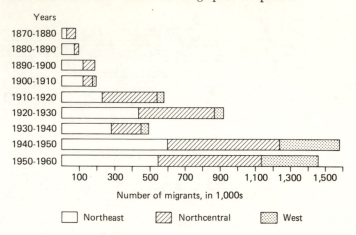

Figure 3.2 Net Migration of Blacks, 1870 to 1960. Length of Bars Represent Totals Leaving South, and Patterns Represent Percentage of This Total Entering Other Regions of the Country.

(From various Bureau of the Census Reports.)

Even though the average, annual net out-migration of Blacks from the South has remained virtually stable (147.3 million from 1950 to 1960 and 147.4 million from 1960 to 1970), the southern black population has continued to increase due to relatively high birthrates and a drop in the mortality rates. Within metropolitan areas natural increase accounted for 3 million of the total 5.1 million increase; the remainder was a result of net in-migration.

The second important characteristic of this South to North black migration was that it was rural to urban. But, as with the directional trends, rural to urban movement did not take place uniformly from 1860 to 1970. There was little change from 1860 to 1910. For example, in 1860 the rural South accounted for 83.3 percent of the total black population. This dropped only to 67.7 percent by 1910. It was not until the second half of the period that Blacks migrated in great numbers. The rural black population of the South dropped to 23.7 percent of the total black population in 1960. But within the South, nonmetropolitan areas still accounted for a large proportion (44 percent) of the region's black population in 1970. This rural to urban redistribution of black population was directed at three groups of cities, in the North, the South, and the West. Most of the migrants went to northern cities and, within the North, to the larger cities. The spectacular numbers associated with the black movement to the urban North have obscured the significant social and spatial fact that southern cities also were important destinations for rural black migrants. This southern movement actually began earlier than its northern counterpart.

Prior to 1910 black migrants moved shorter distances and tended to stay within the South; it was the later movements that were longer and to northern destinations. Rubins' study of black migration from rural, northeastern Missis-

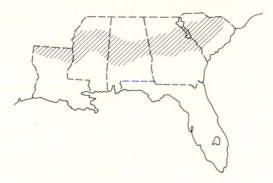

Figure 3.3   The Black Belt South.

sippi supports the view that black migration out of the South has been hier-
archical through time. Prior to World War I black migration was directed to
the towns and cities of the South. In the area studied by Rubins, the shift was
to the cities of the Mississippi-delta region. After the war the gateway cities and
the more industrial cities of the North (Chicago, Detroit, St. Louis, Kansas
City, became major destinations. Finally, the smaller industrial cities received
larger numbers of black migrants. The same kind of rural-urban hierarchy in
migration was found by Dubois in 1898 in Farmville, Virginia; by Wright in
1903 in Xenia, Ohio; and more recently by Woodson in 1930. Dubois noted
that Farmville acted as a clearinghouse for country people who later moved on
to eastern and northern cities.

   "I'm taking a ride, almost anybody in Williamsburg County, South Carolina, knows what it means—almost anybody who is Black and who has raised
a son or a daughter to the age of sixteen or seventeen. Otis Gibson, for
example, watched his three daughters and two of his four sons join this migrant
stream to the North right out of high school" (Walls, 1971).

   In the fall, when the last crops are harvested in North Carolina, probably
90 percent of the region's black high school graduates go "up the road." They
leave via old family cars, Greyhound and Trailway buses, and the two seaboard
trains known as "the Chickenbone Special." During the 6 weeks following
the first Saturday in June, the Chickenbone Special carries around 12,600
people out of the rural Southeast and into the urban Northeast. The trains
get their name from the fact that most of its riders are young Blacks who are
migrating North and cannot afford the meals on the train and carry bag lunches
with fried chicken as the staple food.

   Black migration in the Black Belt was especially interesting. The Black Belt
is an expanse of land extending from northern South Carolina, through central
Georgia, Alabama, and Mississippi, to northern Louisiana (see Figure 3.3).
The name Black Belt seems to have originally been derived from the rich, black
soil characteristic of parts of the region. This rich soil was also the location
of plantation agriculture and large numbers of black people. As a result, the
designation "Black Belt" has come to be popularly associated with black pop-

Figure 3.4   Alabama Black Belt.

uladion. The discussion that follows is concerned primarily with the portion of the Black Belt in Alabama which is a strip of land 25 miles or less in width that curves from the Georgia state line to Mississippi on the west (see Figure 3.4).

Former slaves were leaving the Black Belt soon after the Civil War, especially in the 1870s. In 1873, Blacks were reported leaving Hale County for Mississippi, where they hoped to improve their pecuniary condition (*Alabama Beacon*, 1873). In the late 1870s many Blacks migrated from all over the South (including the Black Belt) to Kansas. They did so mainly because of the agricultural depression and the maltreatment they received as freedmen. Fear of labor shortages in the South was manifested in 1880 and 1881, and heavy license fees were required of labor solicitors (*Haynesville Examiner*, 1881). One of the more disturbing migration episodes, however, came in

YEAR	BLACK BELT COUNTIES		ALABAMA	
	White	Black	White	Black
1860	64,474	171,176	526,271	437,770
1870	67,141	211,176	521,384	475,510
1880	70,728	260,965	662,185	600,103
1890	69,226	267,214	833,718	678,489
1900	77,002	310,912	1,001,152	827,307
1910	80,080	301,821	1,228,832	908,282
1920	91,266	255,542	1,447,032	900,652
1930	107,140	250,143	1,700,775	944,834

Table 3.1: White and Black Population in the Black Belt Counties and in the State of Alabama during the Years 1860 to 1930.

(U.S. Census Reports, 1860-1930)

1895, when labor agents recruited workers for cotton raising in Mexico. The migrants were told fabulous tales of new paradises which never materialized (*Alabama Beacon*, 1895).

Table 3.1 indicates the trends of population in the Black Belt counties and in the state of Alabama during the years 1860 to 1930.

By 1900 Blacks had begun a constant movement out of the Black Belt, so that the period from 1900 to 1910 showed a significant decline in Black population. This was a part of the "field-to-factory" movement of population which affected the entire nation and was accentuated by the extremely rapid growth of industrial cities such as Birmingham. These cities offered increased industrial opportunities for Blacks. In fact, this movement of population from field to factory was a basic phase of the overall transfer of population, wealth, and power to the industrial areas.

Horace Mann Bond has shown that the Black Belt declined steadily from payment of 34.6 percent of the total state taxes in 1870 to 11.3 percent in 1930. The mineral region increased from paying 1.7 percent in 1870 to 31.8 percent in 1930. The migration of Blacks to the factory areas was only one aspect of the more industrial development of the Piedmont section in the state of Alabama at the expense of the rural sections. Other aspects of the movement were the migration of Whites, the development of wealth, and the growth of the coal, steel, and textile industries.

A study of the counties that lost population between 1870 and 1930 with the counties that gained population clearly shows that the departures were occurring most severely in the rural counties with heavy black population, and that the greatest gains were shown by urban and industrial counties (see Figure 3.5).

From 1900 and 1910 the number of Blacks living in cities in Alabama increased from 98,154, or 11.9 percent of the state's black population, to 156,603, or 17.2 percent of the Blacks in the state. By 1920 the numbers had gone to 196,833, and the percentage to 21.9.

Birmingham was one of the principal centers in the South for recruiting

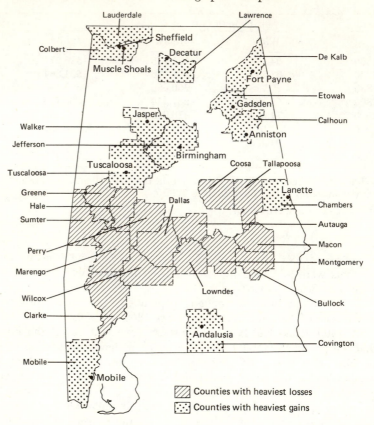

Figure 3.5 Black Population Gain and Loss in Alabama by County, 1923.

(From Alabama Statistical Register, 1923, pp. 297–298.)

labor to send North. Thousands of former slaves gathered there from smaller towns and the rural areas, acquired skills, and then went North (see the case study at the end of this chapter). Many, however, went directly to northern points. A survey of Bullock County made during the migration of 1917 revealed that migrants had gone to the following places: Birmingham, Alabama; Richmond and Norfolk, Virginia; New York City; Philadelphia and Pittsburgh, Pennsylvania; Cincinnati and Columbus, Ohio; Detroit, Michigan; Gary, Indiana; and Chicago and Cairo, Illinois.

After thousands of Blacks had migrated, the Black Belt changed in many respects. In fact nearly all aspects of the town looked different. The usual Saturday crowd of Blacks filling the sidewalks and Sunday morning churchgoers of Union Springs dwindled noticeably, for about one-third of the Blacks were gone.

At first black businesses and professions were hurt, but as money began to come in from the industrial areas, they thrived. In Bullock County, crime—at least, court convictions—decreased by almost half between 1915 and 1917. The black churches lost from 25 to 70 percent of their memberships. The exodus of Blacks made farm labor scarce, so that farmers were forced to diversify their crops and use methods that required fewer laborers.

In districts from which the Blacks moved there came to be a more liberal attitude of Whites toward Blacks. This lessening of race prejudice resulted from the combined effects of sympathy for the complaints of the black man, from the lessening of the threat of black domination because of fewer Blacks, and from the urgent need for keeping laborers on the farms.

Even though the base figure was small, the urban black population of the South quadrupled from 1860 to 1910 (see Table 3.2). And unlike the northward population stream, it did not decline drastically from 1930 to 1940. By 1960, almost a third of the total black population lived in the cities of the South.

Even though the exodus of Blacks from the South after 1915 resulted in a drop in the black populations of some southern cities, the total urban black population for most of the South continued to rise (see Table 3.1). Those cities losing black population from 1910 to 1920 included Danville and Lynchburg, Virginia; Tyler and Austin, Texas; Vicksburg, Jackson, and Meridian, Mississippi; Louisville, Kentucky; and Nashville, Tennessee. The urban black population in the South rose from 18.5 percent in 1920 to 29.3 percent in 1960.

MEDIAN MIGRATION FIELDS

Migration is a form of adaptation to the perceived changes in one's environment. One's "field," or the destinations which make up the alternative choices, is not usually limitless. The individual or group makes a decision to move or stay; a decision in which, either explicitly or implicitly, his present site is compared to a number of potential sites. The choice of a new site is the product of many decisions on the part of the mover. Recent migration studies suggest that distance must be measured by a wide variety of transformations of the linear distance scale and by an equally varied collection of value scales. Experience, economic, sociocultural, and psychological factors influence the range of possible choices that an individual sees open to him. A sampling process is implicit in people's movement patterns. These potential destinations may be called the individual's "migration field."

It is known that northern urban centers have been destinations and that the South is the area of origin of black migrants; there are three regional migration systems within this broad pattern. One is found along the Atlantic seaboard directed to New York and Boston, a second from Mississippi toward Chicago, and a third west from Texas toward California. This stream pattern, however, has not been of recent origin. The two streams in the eastern half of the country were functioning at least by 1930. The Atlantic coastal cities attracted migrants from the southern coastal states; the northcentral cities drew

From field to factory: harvesting the peanut crop in Richmond, 1870 (top).

Bettman Archive, Inc.

The Reynolds Tobacco factory, 1875 (bottom).

Valentine Museum, Richmond, Virginia.

migrants from the Mississippi delta. Black migrants from St. Helena, South Carolina, for example, moved to the seaport of Savannah and then on to the northern cities of New York and Boston. Rochester, New York, has been one of the stops along the East Coast migrant labor stream. With time the demand for the labor decreased, but the flow of migrants did not stop. From 1950 to 1970 the black population in Monroe County grew over 550 percent, from 8,000 to an estimated 45,000. By far the largest proportion of these migrants came from two points of origin on the stream: Sanford, Florida, and Williamsburg County, South Carolina.

The purpose of the following tables and maps is to examine individual median migration fields for certain states and to combine these fields into a composite in an attempt to reveal regional migration patterns for nonwhites from 1955 to 1960 in part of the United States. The complete state to city nonwhite migration matrix would indicate that most states have migrants moving to most large cities. It is felt that the median field reveals the major orientation of black urban-rural migration.

The median field is defined as that group of cities which receive at least 50 percent of the state's nonwhite out-migrants. In order to find the median field the total number of out-migrants from a state in 1955 to the 100 SMSA's* over 250,000 in population in 1960 was found. Then the percentage contribution of each city to the total out-migration from the state was calculated. For each state the city accounting for the greatest percentage was found, then the second and third highest, and so on until the combined percentage total reaches or exceeds 50 percent. The migration fields for twenty-one states are found in Table 3.2 and in Figure 3.6.

Median fields could have been calculated using the number of in-migrants to each city as a base from which to work, but this process obscures the influence of cities from the perspective of the point of origin. Alabama, for example, is the origin of the greatest percentage of nonwhites moving into Detroit, yet Detroit is not the prime attraction for nonwhites from Alabama; Detroit ranks third behind Birmingham and Chicago.

Although we are aware of the problems involved in using census data on migration, it is peripheral to the purpose of this book to discuss them here.

In order to identify regional migration patterns, the cities making up the median fields are grouped into five regional categories: West Coast, North-central, Northeast Coast, South Coast, and other. The regional migration systems are shown in Table 3.3 and in Figure 3.6.

As seen in Table 3.2, the number of cities making up the median fields ranges from three to eight. In those states with more cities in their median fields, the percentage contribution of the highest city tends to be less. For example, in those states with from five to eight cities in the median field, in only three out of thirteen does a city receive greater than 8 percent, yet in those states with three or four cities in the median field none of the highest ranking cities receives less than 18 percent of the migrants. The state with the single

* Standard Metropolitan Statistical Area: an area which includes at least one city of 50,000 inhabitants or more.

ALABAMA		ARKANSAS		FLORIDA	
City	%	City	%	City	%
Birmingham	11.8	Chicago	19.3	Miami	11.6
Chicago	9.4	Los Angeles	15.6	Tampa	10.9
Detroit	7.5	St. Louis	6.9	New York	10.5
Cleveland	7.4	San Francisco	6.1	Fort Lauderdale	9.0
Mobile	7.3	Memphis	4.8	Orlando	6.0
New York	7.2		52.7	Jacksonville	5.8
Los Angeles	6.8				53.8
Buffalo	3.2				
	60.6				

GEORGIA		ILLINOIS		INDIANA	
City	%	City	%	City	%
Atlanta	12.9	Los Angeles	18.0	Chicago	24.6
Miami	11.9	Chicago	10.8	Los Angeles	10.2
New York	9.9	Gary	7.3	Indianapolis	7.6
Tampa	5.5	San Francisco	4.3	St. Louis	5.3
Fort Lauderdale	4.9	St. Louis	3.8	Detroit	4.8
Jacksonville	4.4	New York	3.8		52.5
Philadelphia	4.2	Detroit	3.7		
	53.7		51.7		

KENTUCKY		LOUISIANA		MARYLAND	
City	%	City	%	City	%
Louisville	13.2	Los Angeles	20.5	Washington, D.C.	23.8
Indianapolis	8.6	Houston	12.4	New York	14.3
Chicago	8.1	New Orleans	10.9	Baltimore	13.0
Cincinnati	6.3	San Francisco	8.9		51.1
Dayton	6.0		52.7		
Detroit	4.6				
Cleveland	4.4				
	51.2				

MICHIGAN		MISSISSIPPI		MISSOURI	
City	%	City	%	City	%
Los Angeles	13.5	Chicago	32.9	Chicago	16.7
Chicago	12.1	Memphis	10.9	Los Angeles	16.6
Detroit	7.7	Los Angeles	7.7	St. Louis	6.5
Cleveland	5.4		51.5	Kansas City	6.0
New York	5.1			San Francisco	5.3
San Francisco	3.4				51.1
St. Louis	2.8				
	50.0				

NORTH CAROLINA		OHIO		OKLAHOMA	
City	%	City	%	City	%
New York	26.7	Los Angeles	10.1	Oklahoma City	24.7
Washington, D.C.	13.6	Cleveland	7.5	Los Angeles	18.9
Philadelphia	8.4	Chicago	6.6	Tulsa	14.8
Newark	7.9	Columbus	6.5		58.4
	56.6	Dayton	6.1		
		Detroit	5.5		
		New York	5.0		
		Akron	3.2		
			50.5		

PENNSYLVANIA		SOUTH CAROLINA		TENNESSEE	
City	%	City	%	City	%
New York	14.2	New York	28.2	Chicago	17.7
Washington, D.C.	7.4	Washington, D.C.	8.9	Nashville	10.5
Philadelphia	6.9	Philadelphia	8.5	Los Angeles	8.5
Pittsburgh	4.8	Columbus	8.5	Memphis	7.6
Cleveland	4.7		54.1	Detroit	5.7
Los Angeles	4.6				50.0
Harrisburg	4.1				
Baltimore	3.6				
	50.3				

TEXAS		VIRGINIA		WEST VIRGINIA	
City	%	City	%	City	%
Houston	18.0	Washington, D.C.	18.5	New York	13.4
Los Angeles	17.7	New York	17.7	Cleveland	11.0
Dallas	15.3	Richmond	10.5	Columbus	10.5
	51.0	Philadelphia	9.0	Charleston	8.3
			55.7	Washington, D.C.	7.7
					50.9

Table 3.2:   Median Migration Fields of Selected States, 1955 to 1960.

most concentrated flow is Mississippi with 32 percent of the 1955 nonwhite out-migrants living in Chicago in 1960.

There are two major systems focusing on the cities of the Northeast Coast. One path moves eastward from the states east of the Mississippi River and north of the Ohio River. This is the weaker of the two paths, and its magnitude decreases greatly west of Pennsylvania. This westward decline is a reflection of the increasing importance of regional cities and Los Angeles. The other

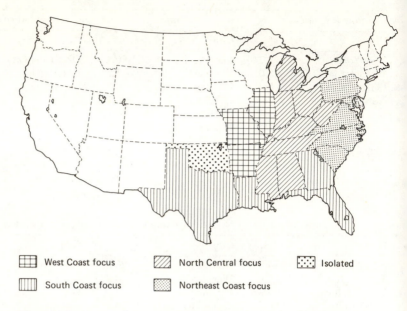

	West Coast focus		North Central focus		Isolated
	South Coast focus		Northeast Coast focus		

Figure 3.6   Regional Migration Systems, 1950–1960.

stream lies east of the Appalachian mountain system; Philadelphia and Baltimore act as secondary centers in terms of percentage of migrants attracted.

Los Angeles is the primary focus on the West Coast for nonwhite migrants from the states used in this study. Its influence is largely restricted to the ring of states west of the Mississippi and north of the Ohio Rivers. In those states north of the Ohio River the attraction of the West Coast declines going eastward from 22.3 percent in Illinois to 4.6 percent in Pennsylvania. Los Angeles and San Francisco seem to act like opposing magnets to the influence of New York and other northeastern cities, as the attractive power of one increases the other decreases. The West Coast attraction is proportionately strongest in Illinois and the states on the western side of the Mississippi River.

The Northcentral cities receive the greatest percentage of migrants from the states used in this study. This migration system has a north-south axis. This area's attractive power is greatest within the region itself and in those states directly south—Kentucky, Tennessee, Mississippi, and Alabama. The flows from the states of Illinois and West Virginia are almost equally divided among the Northcentral focus and the West Coast and Northeast Coast respectively. Chicago is the major receiving city in the Northcentral group; other important cities include Detroit and Cleveland.

Of the four areas, the South Coast receives the lowest percentage of nonwhite migrants, and its influence is limited to some of the states within the region itself. Cities in this region are largely local in influence. Houston, for example, is important for both Texas and Louisiana; Miami is a focus for Florida and Georgia.

REGION*	ALA-BAMA (%)	AR-KAN-SAS (%)	FLOR-IDA (%)	GEOR-GIA (%)	ILLI-NOIS (%)	INDI-ANA (%)	KEN-TUCKY (%)
West Coast	6.8	21.7	0.0	0.0	22.3	10.2	0.0
Northcentral	27.5	19.3	0.0	4.2	21.8	37.0	38.0
Northeast Coast	7.2	0.0	10.5	9.9	3.8	0.0	0.0
South Coast	19.1	0.0	44.1	39.6	0.0	0.0	0.0
Other (local— within state and not covered by other definitions)	0.0	11.7	0.0	0.0	3.8	5.3	13.2

	LOUI-SIANA	MARY-LAND	MICH-IGAN	MIS-SIS-SIPPI	MIS-SOURI	N. CARO-LINA	OHIO
West Coast	29.4	0.0	16.9	7.7	21.8	0.0	10.1
Northcentral	0.0	0.0	25.2	32.9	16.7	0.0	35.9
Northeast Coast	0.0	51.1	5.1	0.0	0.0	56.6	5.0
South Coast	33.3	0.0	0.0	0.0	0.0	0.0	0.0
Other (as above)	0.0	0.0	2.8	10.9	12.5	0.0	0.0

	OKLA-HOMA	PENN-SYL-VANIA	S. CARO-LINA	TEN-NES-SEE	TEXAS	VIR-GINIA	W. VIR-GINIA
West Coast	18.9	4.6	0.0	8.5	17.7	0.0	0.0
Northcentral	0.0	9.5	0.0	23.4	0.0	0.0	21.5
Northeast Coast	0.0	32.1	44.6	0.0	0.0	45.2	21.1
South Coast	0.0	0.0	0.0	0.0	18.0	0.0	0.0
Other (as above)	39.5	4.1	8.5	18.1	15.3	10.5	8.3

Table 3.3: Cities in Median Migration Fields of Selected States Grouped by Regional Location.

* Regions used are defined as follows: West Coast—Los Angeles and San Francisco; North-central—Chicago, Detroit, Dayton, Columbus, Akron, Cleveland, Gary, Pittsburgh, Indianapolis, and Cincinnati; Northeast Coast—New York, Philadelphia, Washington, D.C., Newark, and Baltimore; South Coast—Houston, New Orleans, Mobile, Birmingham, Atlanta, Miami, Tampa, Orlando, Jacksonville, and Ft. Lauderdale.

The major findings of this analysis are as follows: (1) the influence of the Northeast Coast cities is greatest along the Atlantic seaboard and is present, but weaker, westward across the northern tier of the states; (2) the Northcentral cities exert their influence locally and in those southern states on the eastern shore of the Mississippi River; (3) Illinois and the states on the west shore of the Mississippi are primarily oriented toward the West Coast;

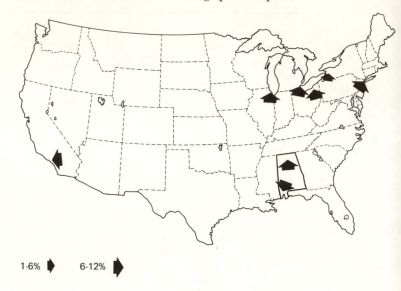

1-6% ▶   6-12% ▶

Figure 3.7   Black Migration from Alabama, 1950–1960.

(4) the influence of the cities along the South Coast is largely limited to the states bordering the Gulf of Mexico; (5) St. Louis and Memphis are important local destinations. Thus, there seems to be definite regional migration systems in the pattern of nonwhite movement in the states studied.

The Figures 3.7 through 3.13 illustrate the regional orientation of the black migration patterns. The northward trend of black migrants from Alabama and Mississippi to Chicago and Detroit is shown in Figures 3.7 and 3.8. Figures 3.9 and 3.10 indicate the tendency of Blacks from the Southeast to move up the coast to New York, Boston, and other eastern cities. Black migrants from Louisiana, however, move westward to California cities (see Figure 3.11). Figures 3.12 and 3.13 are interesting because they show that nearby Chicago and much more distant Los Angeles both exert a pulling effect on Blacks from Arkansas and Missouri.

CENTRAL CITY CONCENTRATIONS

As with the national pattern of black migration, the significant fact about the urban black population is not numbers but location. Blacks are contained— in both a spatial and a social sense—in the central cities of America. The number of Blacks in the cities increased more than eight times from 1900 to 1970. In 1960 more than 50 percent of the black population lived in census tracts in which the population was at least 90 percent Black. Figure 3.14 indicates that the concentration of Blacks in central cities has increased since 1900 and has been accompanied by a consequent decentralization of white population.

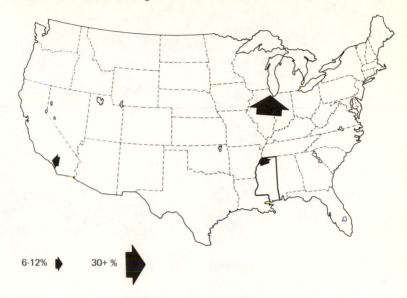

Figure 3.8 Black Migration from Mississippi, 1950–1960.

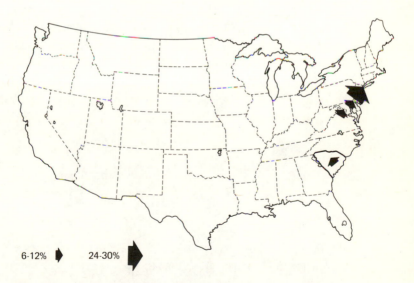

Figure 3.9 Black Migration from South Carolina, 1950–1960.

This is true for all but those SMSA's of less than 100,000 in which both Whites and Blacks are concentrating in the central parts of the cities. Over 5.5 million Blacks, or 86 percent of the increase in black population from 1950 to 1960, are located in the central cities. The larger the urban area, the greater the proportion of Blacks living in the central cities. In 1960, 71.7 percent of all nonwhite families, 2,481,000, were contained in the poverty areas in 100 of

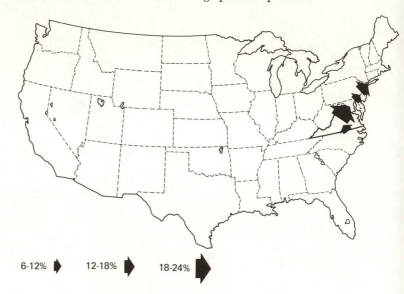

Figure 3.10   Black Migration from Virginia, 1950–1960.

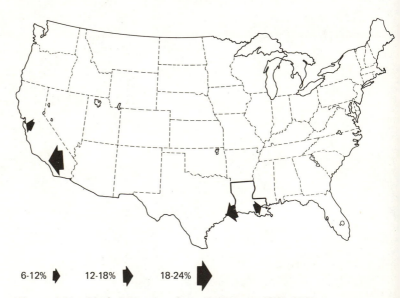

Figure 3.11   Black Migration from Louisiana, 1950–1960.

the 101 SMSA's of over 250,000 total population. These trends continued in the decade 1960 to 1970. Black population increase since 1960 has been almost completely within the central cities; 82.5 percent of the 4-million increase in metropolitan black population occurred in the central cities. This contrasted with the continued white exodus to the suburbs during the same period.

In those northern, western, and southern cities in which there was a net

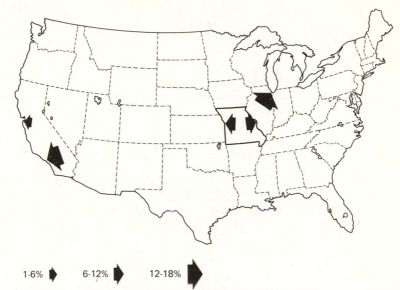

Figure 3.12   Black Migration from Missouri, 1950–1960.

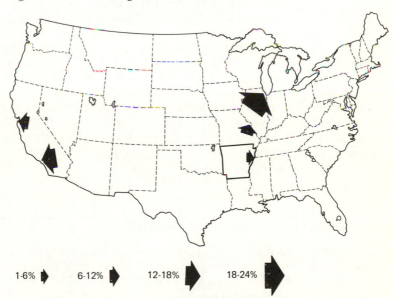

Figure 3.13   Black Migration from Arkansas, 1950–1960.

increase of black migrants from 1960 to 1970, there was a corresponding increase in the net black migration into the central city, with a consequent out-migration of Whites from the central city to the suburbs (see Table 3.4). New Orleans, Birmingham, and Jackson, however, are examples of cities losing black population through migration; in these cities Blacks as well as Whites are leaving the central city (see Table 3.4).

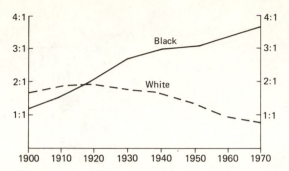

Figure 3.14 Ratio of Central City to Outside Central City Population, Black and White, 1900 to 1970.

(From various publications of the Bureau of the Census.)

During the decade from 1960 to 1970 the racial pattern of Washington, D.C., went through some changes that are typical of many other cities. In 1960 the racial pattern in metropolitan Washington was that of a "white doughnut"; that is, there was a heavily black-populated central city surrounded by a ring of white suburbs which in turn was encircled by higher concentrations of Blacks in areas composed of farm communities and small towns that are remnants of the old plantation pattern. During the decade from 1960 to 1970 the black inner-ring expanded into the adjacent white suburbs; this caused the white suburban ring to move further out into the country.

Blacks are less concentrated in the central cities of the South than they are in the North and West. Forty percent of the southern black population lived in central cities in 1970; whereas in the rest of the country, the proportion was in excess of 66 percent.

A CASE STUDY OF BLACK MIGRATION*

The following brief case study is not meant to be a study of an average or typical black man, nor on the other hand, do we believe it to be rare or unique. It points out some of the many important problems and principles involved in the migration of black Americans.

If it is true that Bessie's mother was an immigrant, this short narrative captures parts of most of the major migrations of black Americans. Not only do we see a great deal of movement in space, but we also see reflections of the overall economic activity of the country. Born in an agrarian era where he worked as a farm boy and before moving on to the mining scene, James Mills

* Based on an interview with James Mills at his home in River Rouge, Michigan, on June 15, 1970.

REGION, BY CITY	NET MIGRATION	INSIDE CENTRAL CITY black	white
North			
Chicago	16.2	13.5	−23.8
Philadelphia	9.9	7.4	−16.8
Detroit	19.3	20.0	−32.7
Washington, D.C.	23.0	9.2	−40.1
Newark	32.4	22.6	−40.1
West Coast			
Seattle	33.2	21.1	−11.4
San Francisco– Oakland	38.2	28.7	−17.7
Los Angeles– Long Beach	47	29.6	− 2.8
South			
Atlanta	16.6	17.5	−27.4
Louisville	10.5	9.9	−24.4
New Orleans	− 3.0	− 4.5	−23.3
Birmingham	−16.3	−17.0	−25.2
Jackson	−12.3	− 6.9	−11.8

Table 3.4: Rates of Black Migration, 1960 to 1970, by SMSA for Selected Cities.

Source: *1970 Census of Population and Housing, General Demographic Trends for Metropolitan Areas, 1960–1970.*

became involved in the initial stages of the great industrial revolution in the United States. After that he moved to Birmingham, where he worked in an iron foundry, another developmental area of the industrial revolution. Finally, Mr. Mills migrated to Detroit where he participated in the most glamorous phase of the industrial revolution, the mass production of the automobile.

Sometime early in the nineteenth century, probably between 1806 and 1810, a young Irishman by the name of Barry McClanahan moved to Hillsdale, Alabama, in Shelby County and staked out a claim. As soon as he was able to, some five or seven years later in 1815, he began to purchase slaves. He became a planter, and as his fortune increased, so did his holdings and his slaves. At some point prior to 1820 he became the owner of a female slave from the Gold Coast who was called Bessie. Bessie bore six children between the years of 1820 and 1830, one of whom was John Mills. When the Emancipation Proclamation became official, Barry McClanahan divided his holdings of nearly 1,000 acres equally among Bessie's six children. This leads to the assumption that the six children may have been his. To support this conclusion, even though Bessie and her children were legally slaves, it appears that they were never subjected to the kind of treatment that was common for the other slaves on the McClanahan plantation. The boys at worst were overseers, and the girls worked in and around the big house. John's share of the holdings was 166 acres. Most of the six children (including John) remained on the plantation. Two brothers, Jim and Sam, went to Birmingham in the late 1860s seeking work.

Before John was emancipated he took a wife who was called Willie. She bore him two sons and two daughters, the youngest of whom was James Mills, born March 16, 1880. As a boy, Jim helped his father to work cotton (the staple crop) which provided an adequate livelihood. But in the late 1890s (about 1898), Jim sought elsewhere for more lucrative employment. He went to a small mining town some 7 miles away, where he found employment in an iron ore mine. He worked there for several years making a much better salary. A couple of years later in 1900, he tired of the dark, damp, dismal, back-breaking assignment. He moved to Birmingham where he worked in an iron foundry. This was even better than the second job which had been better than his first job as a farmer. Life was exciting in the big city, and the pay was good. But, after eight years, he decided to return to the farm and help his aging parents meet their obligations.

During the summer of 1916, a friend of Jim's who went to Detroit, Michigan for the summer found the weather most pleasant. In fact, he was so enchanted by the total atmosphere that he invited Jim to join him. He assured Jim that the weather was fine and that there was little difference between the climates in Detroit and Hillsdale, Alabama. By now Jim had satisfied what he thought had been his responsibility to his parents and was prepared to make another move. At the age of 37, even though World War I was inching along, he had little worry about the draft. At 37, he was, of course, considered among the lesser desirables as far as military service was concerned. So in February, 1917, Jim prepared to make his journey to Detroit. His friend had promised that he would be able to find Jim a job and "put him up" until he could "get his feet on the ground." Unfortunately, when Jim arrived he neither found his friend nor the warm weather which he expected.

He said that he discovered the weather to be the coldest and the hardest he had ever known. In fact, he candidly said, "I didn't realize it could even get that cold." He finally located a place to live, but failed to find his friend, which meant that he was forced to look for work on his own.

Naturally, he was not too particular about the nature of the work as long as it paid wages. His first job was as a laborer in a foundry doing the same type of work that he had done in Alabama. He later managed to move to the Ford Motor Company where he remained from 1919 to 1949, when he retired.

After the end of World War I, there was an industrial surge that brought hordes of Black people into the industrial cities of the North, such as Chicago and Detroit. In Detroit, as in other areas, there were problems of housing. The big question was, where would the black man live? The Ford plants were located in Dearborn, and the citizens of this tiny community were totally unwilling to accept Blacks. Henry Ford was either helpless or unwilling to face the issue. Finally, as an alternative, Ford bought property in a small town called Inkster, where he rented, sublet, and sold to Blacks. At the same time he attempted to settle some Blacks in a small community called River Rouge, which was the site of the foundries and the place where a large number of Blacks were employed. It was largely an agricultural area, and the people refused to sell. They were unwilling to allow black people to live in their "lily white" River Rouge. In subsequent decades the attitude and other conditions changed, because James Mills lives there now.

This short narrative points out three major patterns common to black migration. First, black migration from the rural South to the urban North follows an hierarchy of movement, first to nearby small towns, then to larger cities within the South, and finally to the large cities of the North. Second, there is the tie to home and family that often keeps the migrants moving back to the South for brief periods. Finally, Mr. Mill's decision to move to Detroit was made easier by a friend who offered to "put him up" and help him find a job; but as often happens, these good intentions did not work out.

SELECTED BIBLIOGRAPHY

1. Bond, Horace M.: "Negro Education in Alabama," New York, Atheneum, 1969.
2. Dubois, W. E. B.: The Negroes of Farmville, Virginia: A Social Study, U.S. Labor Bulletin, vol. 3, no. 14, January, 1898.
3. Katzman, Martin T.: Ethnic Geography and Regional Economics, 1880–1960, Economic Geography, vol. 45, pp. 45–52, January, 1969.
4. Kennedy, Louise Venable: "The Negro Peasant Turns Cityward," New York, Columbia University Press, 1930.
5. Kiser, Clyde: "Sea Island to City," New York, Atheneum, 1969.
6. Meier, August and Elliott Rudwick: "From Plantation to Ghetto," New York, Hill and Wang, 1966.
7. "Report of the National Advisory Commission on Civil Disorders," New York, Bantam Books, 1968.
8. Rubins, Morton: Migration Patterns of Negroes from a Rural Northeastern Mississipi Community, Social Forces, vol. 39, pp. 59–66, October, 1960.
9. Smith, William: "A Political History of Slavery," New York, F. Ungar Publishing Company, 1966.
10. Starobin, Robert: "Industrial Slavery in the Old South," Oxford, Oxford University Press, 1970.
11. U.S. Department of Commerce, Bureau of the Census: 1930 Census of Population.
12. U.S. Bureau of the Census: Current Population Reports Series p. 23, no. 42, 1972.
13. "Urban and Rural America: Policies for Future Growth," Advisory Commission on Intergovernmental Relations, Washington, D.C., April, 1968.
14. Wade, Richard C.: "Slavery in the Cities," New York, Oxford University Press, 1964.
15. Walls, Dwayne E.: "The Chickenbone Special," New York, Harcourt Brace Jovanovich, Inc., 1971.
16. Webber, Melvin M., "Cultural Territoriality and the Elastic Mile," Papers of the Regional Science Association, Vol. 13, 1964, pp. 59–69.

Courtesy of The Negro Almanac.

4 Post-Civil War Black Migration: Part Two

BLACK MIGRATION CONTROLS

Obviously there are numerous reasons behind the movement of large numbers of people over a long span of time. It is difficult to make an inclusive list of all the causes for the migration of such a group, but some major reasons can be outlined. In general, we can identify "pull" factors in the North, more specifically the urban North, and "push" factors in the rural South, as these are respectively the points of destination and origin for the vast majority of black migrants leaving the fields for the factories.

Some authors stress racism as a factor separate from economic conditions, social conditions, mechanization, etc. This isolation is inaccurate since racism is an integral part of all these factors. Racism will thus be dealt with as an element in each of the push-pull factors or conditions.

Black migration during the 100 years following the Civil War nationalized a southern "problem." Before the war, the question was how to free Blacks from the violence of the southern slaveholders; after the war, the question became how to free Blacks from the discrimination and violence of white society, nationwide. Historically, the simplest resolution of problems of socioeconomic deprivation and intolerance has been migration, more often than not to urban places. But this sociospatial process has been delayed, if not altogether blocked, for Blacks in the United States. Since 1865, the relative economic well-being of Negro tenants, sharecroppers, and independent farmers has declined. The effects of the economic and social controls have been twofold: to keep the Black person in his place or to force him to flee.

Several push factors, singly or in combination, provide the impetus for black out-migration from the rural South. But it must, also, be remembered that the individual migrant may have been influenced by additional personal factors that do not lend themselves to categorization.

The general factors may be grouped into economic and social classes. The economic causes of out-migration include the mechanization of agriculture, general economic depression, reduction of cotton acreage, the depredation of the boll weevil and floods, and discriminatory agricultural programs.

Economic "Push" Factors

MECHANIZATION OF AGRICULTURE

Technical innovations in agriculture were a major cause for the poor economic condition of southern Blacks, which subsequently led to massive out-migration. Traditionally southern cotton growers had relied on manual labor. Laborers, both wage hands and resident sharecroppers, were prevalent and did not demand high, or even moderate, wages.

The nature of the cotton plant made hand labor particularly useful. The plant is delicate and very susceptible to injury. It requires a long growing season, thus promoting the growth of weeds which need to be removed by hand. Also, the rolling land of much of the Southeast did not lend itself to the use of mechanized production as readily as the more level land of the Southwest.

Technical innovations were adopted by southern agriculture slowly. Up to the 1940s mechanization had not been important. The mechanical cotton picker, for example, became available in 1943. For a long time the low level of mechanization required a dependence on cheap labor, which, so long as available, made mechanization unprofitable. The growers were reluctant to introduce tractors because they felt that such a policy would not only alienate the portion of their labor that drove the mules but reduce the earnings of the labor forces sufficiently to drive them to seek employment in towns or in the North, thus leaving the grower without the labor needed to pick and weed the cotton. It seems that the fears of the planters were at least partly correct in that increased mechanization did drive black tenants away from the fields.

Increased use of weed killers, tractors, and mechanical cotton pickers greatly reduced the need for the black laborer. "In 1958, 27% of the Mississippi Delta cotton crop was harvested by mechanical cotton pickers. Six years later, in 1964, this had increased to 81%" (Dillingham and Sly, 1966). This mechanization has affected Blacks more than Whites, as they were more dependent on the cash-crop, cotton plantation economy.

Race prejudice also plays a role in the handling of machines. Operating machinery has been traditionally a "white man's job"; this is true even though Blacks have shown the necessary skill. Only a small fraction of the machines were run by black operators on southern farms.

Crop diversification programs became more popular in the South after the severe losses to the cotton crops brought on by the boll weevil and floods between 1910 and 1920. Although seen as an economic boon to the South in general, this diversification was an added factor forcing Blacks off the land. The racism of the South had largely "contained" Blacks as laborers in the cotton fields, allowing them little knowledge of other kinds of agriculture. White Alabama farmers, for example, were given training and financing to allow them to switch to livestock, poultry, and soy beans. Not receiving this aid, a disproportionate share of small, independent black farmers were left with uneconomical cotton farms. Thus, in 1968 it is assumed that as many as 80 percent of Alabama's black farmers still farmed small plots of cotton, compared to probably 30 percent of the state's white farmers. Whites probably owned four times as much poultry and livestock as did Blacks.

NATURAL DISASTERS

Natural disasters in the forms of the invasion of the boll weevil in 1892 and 1915 to 1916 and floods in 1915 and 1916 also played a role in pushing Blacks to the North. The boll weevil greatly damaged the cotton crops of 1915 to 1916 in Mississippi, Louisiana, Alabama, Georgia, and Florida. Unusually high flooding during the summer of 1915 affected many of the same areas hit by the boll weevil. *The Montgomery Advertiser* said, "The Negro is going because he is the most unfortunate of the victims of the combined disaster this year of the flood and the boll weevil."

The destruction caused by the weevil spread from west to east, passing the Mississippi River about 1910. As the insect moved eastward, the areas previously affected began to recover. Thus, by 1929 the four southwestern states of Texas, Arkansas, Louisiana, and Oklahoma accounted for nearly 50 percent of the national cotton output. This also helped to push Blacks off the land, as the cotton farming improved in those areas which were more mechanized and the planters were less dependent on black labor in the Southwest than they were in the Southeast.

Because of the intervention of the National Guard and the Red Cross, the floods along the Mississippi River did not cause the migration of as many Blacks as otherwise might have occurred. The Red Cross set up temporary holding camps to house the field hands for those planters whose land was flooded. These Blacks could not leave the camps without passes, and the National Guard was used to hold them prisoner.

REDUCTION OF COTTON ACREAGE

The federal government's reduction of the cotton acreage was an additional impetus to black migration. This occurred twice, once in the 1930s and again in 1953. In the latter year the federal government instituted programs resulting in a 40 percent reduction of cotton acreage.

As in other federal efforts, racism was apparent in carrying out these programs. On the surface the soil bank, soil conservation, and restricted cotton acreage programs of the Agriculture Adjustment Administration of the 1930s would not appear to be racist. But such programs had to be carried out within the context of the social relations of the South; the result was discrimination against black field hands and farmers. "A government research team found in 1936 that landlords had received an average of $822 per plantation, compared with $108 per plantation for *all* the tenants put together." The result of the AAA program was a subsidization of the planters. Kester has gone so far as to say, "Indeed it is doubtful if the Civil War actually produced more human suffering and pauperized more individuals in proportion to the population that the AAA has done in its few years of existence" (Kester, 1969).

In the "plow up" program of 1933 cotton producers agreed to plow under between 25 to 50 percent of their acreage for which they were to receive a rental of approximately $11 per acre. The following year the reduction program went into effect. The government rented the land that was retired, giving the money directly to the planter.

The local administration of the AAA programs was under the control or influence of the planters. As is clear from Section 7 of the Cotton Acreage Reduction Contract, even though the tenants were supposed to have rights, these rights were under the jurisdiction of the white landowners. The language of the contract (below) left the laborers powerless.

> The producer shall endeavor in good faith to bring about the reduction of acreage contemplated in this contract in such a manner as to cause the least possible amount of labor, economic, and social disturbance, and to this end, insofar as possible, he shall effect the acreage reduction as nearly ratable as practicable among the tenants on this farm; shall, insofar as possible, maintain on this farm the normal number of tenants and other employees; shall permit all tenants to continue in the occupancy of their houses on this farm, rent free for the years 1934 and 1935 (unless any such tenants shall so conduct himself as to become a nuisance or a menace to the welfare of the producer); during such years shall afford such tenants or employees, without cost, access for fuel to such woods land belonging to this farm as he may designate; shall permit such tenants the use of an adequate portion of the rented acres to grow food and feed crops for home consumption and for pasturage of domestically used livestock; and for such of the rented acres shall permit the reasonable use of work animals and equipment in exchange for labor (Kester, 1969).

The decision as to tenant or wage laborer status was up to the producer, and he gained by reducing the status of tenants to wage laborers, reducing the income of the laborers at the same time increasing that of the planter. Table 4.1 indicates that the planters received not only a greater income from AAA payments but a larger percentage of their yearly income came from the federal government.

One need only understand one point to see how a program, even if originally established to benefit both Black and White, planter and laborer, resulted in discrimination against the black laborer. This point has been made by Myrdal in his discussion of the allotments and benefit payments from the administrators of the AAA. "The accuracy of the records and calculations depends on the good-will, conscientiousness, and competence of those in charge of the local control" (Myrdal, 1944). The result was that the programs were fitted into the local fabric of racial injustice.

With time rural poverty has become institutionalized. "The poorest 10 percent of the nation's cotton farmers received only 1 percent of the federal benefits, while the richest 10 percent were paid 50 percent of the cotton benefits.

| | 1934 | | | 1937 | | |
	Net cash	AAA payment	% AAA of net cash	Net cash	AAA payment	% AAA of net cash
Planter	$2,528	979	38.7	$3,590	833	23.3
Tenant	263	11	4.2	300	27	9.0

Table 4.1   Net Cash Incomes of Planters and Tenants on 246 Southern Plantations in 1934 and 1937, and Proportion Coming from AAA Payments.

From: *W. C. Holley, Ellen Winston, T. J. Woofter, Jr., The Plantation South, 1934–1937.* Freeport, L.I., N.Y., Books for Libraries, 1971, reprint of 1940 ed.

| | 1961 | 1963 | | | | 1964 | | |
Region	Lower 10% of farm- ers	Upper 10%	Upper 1%	Lower 10%	Upper 10%	Upper 1%	Lower 10%	Upper 10%	Upper 1%
Southeast	2.6	34	4.6	1.9	47	14	1.9	47	14
Delta	1.4	44	6.4	1.2	58	21	1.2	58	21

Table 4.2   Distribution of Upland Cotton Price-Support Benefits, 1961, 1963, 1964, by Percentile, by Region.

From: *"The Distribution of Benefits from Selected U.S. Farm Programs," by James T. Bonnen, in Rural Poverty in the United States, Tables 16, 17, 18, pp. 484–486.*

In 1959 the highest average level of living index for Negro farmers in any of the 14 states studied by the U.S. Civil Rights Commission was lower than the lowest state average level of living index of white farmers" (Good, 1968a).

The facts shown in Table 4.2 are similar to those in Table 4.1 from 30 years earlier.

It is obvious from Table 4.2 that the richest cotton farmers continue to receive a greatly disproportionate share of the federal subsidies. In fact, while the richer farmers have increased their share from 1961 to 1963/1964, the shares of the poorest farmers decreased. Proportionately more black farmers are in the lowest level of farming. Only 44,000, or 17 percent, of the black farmers earned more than $2,500 per year in 1960.

DISCRIMINATORY AGRICULTURAL PROGRAMS

The U.S. Commission on Civil Rights found, in 1965, that the four major federal farm programs [ASCS (Agricultural Stabilization and Conservation Service), Farmers Home Administration, Federal Extension Service, and the Soil Conservation Service] were guilty of not providing equal opportunity and treatment to black farmers. The Commission found no significant improvement when it went back to Alabama in 1968.

	Regular county committeemen	Regular community committeemen	Alternate county committeemen	Alternate community committeemen
Totals	4,150	26,400	2,648	17,600
Black	1	116	8	380

Table 4.3   ASCS Committeemen in Fourteen Southern States, Totals and Black, 1968.
Data from Civil Rights Digest, spring, 1969, p. 26.

The programs of the ASCS include cotton diversion and allocation of federal funds. As in the earlier programs the allocation of these funds and the benefits of the programs are put into the hands of local committees, with the expected results for Blacks.

A white man and a Negro were farming the same crop, cotton, side by side. The Negro had 100 acres, the white man 50. The county committee took 80 of the Negro's acres out of production but let the white farmer produce on all 50 (Ray, 1963).

This county committee system began in 1933. Research in 1967 by the National Sharecropper's Fund showed fifty-eight southern counties in which Blacks outnumbered Whites and 320 counties in which black farmers comprised 20 percent or more of the farm operators; yet, as of April, 1968, not a single Black was serving on a single county committee in the entire South. In September, 1968, an historic first occurred; Mr. Otis Pinkard became the first Black man to ever serve on a county ASCS committee in the South. There are about 4,150 such county committeemen. Progress for Blacks is measured in small degrees.

In 1965 the Department of Agriculture was taken to court to prevent the rerunning of the 1965 election of ASCS committeemen in Lowndes County, Alabama, as well as the planned 1966 county elections. Black farmers won a month's delay of the election. The time was to be used to explain the importance of ASCS and the local elections to their neighbors. This is an important situation because, as in most civil rights problems, Blacks not only had to bring suit to obtain rights set forth in the first place, but they then had to take over functions of the federal government which it was either unwilling or unable to undertake. Under the law tenants are not to be put off the land in order that it may be retired from cotton, and they are to receive a share of the subsidy paid by the government. Yet in practice neither of these measures is carried out.

Mr. Charlie White, a black tenant farmer in Panola, Sumter County, Alabama, went to "the Man" to see about getting his ASCS check. Instead of a check, he got an eviction notice. The following letter sent to Mr. White is representative of the type received by many farmers. Notice that it is addressed, in keeping with white racial etiquette, to Charlie and not to Mr. White.

Nov. 25, 1966

Charlie White
Route 2, Box 80
Panola, Alabama

Charlie:

This letter is to advise you that the land which you have been renting from me for the past several years will no longer be available to you for rent. I have rented this land to _____ Paper Co. and they are going to grow timber on the lands.

This is to give you notice that you will not be able to have the acreage formerly cultivated by you for the years 1967 and thereafter, and you can make arrangements to get acreage elsewhere.

If you wish to live in the house which you have occupied you can continue to do so for a monthly rental of $15. The first rent payment will be due on or before the 5th day of January, 1967.

Under my contract with the paper company, you will not be able to have a garden or any cultivable land, or have any pasture or run any livestock, nor will you be able to cut any wood from the woods.

This is to advise you that if you do not wish to rent the house, then you must immediately make your arrangements to vacate the property before January 1, 1967, when the _____ Paper Co. will take charge of the property.

Yours very truly,
Mrs. Deborah Calhoun

The payment of soil diversion checks by the government has guaranteed the planter collection of the debts of his tenants. Eviction is not uncommon. The White family and twenty-three other families were evicted from their Alabama plots in 1966. The reason given was that it was more profitable to put cotton land into other crops. The reason not given was that Mr. White and the others had voted.

The Federal Extension Service is supposed to offer programs ranging from 4-H programs and homemaking to crop counseling, soil testing, and insect control information. Yet this type of service does not reach black farmers. Extension agents work according to the custom of segregation; thus, there are fewer black extension agents to serve a larger proportion of black farmers. When asked why his office had never named a Black to a county extension chairmanship, Dr. Fred R. Robertson, Director of the Alabama State Extension Service, replied that it is a basically sound idea to stay with the power structure in order to keep the communications going and the rent coming. But he has "no built in prejudice against having a Negro chairman if he is qualified." But the prevailing power structure Dr. Robertson was so intent upon pleasing has by its very nature a built-in prejudice against Blacks.

The Farm Home Administration is another agency in the Department of Agriculture that is supposed to help the rural poor without regard to race. But there has been discrimination in the loans given out by the agency. Blacks received smaller loans, both absolutely and in relation to their net worth, than did their white counterparts. This agency has a heritage of racism that deters Blacks from applying for loans. Its committee structure and functioning is similar to that of the ASCS, that is, virtually all-white. The regulations set up by the agency are such that those most in need of help cannot receive it. The one program under its administration that seemed to reach the poor—Self-Help Housing—has apparently been abandoned.

Another important, yet often overlooked, factor in the economic geography of the rural South is the road network. Again the black farmer is at a disadvantage. He has been more isolated than the white farmer. In 1959, for example, 43 percent of all nonwhite farmers selling a minimum of $2,500 per year were still located on dirt roads compared to 28 percent of white farmers. This disparity was even greater for smaller farmers.

In an attempt to fight the discrimination of the federal agricultural programs, black farmers in parts of the South have formed agricultural cooperatives. In 1966, approximately 700 small black farmers from ten counties in Alabama formed the Southwest Alabama Farmers Co-operative Associations (SWAFCA). This is one of a number of cooperative movements which have tried to make agriculture work for Blacks in the rural South. In 1969 there were at least forty poor people's cooperatives with about 15,000 people, almost all-black. Some of these cooperatives were:

1. SWAFCA
2. Grand Marie Vegetable Growers Association
3. Poor People's Corporation
4. Mid-South Consumers Oil Corporation
5. Southern Consumers Co-op
6. "Cut-and-Sew" Co-ops
7. Grenola Citizens Federal Credit Union

Ulmer sets out nine basic needs which the cooperatives are trying to meet. These are: "(1) more money; (2) decent housing; (3) land for farms, industry, and recreation; (4) adequate food; (5) education, or the chance for self-development; (6) political and economic power; (7) adequate circumstances to keep young people from leaving the rural areas; (8) strong, organized communities; (9) a measure of security in terms of such things as insurance against bad health, unemployment, and death" (Ulmer, 1969).

But the black cooperative movement has many very difficult problems to overcome. Some of these are internal. Some, which seem to be endemic to small businesses in a big business economy, include insufficient operating funds and development capital. Lack of previous business experience has led to poor management and accounting practices and conservative leadership.

Other problems come from outside of the cooperative. Harassment from local officials and complacency on the part of federal agents hinder its work. There is a curious white attitude reflected here; white officials preach that Blacks are incapable of taking care of themselves, yet when they attempt to do so, the same officials become indignant. SWAFCA, for example, received an OEO grant of nearly $400,000 which was vetoed by Governor Wallace. Sargent Shriver, then head of OEO, waited until July to override the veto. Later, this cooperative was served with an injunction that would have stopped its business. Also, the white county extension agent was curiously ignorant of the operations of SWAFCA. The Mid-South Consumers Oil Co-op had to survive a "gas war" to maintain its business.

There had been a rural cooperative earlier in Alabama. During the late 1930s the Gee's Bend Co-op was organized by regional officials of the Farm Security Administration. This seems to have been a relatively prosperous operation with a cotton gin, general merchandise store, community center, school, and health center. But this cooperative was organized from without and managed by a white man.

Many have argued that it is economically unfeasible for the government to help these cooperatives; but as Paul Good has written, "the average poor black person's life in the rural South is *not feasible*" (Good, 1968a). Many also argue that it is wrong for the federal government to pay the way of black farmers, whereas federal payments to rich Whites are seen as subsidies, not as welfare. In 1967 45 percent, some $90 million, of the government money spent in Alabama went into price subsidies and soil diversion checks. The federal government also pays the salaries of the FHA, the ASCS, and 40 percent of the Federal Extension Service employees, who are virtually all white.

In conclusion, the main difference between black conditions in the rural South in 1910 and in 1970 is that the shacks and the people have become 60 years older and a new generation has entered the poverty cycle. One of the problems with an extended discussion of these problems is that a certain degree of impersonalization becomes evident. The human being becomes a percentile, but ultimately these statistics and programs are reduced to the day-to-day struggles of real men, women, and children.

> The lone witness was Peter Agee, a sweet-faced, slight Negro farmer and sculptor, aged 50. A nominee for election to his community Agricultural Stabilization and Conservation Service committee, he told the court how a white member of the county ASCS committee had offered to give him ten acres of "the best land" and to show him how to get a loan to buy cows if he would "jump out" of the race.
>
> A white man that he was raised with, he said, came to see him when he wasn't home. "If he comes back," he told his sister, "tell

him I ain't here." And he went away. When he approached his home again later in the evening, "the white man was sitting on the porch. So I dodged him."

"But I thought you said you didn't know him," Assistant U.S. Attorney Gil Zimmerman questioned.

"Sure I knew him. I was raised with him. I didn't know he was on the committee."

"Then why did you dodge him?"

In the entire courtroom probably only the man who asked the question doesn't know the answer.

"Because if you see a white man sitting on your porch, you don't know what he has in mind."

Under searching and persistent cross-examination, Mr. Agee, clasping and unclasping his hands, repeats the details again and again, with the patience of a good grandfather.

"Now listen carefully, I want you to understand this. . . . Let me explain it to you good. . . . You have to understand me because my life is mixed up in this."

In the cool and decorous courthouse down the hill from the Capitol, the implications of the last remark are all but lost. But when Negro farmer Peter Agee returned to the green hills and red earth of lovely Marengo County the next Saturday, a group of white men drove by his store and fired shots into the air. Agee fled the state without telling folks where he was going. He has since returned (Wasserman, 1967).

Social "Push" Factors

SOUTHERN JUSTICE

From the black point of view southern justice has meant lawlessness and disorder. For the black person living in the South, laws have been white made and white enforced. The internal social controls that may exist within the black community are only vaguely related to the system of law used by the surrounding white community. It is important to note that even though extralegal activity by whites—such as lynching and other forms of terrorism—were significant factors in causing Blacks to move North, white laws and their enforcement have been causes of equal weight.

In the communities that he studied, Johnson found the courts to be outside the scheme of life for Blacks.

> Instead of providing security as the arbitrator of personal differences, the courts are an institution to be feared, a medium through which justice is to be secured only by recourse to some individual white protector (Johnson, 1934).

This keeps the black person in a continual state of impotence with respect to the achievement of justice; what justice he is able to obtain is at the hands of

Whites to whom he is then beholden. In effect, local Whites act as mediators between Blacks and the courts; the roles of the courts and the local Whites become reversed from what is normally expected. Law represents white domination throughout the process of justice—from the police to the courts. Lewis found the same type of conditions in the black community that he studied. Differential treatment, brutality, and lack of respect as an individual have been hazards of being Black in the South.

This type of treatment has been given as a significant cause for black migration. It is important to note here that both individual and institutional legal racism under the guise of law are involved. It is not only the white individuals *qua* policeman and judge but the legal structures themselves that are racist.

In 1964 in the 289 county prosecutor's offices in the southern and border states there were only seven black lawyers. In the same year there were no black judges in the southern or border states. In 1961 a survey by the U.S. Commission in Civil Rights in seventeen Black Belt counties found that "the only service rendered by Negroes in the courts of justice is janitorial" (Knowles and Prewitt, 1969).

There are many ways that Blacks have been kept off juries in the South. In some states jurors may have no criminal record, must own taxable property, and must pass literacy tests. Blacks may be summoned for service but never put on the panel. Also, there is often agreement among counselors that any Blacks on the panel will be removed by the use of peremptory challenges.

Four standards of justice exist in the South.

> First, where White is against White (apart from the absence of sufficient aid to the poor), there is equal protection of the law. Second, where Negro is against Negro, the common complaint is that Southern courts and police are too lenient. . . . Third, where a White commits a crime against a Negro, he will be punished lightly if at all, and the Negro complainant may expect reprisals. Fourth, where a Negro commits a crime against a White, especially an offense against the person, retribution is swift and severe (Lester, 1965).

LYNCHING AND TERRORISM

Not only have Blacks been the victims of the legal systems of the South, but they have also been murdered and lynched without recourse to any system of laws or law enforcement. For a long period in the South lynching and murder were expected white responses to any perceived black trouble. Between 1882 and 1951 there were 3,437 Blacks lynched in the United States; 92 percent of these took place in the twelve southern states. Figure 4.1 and Table 4.4 indicate that lynching was a primary reason for the period 1880 to 1905 being called the "nadir" of American black history. The press in Georgia, for example, was of the opinion that lynchings were driving Blacks out of the state. The *Atlanta Constitution* on December 10, 1916, said, "Lynching was indeed a cause behind the black exodus. . . . The heaviest migration of Negroes has been

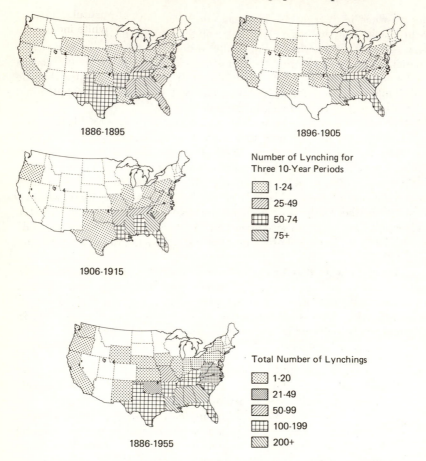

1886-1895   1896-1905

Number of Lynching for
Three 10-Year Periods

▢ 1-24
▨ 25-49
▦ 50-74
▧ 75+

1906-1915

Total Number of Lynchings

▢ 1-20
▨ 21-49
▨ 50-99
▦ 100-199
▧ 200+

1886-1955

Figure 4.1 Lynchings of Blacks in the United States for Three Ten-Year Periods.

(*From Ginsberg, Ralph, "100 Years of Lynchings," Lancer Books, New York, 1969.*)

from those counties in which there have been the worst outbreaks against Negroes."

To understand the role of lynching as a factor in pushing the Blacks out of the South, one has to realize the nature of the relationships existing among the black person, law, and terrorism. Lynching, terrorism, and "nigger-hunts" have been used as a social mechanism to keep the black person in his place. "The manhunt tradition rests on the assumption of the unlimited rights of white men and the absence of any rights on the part of the accused Negro" (Raper, 1936). Lynchings may not be pleasant, but they were seen as necessary by many "good Christian" whites to keep the Black in his place. Such was the sentiment found by Powdermaker in her study of a small southern community.

In many places it was the threat of this form of extralegal violence that acted as a social control upon the behavior of Blacks. Older Blacks could remember

State	1886 to 1895	1896 to 1905	1906 to 1915	1916 to 1925	1926 to 1935	1936 to 1945	1946 to 1955
Alabama	90	87	56	10	2	3	
Arkansas	56	76	35	10			
California	1	2					
Delaware		1					
Florida	40	56	52	11	2	7	1
Georgia	86	123	106	42	6	5	6
Illinois	3	6	6	1		1	
Indiana	3	5			2		
Iowa	1	2					
Kansas	6	5					
Kentucky	49	37	21	4			
Louisiana	17	95	69	18	1	1	1
Maryland	1						
Mississippi	37	138	91	10	6	10	4
Missouri	15	23	15	2	1	1	
Nebraska	2						
New Mexico		2					
New York	1						
N. Carolina	13	16	9	4	1	1	
Ohio	5	2	1				
Oklahoma	4	3	23	7	1		
Oregon	2	1	1				
Pennsylvania	1	1	1				
S. Carolina	38	50	26	3	2	1	1
Tennessee	67	55	29	9	1	3	
Texas	50		16	27	3	1	
Virginia	7	10	3	3			
Washington		1					
West Virginia	10	12	2	1			
Wyoming	1	1		2			

Table 4.4   A Partial Accounting of the Number of Black People Lynched in the United States from 1886 to 1955.

From: Ginsberg, Ralph. 100 Years of Lynchings. New York: Lancer Books, 1969, pp. 253–270.

lynchings, but none from recent years: "The onliest places that is uncivilized now is Georgia and Mississippi" (Lewis, 1955).

Rather than worrying primarily about attacks from outside the law, Blacks now became afraid of the legal sanctions. "Whatever can be said of his brothers in the Deep South, the Black in the mid-South and upper South is far more concerned with legal harassment and denial by established authority than he is with the illegal intimidation, reprisal, and cow-pasture bombast of

A Ku Klux Klansman in full Klan regalia. A white supremacist organization founded in 1915, the Klan's typically terrorist methods were used to
keep Blacks "in their place".

Courtesy of the Giles County Public Library, Pulaski, Tennessee.

Klansmen" (Vandiver, 1966). The implicit sanctioning of terrorist practices of
previous years has become legalized. Only a change in form occurred: illegal
lynching became, in effect, legal hanging.

Lynching in the South has not been principally an attack upon an individual
black person but rather against Blacks as a group and, as such, almost any
black person will do for the victim. Lynching is an outgrowth of the extralegal place of the Black in southern society. The use of force against Blacks
who get "uppity" is sanctioned by the general populace, the legacy of history,
and the legal structures. "Lynching is not punishment; it is racial aggression"
(Cox, 1948). Cox has pointed out that migration is an alternative response for
Blacks during a period of lynching.

FEE AND CONVICT LEASE SYSTEMS

Another facet of the southern legal system which has acted as a push factor for black migration is the combination of the fee system and the convict lease system; these were two of the most effective causes of migration. In a sense, these systems combine to form a more modern counterpart to the patrols of the slavery era. The newer vagrancy laws have been substituted for the earlier Black Codes. The fee system is the method used by local sheriffs to obtain an income. The convict lease system is the means by which local planters receive additional labor.

In the fee system, the sheriff received a certain fee for each prisoner; the greater the number of prisoners, the greater his income. In Jefferson County, Alabama, for example, in 1917 the sheriff's fee bill was $37,688.90. This was based on 30 cents a day to feed the 6,340 prisoners (73 percent of whom were black). He fed them for 10 cents a day and made a profit of $25,125.94 during the year. In 1944 this system was still in use in over half the South.

The prison road gangs reached their high point in the 1930s. The American Correctional Association said that 100,000 men were working on road gangs in 1934 to 1935. The road gang has declined through the years. As of 1972 there were five states in which they were still sanctioned: North Carolina, Virginia, Alabama, Florida, and Georgia. In these states the use of road gangs is declining. Florida used 3,000 men in 1960 and 1,500 in 1970; in the same period the drop in Georgia was from 2,400 to 800.

The following excerpts from *Georgia Nigger* by John L. Spivak illustrate the process by which convict labor was obtained in Georgia in 1930.

> There was difficulty with labor each year and each year at planting time the sheriff, placed in office by the politically influential land owner, picked up foot-loose niggers in the county who, rather than serve time on the chain gang for vagrancy, usually agreed to work off the fines the planter offered to pay (Spivak, 1969).

> When the justice of the peace solemnly imposed a fine for vagrancy on him the boy kept his eyes on the wooden floor of the court room.
>
> A white farmer approached with a grin.
>
> "I need a lit'l he'p out on my place," he said amiably, "an' I'll advance you the fine if you'll come an' work it off. Pay you twenty five dollars a month."
>
> David did not answer.
>
> "Whut say, boy?" The sheriff poked his shoulders. "Hit's a lot better'n workin' it off on de roads."
>
> "I ain' goin' tuh sign nothin'," David said sullenly.
>
> "Make him sign," the sheriff laughed.
>
> "It's against the law. This buck mus' a-worked fo' a farmer befo'!"
>
> His belly shook with laughter.

"I don't want him after the second pickin'," the planter protested.
"Tell it to him," the sheriff grinned.
"There's plenty work in this county. We kin use'm. We're short
o' convicts anyway to finish the road to Jeff Beacon's place" (Spivak,
1969).

When Spivak's book became public, the Georgia State Prison Commission
sought a federal indictment against him.

The convict lease system began after the Civil War as a means of controlling
Blacks and providing labor for local projects. It disappeared as such in the
1920s but was replaced by the work camp system of the Southeast states and
the state farm system in the Southcentral states. The camp systems, however,
were as inhuman as their predecessors. The convicts are still used to maintain
roads and other public works, as well as labor for private individuals. For the
laborers, conditions include chain gangs, housing more accurately described
as caging, and food known as "weevils and beans."

This work camp system evolved out of slavery and the subsequent convict
leasing system. The great majority of the prisoners are black. In the late
1960s there were more than 8,000 convicts in the work camps of South Carolina,
Alabama, Georgia, and Florida. In South Carolina some camps use the "chain-
gang" method of labor. In Georgia in 1969, 3,400 prisoners were in county
camps with another 1,050 in camps operated by state prisons. Seventy-five
percent of the prisoners in the county camps were black. In Florida the figure
was 65 percent black. The great majority of the prisoners in the South Carolina
system were also black. And in Alabama all the convicts leased to the state
highway department were black. These county camps in many cases are run
autonomously with no supervision from the state prison system or any other
outside agency.

The legal systems of the South were not the only social factors that acted as
push factors. Exclusion from employment opportunities, quality education, and
adequate health care have also been significant causes for black migration.
Again, it is important to keep in mind that those aspects of life that most of us
take for granted just simply cannot be so taken by Blacks.

EMPLOYMENT

The opportunity to earn a better living has been one of the major, if not the
primary, reasons behind the black movement out of the South. The North
offered not only a chance to get out of the field but a chance to increase one's
income by at least two times. Respondents in northeastern Mississippi said
that the lack of economic opportunities in southern industry was more important
in their decision to migrate than other social conditions. Articles in southern
papers like the *Montgomery Advertiser* and the *Atlanta Independent* stated
that low wages in the South were the cause of the exodus of Blacks. The Blacks
migrating from St. Helena, South Carolina, voiced economic considerations as
the prime cause for their move northward, although it was by no means the
sole motive.

The difficulty in leaving is much more than just economics, however. To Creola and Wash Alston, their little patch in Warren County, North Carolina, is theirs; it is deeply part of their lives. Home is often:

> . . . a nail beside the kitchen door where the hat has been hung for 30 years. It is the old cane-bottomed chair under the shade tree, where ice water tastes so good at the end of a summer day. It is the smell of manure and old harness leather, and the memory of young love carved on the barn door: ABS & JT Aug. 1930. It is the church and the graveyard, where parents and brothers and sisters and babies are buried (Walls, 1971).

Leaving is usually easier for the teen-ager just graduating from high school than it is for his or her parents. The younger people have not yet become as deeply entangled in the web of intense feelings and frustrations that bind adults to their homes. Indeed, it is the recognition of what these emotions have done to their parents that helps to drive the teen-agers to the hoped-for progress in the North.

For the parents there never is a good time to leave.

> In winter, there is not even enough money to buy food, and so it is better to stay where you can get food on credit until the crop is sold next year. In spring and summer, there is a crop in the ground; a man cannot leave a crop to rot in the fields. In the fall, when the crop is harvested and sold and there is a little money, there is still the debt (Walls, 1971).

And the yearly cycle begins anew.

The north-south differentials in employment opportunities for Blacks have continued since 1915, although the South as a whole has undergone substantial change and economic improvement. The relative role of agriculture in employment has declined while that of manufacturing has increased. The southern employment structure has become more diversified. But these conditions are for the South in general and Whites in particular.

For the Black, progress has not occurred at such a rate. In fact, the economic position of the southern Black has deteriorated relatively. More Blacks are working, and their incomes have increased; but when these increases are measured against the white increases, they become relative decreases. The fact that the proportional growth of wages and salaries has been greater for Blacks than for Whites is less a measure of black economic progress than of the initially extremely low income against which the black increase is measured. The absolute dollar difference between white and black incomes in the South has increased markedly, more than in other regions (see Table 4.5).

Many of the southeastern counties which have lost black population simply do not have opportunities for employment. For the young and old alike the routine is the same: the land has been long since worn out; crop allotments keep getting smaller; and there are no present or foreseeable openings in the few mills. Donnie Gibson made the rounds before leaving his home in Williamsburg

Region	1960			1970		
	White	Nonwhite	Dollar difference	White	Nonwhite	Dollar difference
Northeast	$6,318	$4,371	− $1,947	$11,291	$7,601	− $3,690
North	5,994	4,371	− 1,674	11,019	7,603	− 3,416
South	5,009	2,322	− 2,687	9,708	5,414	− 4,292
West	6,444	4,937	− 1,507	10,803	7,623	− 3,180

Table 4.5 Median Income of Nonwhite and White Families, by Region, 1960 to 1970.

Sources: *Henderson, Vivian W.,* The Economic Status of Negroes: In the Nation and in the South, *p. 14.* The Southern Regional Council: *Southern Regional Council, 1963.* The Social and Economic Status of the Black Population in the U.S., *1971, 1972, p. 32.*

County, South Carolina. He went to Albany Felt and the Douglass plant in Saint Stephen and to Georgia Pacific in Russelville; he was told he would be notified if a suitable opening became available. Donnie's father had to go to North Carolina to find a job; it was so far that he took board there during the week and returned home on the weekend, and this for $45 to $50 a week.

The expanding labor market of the 1950s to 1960s was much different from that of the period 1910 to 1920 when Blacks could find unskilled jobs in northern factories. Technology expanded the opportunities at the upper levels of employment and decreased the need for labor in the lower echelons of employment categories, exactly those levels in which Blacks are most numerous. Between 1947 and 1961 those industries which absorbed Blacks showed a declining rate of employment. Although there were increases in the percentage of Blacks employed in white-collar occupations, these increases were very small both in absolute figures and in comparison to white gains. Table 4.6 illustrates two important characteristics of black employment structures in the South. First, a much higher percentage of Blacks than Whites was employed in the lower levels of employment. Secondly, the gains for the black female in white-collar employment are greater than those for the black male. This is probably a reflection of an increase in the number of black secretaries.

> In sum it appears that penetration of higher echelons of the occupational scale by Negroes has been relatively limited (up to 1960), and much more so in the South than outside the region (Henderson, 1963).

The result of the lack of adequate employment opportunities in the South through the 1960s has continued to drive Blacks to the North.

Black unemployment and underemployment in the South has also been the result of discriminatory hiring. Much of the industry moving to the South excluded Blacks from their new jobs. Such was the case in northeastern Mississippi. Contrary to federal law a number of major companies with mills in the South have continually discriminated against Blacks in employment. In 1964, for example, Dan River Mills in Alabama employed only three Blacks out of 100 employees, and they were in menial jobs. The same has been true of the Alabama Power Company. It employed 5,400 people, 472 of whom were black, and 75 percent of these were laborers and janitors. Both of these companies do business with the federal government. In the case of the McGregor Printing Corporation (which does 70 percent of its business with the federal government), all job applications are screened by the white mayor of the town in which the company is located. "In his capacity as mayor he keeps a photo file of demonstrators and he affirms that no one in that file would make a good clerk because many are trouble makers" (Good, 1968). Since the hearing of the U.S. Commission on Civil Rights in 1968, this practice is supposed to have stopped.

In some cases companies go so far as to operate segregated towns. Such was the case with the American Can Company in Bellamy, Alabama. This company is a government contractor and as such is subject to nondiscriminatory laws, but that is on paper and the reality is much different. As of April, 1968, the federal government, required by its own law to insist on non-segregated, equal job opportunities from its army of more than 100,000 contractors and unnumbered subcontractors, has never cancelled a contract for civil rights violations in Alabama or anywhere else in the country.

A survey of American Can Company uncovered the following problems:

A rickety all-black school with outdoor privy

Forty-five company houses inhabited by Whites had bathrooms and running water, but only eight of the 123 inhabited by Blacks

The other 115 black families had to use outdoor privies, and there was only one water spigot for every two families

The plant had separate bathrooms

Only one black office worker, an office boy

A company store from which Blacks received no bills, just deductions from their checks

One black man received a gross income of $139.43 for 2-weeks' work ending April 12, 1968, for 6 days' work he pockets $5

The night before the Hearing of the U.S. Commission on Civil Rights the company had a meeting of its workers. It said that open housing would be discussed at the hearing and warned that "there is a chance because of the law, we may have to stop all renting soon" (Good, 1968).

After the hearing in May, 1968, American Can Company began to improve the conditions in the town. There have been some black promotions, although these gains have meant little for the majority of workers. Another improvement has been that the quasi company store and gas station have been turned over to a cooperative of black and white workers. However as of 1969 the school remained all-black and in poor physical condition.

EDUCATION

Lack of educational opportunities has been an additional factor in the low-employment figures and the desire to move North. Improved occupational mobility for Blacks depends a great deal on better educational opportunities and manpower development. Vocational training that is available to Blacks,

| Occupation group | WHITE | | | | | |
| | MALE | | | FEMALE | | |
	1950	1960	1970	1950	1960	1970
White collar	30.9	36.9	43.8	58.8	59.8	64.7
Blue collar	36.7	39.7	44.4	20.6	18.6	18.0
Unskilled and service	9.8	9.8	11.9	13.8	15.1	16.5
Farm occupations	21.5	10.2	0.5	3.8	1.7	0.8
Not reported	1.3	4.0	—	2.9	5.2	—

Table 4.6   Major Occupation Groups of Employed Persons in the South, by Race and Sex, 1950, 1960, 1970* (percentage).

* 1970 figures represent Blacks; 1950 and 1960 figures are for Nonwhites.
Source: *U.S. Department of Commerce, Census of Population 1950, 1960, 1970.*

for example, is limited to those types of jobs traditionally held by them. In the vocational training schools of Atlanta, Houston, and Nashville, Blacks received training in courses such as cooking, cleaning, and some mechanics while Whites received training in machine shop, tool-and-die, and metal working. The state of Alabama set up only one Manpower Development and Training Center by 1964 in central Alabama—for nurses' aides.

Not only the vocational but the general educational systems for Blacks in the South have been inadequate and as such have served as another element in the push of Blacks out of the South. Figure 4.2 indicates quite clearly why the lack of educational opportunities in the early decades of the century has been such a common motive given by Blacks for their northward migration. As schools become more black, the percentage of funds spent per pupil decreases in those schools, while the reverse occurs in those schools with a majority of Whites. From the black point of view, it is obvious that more money is spent on black children if they are in predominantly white schools. The more black the county population, the less was spent on the education of the black children.

We are now going to examine briefly an educational program that began in Mississippi in the mid-1960s. It is called the Child Development Group in Mississippi (CDGM). The purpose of our discussing CDGM is not to pretend to understand the complicated problems of the group but rather to indicate that if you are poor and black in the South, sending your children to school is not simply packing a sandwich and an apple and kissing them on the head and scooting them off to school. That is what makes education such an important factor in black migration. Black education in the South is not a simple matter, especially when the federal government is ostensibly involved in seeing that the education is improved.

The history of the CDGM is a good example of the complicated, frustrating interworkings of Washington officials, southern politicians, social activists, and poor people all trying, or not trying, to provide black children with an education. It was founded in 1965 as one of the first large poverty programs in the country in which the formation of grass-roots political and economic organizations was emphasized. It was as well a Head Start program involving 6,000

Occupation group	NONWHITE					
	MALE			FEMALE		
	1950	1960	1970	1950	1960	1970
White collar	5.8	8.3	14.6	10.6	13.2	27.0
Blue collar	24.6	30.8	43.2	9.6	9.0	17.8
Unskilled and service	34.3	36.3	34.8	64.0	66.4	53.2
Farm occupations	33.8	18.6	7.4	13.9	5.9	2.0
Not reported	1.3	5.9	—	1.7	5.6	—

Table 4.6 Continued

to 12,000 children. When asked about the issues of CDGM, Marion Wright answered, "Eating and kids. They're basic" (Wasserman, 1967). When the educational director, Polly Greenberg, set up the program, it concentrated on involving both parents and children in the education process at each stage. This parental involvement was a social as well as an educational goal, as the children saw their parents as part of, indeed leaders in, their education, and the school became a part of their community.

It is indeed a curious phenomenon that Mississippi, a state in which education of black children had been of so little concern to the public officials, all of a sudden became concerned about the schooling of the "nigger kids." The problem with CDGM was that it was doing exactly what it was supposed to do, reach and involve poor people in the process of eradicating the socioeconomic, political, and educational legacy of slavery. Under normal Mississippi conditions:

> A black child is taught "not to get into things" around the yard. A bigger child is taught "not to get into things" at school—not to think or question. An adult is taught "not to get into things" affecting his life—white things, decision making, the greater society, social change (Greenberg, 1969).

There is an extremely important point here: a seemingly simple task of educating poor black children is not so simple in Mississippi, or in other states for that matter. Education is a political issue. Although CDGM is an educational program; much of its time is spent in the process of dealing with Washington and with southern politicians.

The geography of the program was one example of the conflict between meeting the needs of the people involved in the program and meeting the needs of those who sit in state houses and in Washington. It was political power, not the locational principle of nearness, that ultimately decided the location of the CDGM offices. In Mississippi, federal programs are located in white territory, even when they are ostensibly for Blacks. Obviously, this helps keep them under white control. The location of the CDGM headquarters was a good example of the importance of spatial positioning in the geography of race and poverty. At first, CDGM decided to locate at Mount Beulah, Mississippi, in the center of civil rights activity, but in 3 months was forced to change its location to a downtown office. This move not only increased the spatial distance between

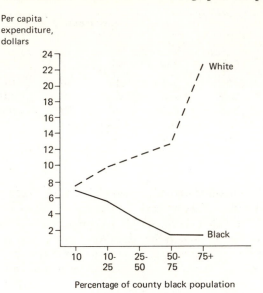

Figure 4.2   Per Capita Expenditures for White and Black Pupils by Percent of Country Population That Is Black for Fifteen Southern States and the District of Columbia, 1916–1918.

(From Bracey, Meier, Rudwick, 1971, p. 48.)

the program and its recipients but also increased the social distance between them. The percentage of poor people who visited the center in its new location dropped drastically. There were a number of reasons for this. The new office-type physical environment with its cubicles, waiting room, and receptionist did not look comfortable to the poor, rural Blacks. In addition, the new surroundings were more in tune with the environment of the white town in which the new building was located. "There were no mowed fields and mud driveways for parking. There was no community dining room that served cheap familiar food, in an intimate family setting. There was nowhere to put the children who accompanied their parents" (Greenberg, 1969).

HEALTH

Health and welfare are not usually categorized among the reasons given for the large black migration of the period 1910 to 1970. We do not mean to suggest that they have been as significant a cause as the search for better jobs. But on the other hand, health and welfare, or the lack thereof, obviously form a major portion of the life experiences of poor Blacks in the South. And as such, they become important components in black migration. Dr. Krumdick's research, for example, supports the view that malnutrition in rural areas plays an important causative role in urban migration. At the Poverty Subcommittee Hearings Dr. Raymond Wheeler and Marian Wright accused the federal government and southern white power structures of withholding food aid from

Makeshift "classrooms" like the one in this Louisiana home reflect the abysmal state of black education, one of many motivating factors in the black migration to the North.

The Bettmann Archive, Inc.

the poor in order to drive an unwanted black population out of the South. Anzie Moore, a southern black woman concurred: "It seems you either have to starve or go to Chicago" (Payne, 1969). The decisions of white political leaders and bureaucrats have driven many Blacks out of the South.

There was also feeling among some Mississippi Blacks, as well as in the Civil Rights Advisory Committee, that the switch from surplus commodities to food stamps was aimed at driving Blacks out of the state. The government food programs of the 1960s drove Blacks northward just as the government's cotton programs had done some 30 years earlier. Curious relationships between black migration and disease have been described by doctors. In both cases, one during slavery, the other in 1935, black migration is linked with the racial ideology of the period. In the first of these cases, Dr. Samuel Cartwright of New Orleans "discovered" a disease peculiar to Blacks, called drapetomania (the urge for

Blacks to run away). The southern ideology of the time would not acknowledge that Blacks ran away to escape from slavery, thus they must be sick. In a
more recent statement Dr. Mills warns against the dangers caused by the
northward black migration.

> In many ways the Negro shows his lack of physical fitness for
> existence in the more energizing areas of the world. Should we not
> attempt some sort of a campaign to bring these facts home to the
> people of the South, emphasizing the dangers that have shown up
> from the past fifteen years' migration.

He continues,

> Higher wages and levels of living in the more energetic northern
> areas are always viewed with envy by people of the South, but it
> would seem that the lesser stress of life under which they live in
> the South—their greater relaxation and more complacent existence
> —should compensate in large measure for their lowered vigor and
> productiveness.

And,

> There should be a curb to free migration according to economic
> origins when we enter another era of industrial expansion. Since
> individuals of the class that migrates are seldom capable of heeding
> such a warning, the question arises as to whether there should
> be some degree of Federal control of such population movements.
> From both economic and health viewpoints it would seem
> desirable (Mills, 1935).

There are a number of examples of racist thought in Dr. Mills's article.
What makes the article even more dehumanizing is that on the surface he
seems to be concerned about the health of black people. But his racism is
strong. First the deaths of Blacks are attributed to climate, and there is no recognition of the effects of poverty and racism on the health of Blacks. He also
smoothly equates Blacks with "stagnation" and Whites with "energization."
When he suggests that Blacks show a lack of physical fitness, he is completely
ignoring the fact that the South was built by black labor. In the second para-
graph he speaks of black life in the South as complacent and relaxing. Again,
he is ignoring the actual conditions of toil and tragedy of black life in the
South. Finally, he points out that these relaxed people are incapable of heeding
his warning and thus they should be forced to do so. More recent ideology continues to describe these problems as traits of the people involved. If the
accuser is blatantly racist, the black poor are that way because they are born
that way; if the accuser is more paternalistic, the black poor acquire these traits
through living. There is a strong tendency in this kind of thinking to blame
the poor themselves for their problems. We are not saying that the black person
is just a puppet with no humanity of his own, working at the whim of society.
The point is that the black poor are responsible, striving people in a society that

puts innumerable barriers in front of them. Both white and black parents want their children to be healthy; the difference is that for Whites the desire can be and is translated into health care. But for too many Blacks the desire ends there. The goals are the same, yet their views about their ability to obtain these goals realistically differ. While systematically withholding the means of obtaining these goals, society upholds these values and goals as ends. Society then calls the inability of the black poor to achieve these goals apathy. Again the poor are at fault. "The attitudes of the poor Black arise in no vacuum, but are logical results of real life circumstances" (Irelan, 1968).

If we re-examine Oscar Lewis's definition of the "culture of poverty," we find that it implies that the responsibility for their poverty lies with the poor. As defined by him, the "culture of poverty" is a design for living which is passed down from generation to generation. We suggest, however, that there is an additional dimension which needs to be added to the definition. We suggest that the "culture of poverty" is a design for living under the constraints that society passes down from generation to generation.

The health conditions of Blacks in the South come as a shock only to those unaware of the legacy of poor health from slavery. Health care for Blacks following slavery may have been worse than during the days of slavery, for at least under slavery there appears to be some question about whether masters did provide some care for their slaves. But after the Civil War, Blacks were on their own. In the rural areas of the South, the states did practically nothing. Blacks were denied admittance to hospitals. Hospitals available to Blacks were sometimes 100 to 200 miles away. The hospitals were segregated. Of the 183 black hospitals in 1928 only seven were approved by the National Hospital and National Medical Associations. Change takes time. In 1967, only sixty-eight of the 138 hospitals in Alabama would sign the necessary compliance forms making them eligible for federal funds; they preferred segregation to money. Change takes more than 40 years. Clinics closed their doors to Blacks in Alabama; this action was supported and condoned by the U.S. Public Health Service.

Before examining the reasons behind the maintenance of hunger and poor health for Blacks in the South, we will look briefly at who is hungry. It is important to note that health and hunger are not synonymous; hunger is just one important factor in one's total health.

> Mrs. Moore lives in a sharecropper's shack on a Mississippi planta-
> tion. Like her parents and grandparents before her, she is a
> reminder that the legacy of slavery has not died in our country.
> She sobs softly as the coffin carrying the body of her 6-month old
> baby boy, Ernest, is lowered into the Delta clay. Mrs. Moore has
> had seven children but Ernest is the third to die before he was a
> year old, the victim of complications rooted in conditions of mal-
> nutrition, poor housing, poor sanitation, and disease (Payne, 1969).

Ernest is not a statistic to Mrs. Moore, but she has no power to alter the health conditions under which she lives. Her only choice is to be hungry in rural

Mississippi or to be hungry in urban Chicago. But Ernest, as we shall see, is only a statistic to the politicians and bureaucrats who control his life chances.

In their 1969 study of nutritional deficiencies in preschool black children in Memphis, Tennessee, Dr. Zee and his colleagues found that the lack of quality in and quantity of food contributed most to the growth retardation and anemia in the children; and these conditions are directly related to poverty (Sugg, 1971). This is perhaps a rather bland and neutral sounding statement until one realizes its impact. The result is simple—poor black children in Memphis and in other areas of the South do not get enough of the right food. Like Ernest they become statistics.

There is a very real health gap between the South and the rest of the country, and between Whites and Blacks. The black infant mortality rates are substantially higher than those of Whites, and black infants are far more likely to die during the first year of life than are white babies. Ernest was one of these statistics.

The federal government has been directing food programs of various kinds for over 30 years. There are at present four major food programs under the Department of Agriculture: commodity distribution, food stamps, school lunches, and special milk (see Table 4.7). In order to understand the inadequacies of these programs, it is crucial to realize that none of them were meant to feed the poor. They were created to boost the agricultural prices of the large commercial farmers. The hungry poor were one means of disposing of this surplus food, and even then they were last on the priority list, coming behind overseas sales for dollars and the Food for Peace plan. The poor around the world need to be fed before those in the South, because feeding the latter yields no propaganda value on the world market. Indeed, in the official policy statements on the disposal of food from the Agriculture Department, hungry Americans are not even mentioned.

Another major problem with food programs is that at their worst they are run for the benefit of the large, racist landowners and southern politicians and at their best they are run by misguided paternalism. It is abundantly clear that the disposition of the government food programs is under the supervision and control of certain southern senators and congressmen. Ostensibly the food programs are under the Department of Agriculture, but they are, in effect, run by four congressional committees and their respective heads: the House Agriculture Appropriations Subcommittee headed by J. Whitten of Mississippi, the House Agriculture Committee run by A. Ellender of Louisiana, the Senate Agriculture Appropriations Subcommittee run by S. Holland of Florida, and the House Agricultural Appropriations Subcommittee run by W. Poage of Texas (see Table 4.8).

When asked to help the hungry poor, government officials like Agriculture Secretary Freeman, HEW Secretary Gardner, and OEO Director Shriver have said that they could not act without clearance from the senators and congressmen mentic ied above. Freeman acknowledged that he declined to use powers that were legally his until he had checked with Congressman Whitten. The reason behind Freeman's return of Section 32 funds to the Treasury rather than using them to feed the poor was because Whitten and Holland felt that

Program	THE UNIVERSE OF NEED		PARTICIPANTS		HUNGER GAP		% BEING SERVED	
	1969	1972	1969	1972	1969	1972	1969	1972
Food stamps	30	26 to 30*	3.2	11.8		11.2 to	NA	49 to 58
Commodity distribution			3.5	3.0	22.8	15.2		
Supplementary								
Food packages	5.8	NA	40,097	NA	5.2	NA	10	NA
Free or reduced price lunches	8.4	10	2.4	8.4	1.8	1.6	79†	34
All school lunches	52	NA	20.1	NA	32.2	NA	38	NA
School breakfast	8.4	3.5 to 6	0.299	1.2	7.9	2.3 to 4.8	6	20 to 34
Special milk	8.4	NA	1.7	NA	6.7	NA	20	NA
Nonschool food services (a) Year-round day care	0.5	0.75	0.042	0.154	0.4	0.596	20	24
(b) Summer recreation	1.2	3 to 5	0.31	1.38	NA	2	26	27 to 46

Table 4.7 The "Feeding Report Card" of the United States Government (figures in millions).

* Lower figure holds if poverty level is $4,110 for family of four; higher figure holds if poverty level is set at $4,476 for family of four.

† Thirty-five percent, in fact.

Sources: *Hunger U.S.A. Revisited, 1972, p. 12 and Action Report of the National Council on Hunger and Malnutrition in the U.S., December, 1969, p. 41.*

these funds should be used only when they would buy an oversupply threatening farmers' profits.

Political control functions at many levels to stop food from getting to the poor. Before the National Nutrition Survey was taken, Whitten was told by Dr. George Irving, Director of the Agriculture Department's Research Service, that Mississippi was on the list of states to be studied. The result was that the hungry of Mississippi were taken off the list in order "to avoid unnecessary political friction." Also, because he responded to the hunger issue with medical exactness, Dr. Arnold Schaefer, the original director of the National Nutrition Survey, was removed from that job; and when he later testified about delays, he was warned that he would be fired if he spoke out again.

Congressional chairman	Population	% of population over 5,000	Number of population over 5,000	$ Average payment	% population in proportion	People in proportion	$ Average payment	°
J. Whitten†	427,468	0.3	1,282	18,380	59.1	234,634	17.00	5+
W. Poage‡	389,954	0.1	390	13,638	37.6	148,382	1.00	23+
A. Ellender§	3,257,022	0.048	1,628	13,505	35.6	1,159,550	4.75	4+
S. Holland¶	4,951,560	0.0065	297	22,374	28.4	1,386,437	3.18	1½+

Table 4.8 Comparison of Federal Money Spent on Agriculture and Food Assistance Programs in the Voting Areas of Four Chairmen of Congressional Agriculture Committees, 1966 to 1967.

° Number of times more money spent on agriculture programs for those producers receiving over $5,000 from the federal government than on food assistance programs for 1 year.
† Chairman—House Agriculture Committee; from Mississippi.
‡ Chairman—House Agriculture Appropriations Subcommittee; from Texas.
§ Chairman—Senate Agriculture Committee; from Louisiana.
¶ Chairman—Senate Agriculture Appropriations Subcommittee; from Florida.

Sources: *Hunger USA, 1968, pp. 82–83; Senate Hearing, Department of Agriculture and Related Agencies Appropriations, 90th Congress, First Session, Fiscal Year, 1968; Part 3, Reports to the Committee on Payments Made to Producers During Calendar 1966, Subsidy Payments for Agricultural Exports; Congressional Directory, 90th Congress, First Session, March, 1967; U.S. Department of Agriculture, Consumer and Marketing Service, Participation in Commodity Distribution Programs, 1966–67 by County (unpublished); U.S. Department of Agriculture, Consumer and Marketing Service, Participation in Commodity Distribution Program, 1966–67 by Year, 1967 (unpublished).*

Another significant problem has been that the poor have not been able to participate in the decision-making process involved in the food program. In fact, the only local involvement has been that of the local political institutions. In 1965 and in 1971 task force and follow-up reports of the White House Conference asked the federal government to include the poor in the running of the food program. But up to 1972 the President and the Agriculture Department have declined to admit the poor into the group that makes decisions. The geography of exclusion dictated that the administration find a location for the "Follow Up" Conference to the White House Conference on Hunger and Nutrition so that the poor people who took over the original conference could not find the follow-up meeting. Thus, it was located at isolated, expensive Williamsburg, Virginia.

The decision to get food programs to the hungry can be stopped or delayed at all political levels except at the level of the people themselves. The President; senators, congressmen, and state officials; county, city, township, and other local politicians can and do make decisions to keep the poor hungry. And even when the decision of one of these politicians is reversible, it may not be reviewed because of the jurisdictional rights and fears of other officials. The federal government, for example, will not intervene to force state, county, or township governments to feed the poor. In fact, it took the intervention of Kobe, Japan, in 1971, to feed the people of Seattle before the federal government would help. It seems that the federal government can stand the humiliation of continued hunger in this country but that it cannot tolerate the help of other nations in feeding the American poor. The pretense of saving face is more important than the saving of lives. The states and counties are even more attached to the principle of nonintervention in helping the poor. No one is responsible for the hungry. This situation is aggravated when the hungry are black and the officials in control are white, and such is the case in the South.

DISFRANCHISEMENT

Disfranchisement was essential to the return of white control in the South after Reconstruction. Between 1870 and 1910 the states of Mississippi, Alabama, Georgia, North and South Carolina, Florida, Louisiana, Arkansas, and Tennessee had, in one way or another, taken the vote away from Blacks.

It was during this period that there was a possibility of bipartisan political competition in the South. This competition raised the possibility that bloc voting by Blacks could greatly influence the balance of power. In order to forestall this, laws were passed to keep the vote from Blacks. "Legal" as well as illegal methods were used, including the restricted primary, the poll tax, the grandfather clause, and terrorism. The history of black voting in the South is the result of the conflict of the basic voting rights set forth in the Constitution and the caste principle of the South which says that Blacks shall not vote. There is, however, an exception to the latter rule; "good" Blacks can vote, when and where it serves the needs of Whites.

At first terrorism and/or the threat of violence was the major method of keeping Blacks away from the polls. This was accompanied by economic pressures such as the threat of the loss of a job, credit, or housing. More sophisticated and subtle measures were adopted as white control was reaffirmed. Such tricks as manipulation of voter registration, rules against voting if one had committed a petty crime, and the "eight-box voting" gimmick were used. The latter involved the setting out of eight unlabeled boxes in which the marked ballots were to be placed. For the Whites this was no problem as the election officials would see to it that their votes counted. But for the black voter the chances were one out of eight that his ballot would be put into the box that he wished.

Other barriers to black voting included having the Whites vote first. They would proceed so slowly that it would be time for the polls to close before the Blacks reached the head of the line. Polling places were also located in places either far from or inconvenient to Blacks. Fraud existed in the form of false-bottom ballot boxes, falsified counts, and tissue paper ballots. The latter could be easily identified if there were more ballots than registered voters and some ballots needed to be removed. As older methods were knocked down by the

State	1947	1952	1956	1968	% registered
Alabama	6,000	25,224	53,366	273,000	56.7
Arkansas	47,000	61,413	69,677	130,000	67.2
Florida	49,000	120,900	148,703	292,000	62.1
Georgia	125,000	144,835	163,389	344,000	56.1
Louisiana	10,000	120,000	161,410	304,601	59.2
Mississippi	5,000	20,000	20,000*	250,777	59.4
N. Carolina	75,000	100,000	135,000	305,000	55.3
S. Carolina	50,000	80,000	99,890	207,509	55.9
Tennessee	80,000	85,000	90,000	228,000	72.6
Texas	100,000	181,916	214,000	540,000	83.1
Virginia	48,000	69,326	86,603	255,000	58.4

Table 4.9   Black Voter Registration, 1947, 1952, 1956, 1968.

* Mississippi total is for 1955.
Sources: Data for 1947, 1952, 1956 from Price, Margaret, The Negro Voter in the South, Atlanta: Southern Regional Council, 1957, p. 5; data for 1968 from Majority Black School Districts in the 11 Southern States, Race Relations Information Center, Nashville, 1970, Table 1.

courts or proved ineffective, southern Whites developed a new method of restricting the franchise of Blacks. This was to discriminate not on the basis of race, per se, but on those conditions common to Blacks. These restrictions were selectively enforced with the use of the grandfather clause. Specifically the grandfather clause excluded the descendants of those people who voted prior to 1865 from having to pass literacy tests prior to registering to vote. At this time most Whites as well as Blacks were illiterate, but the effect of the grandfather clause was to bar Blacks while allowing illiterate Whites to register. This technique survived until 1915, when it was found unconstitutional by the U.S. Supreme Court.

The result of all these methods of restricting the vote of Blacks was predictable: black voting declined. The pattern in Louisiana was characteristic of the other southern states. In 1896 there were 130,344 black voters in the state; this had dropped to 5,320 by 1900 and to 1,718 by 1904.

Registration of Blacks has increased dramatically in the South, especially in the years from 1956 to 1968 (see Table 4.9). Yet, in only one of eleven southern states were more than 75 percent of the black residents registered in 1968. This increase in the number of Blacks registered to vote is largely a result of the extensive and intensive efforts of groups such as Voter Education Project, CORE, NAACP, SNCC, and SCLC. Other factors include the passage and enforcement, though slow and uneven, of the Voting Rights Act of 1965. In Mississippi, for example, black registration increased from 8.1 percent of the voting population before passage of the act to 83.7 percent after passage of the act in those counties examined by federal officials; the increase in those counties not examined was from 4.5 percent to 76.7 percent. Yet this progress has not been uniform. In Georgia, for example, in Taliaferro County 100 percent of the black population was registered in 1968, while in Marion County the percentage was only 18.4. There is another fact that must be realized in conjunction with the low percentage of black registration. There are many areas in the South in which more than 100 percent of the white population is registered. Such was the case in 1968 in two counties in Florida, thirty-eight in Georgia, six in Louisiana, twenty-seven in Mississippi, and four in North Carolina.

New methods of preventing black voting had to be found after the turn of the century. Some southern Whites were embarrassed by the use of force and intimidation in previous years. However, force, or the threat of it, has continued to be a factor in keeping Blacks away from the polls. Visits from the Klan and harassment by the police are among the tactics used to keep Blacks from the polls. When threats are not enough, murder and assassination are used, as in the shotgun death of Reverend George Washington Lee in Belzoni, Mississippi, on May 7, 1954. Intimidation also takes on economic forms. As punishment for registering to vote, Blacks in Fayette and Haywood Counties, Tennessee, were refused credit and loans and forced to leave when the crops were harvested. Other Whites still felt that they needed more "judge-proof" means of keeping Blacks from voting. The white primary, first used in Texas in 1922, was the result. The power of the federal government and its laws did not extend to party primaries, which could then be run by local party officers. These were struck down by the U.S. Supreme Court in 1927 only to be replaced by a more effective block to black voting. In fact, the federal judiciary had, in the 1930s, affirmed the use of two methods of excluding Blacks. One was the once illegal white primary. Through successive court battles, what the state of Texas could not legally do, the Democratic party of the state could. Thus, in the *Grovey v. Townsend* (1935) case, the U.S. Supreme Court reinstated the white primary. In effect, the Court said that although the state cannot deny the right to vote a voluntary, private association can.

Next to the white primary, the poll tax has over the years been the most important method of limiting black voting power. In effect the poll tax is a tax on the right to vote. The effectiveness of this method has declined recently, with the rise of more effective means of limiting black voting. By the 1960s only Alabama, Mississippi, Texas, and Virginia still used the poll tax.

With the fall of the white primary and the decline of the poll tax, white supremacists turned to literacy tests to limit black voter registration. Alabama, Virginia, Louisiana, South Carolina, North Carolina, Georgia, and Mississippi have statutes providing for "reading and writing" or literacy tests. The effects of these tests can be seen from a brief comparison of their differential use in Mississippi. Three Blacks with master's degrees were judged illiterate, while a white Mississippian was judged as literate for interpreting the phrase, " 'There shall be no imprisonment for debt' as 'I think that a Neorger should have 2 years in collage befor voting because he don't under stand (sic)' " (Lewis, 1955).

The Voting Rights Act of 1965 suspended literacy tests in those states or counties in which less than 50 percent of the residents of voting age were registered on November 1, 1964, or voted in the 1964 presidential election. The Warren Court ruled in 1969 that it was not only the intent but the effect of the literacy tests that was crucial and that past discrimination in the public schools had produced higher rates of illiteracy among Blacks than Whites, so the tests abridged the right to vote on the basis of color.

The Boswell Amendment (which follows) was added to the Alabama state constitution in 1945. It is a good example of a law that does not restrict Blacks per se, but bases its restrictions on the socioeconomic conditions of the black population.

> . . .(t)he following persons and no others who, if their place of residence shall remain unchanged, will have, at the date of the next general election, the qualifications as to residence prescribed in Section 178 of this article, shall be qualified to register as electors provided they shall not be disqualified under Section 182 of this constitution: those who can read and write, understand and explain any article of the Constitution of the United States in the English language and who have worked or been regularly engaged in some lawful employment, business, or occupation, trade, or calling for the greater part of the twelve months next preceding the time they offer to register, including those who are unable to read and write if such inability is due solely to physical disability; provided, however, no persons shall be entitled to register as electors except those who are of good character and who understand the duties and obligations of good citizenship under a republican form of government (Bardolph, 1970).

If Blacks can sneak by the conditions of unchanged residence, ability to read and write, understanding and explaining the Constitution, and being regularly engaged in work, then they can be omitted on the basis of the "good character" rule.

The legal structures denying the vote to Blacks began to crumble in the 1940s and 1950s. The white primary was ruled unconstitutional in 1944. Four years later the Boswell Amendment fell. And the Voting Rights Act of 1957 invalidated the literacy and interpretation tests in 1960.

Although there was renewed legislation by some southern states in the 1950s, most could rely on the traditional illegal practices and complicated qualification and registration procedures to withhold the vote. Gerrymandering and other spatial manipulations were used as well as the resignation of voting registrars, leaving no one to sue.

Gerrymandering and manipulation of local political boundaries have been used, for example, in Richmond, Virginia and Adams County, Mississippi. In the latter case local Blacks attacked the County Board of Supervisors' plan to redistrict, arguing that it was racially motivated to dilute the black voting power in the county. The court held in *Howard and Schoby v. Adams County Board of Supervisors* that the charge of gerrymandering must be proved by the Blacks. In the Richmond case, black voting strength had grown from 4,000 in 1962 to 35,000 in 1969. The result was that the city sought to annex two adjoining counties, Henrico and Chesterfield. Part of Chesterfield was annexed, adding 97,000 people, 97 percent of whom were white. Black residents of the city charged that the purpose of this annexation was to dilute black voting strength. The court agreed.

There are two important points that need to be stressed. First, constitutional amendments and voting rights acts are paper. Legislation means nothing without effective enforcement. Enforcement of these laws has been almost wholly dependent on the suits of individual Blacks. Litigation by the Department of Justice has been extremely slow and very inadequate. It brought ten cases to court in the last 3 years of the Eisenhower administration and fifty in the first 3 years of the Kennedy administration. But the approach of the federal government is more to produce acts than it is to initiate action. The deaths of many Blacks in the 1960s produced civil rights acts in 1960, 1964, and 1965. The last of these provided for direct action by the federal government to enable Blacks to vote. But even this new act has not removed all hindrances to black voting. The Voter Education Project office still records that offences are committed against black voters or potential voters. For example, it took almost 4 years for the Mississippi bills restricting black voting to be overturned in March, 1969, even though these bills were contrary to Section 5 of the Voting Rights Act of 1965.

The fact that Whites have not given up the vote to Blacks without considerable trouble has helped drive Blacks to areas where they could vote. As one black North Carolinian put it, "we come where we could vote" (Wooten, 1971).

Socioeconomic "Pull" Factors in the North

As with the push factors in the South, there have been factors in the North that have acted as pull forces impelling Blacks to migrate. Again it should be emphasized that we are not attempting to examine all the causes nor do we say that they operated equally on all migrants. Essentially the North appeared to be a haven of escape from southern racism in its many forms and, at the same time, a land of economic opportunity. The North had its own brand of racism and "Negro jobs." Still, there were several general economic and social as well as many personal reasons for the pulling effect of the North. These can be divided into two groups. First, there were forces that made such large-scale migration possible, including industrial expansion, improved transportation and communication, immigration laws, and a change in the black feeling of attachment to the land. A second group of factors are those perceived by the migrant as reasons to move North. These included improved economic opportunities; encouragement from family, friends, and black newspapers, in particular the *Chicago Defender*; and hope for better social conditions (schools, health care, the vote).

EXPANSION OF INDUSTRY, TRANSPORTATION, COMMUNICATION

The industrial expansion of the North created economic opportunities for people who had no previous industrial skills or experience. These were the fringe jobs that an industrial, commercial society produces—janitors, servants, general laborers, strikebreakers when and where the need arises, and domestic jobs for women—the jobs that had little competition from white workers.

A second general factor was the improvement in transportation and communication. The mails and the trains acted as the messengers and the carriers of the black migrants.

IMMIGRATION LAWS

Prior to World War I European immigrants were filling much of the employment vacuum created by industrial expansion. But World War I and the immigration laws of 1921 and 1924 reduced the migrations from Europe, especially from South and East Europe. It is ironic that the American "nativism" responsible for the exclusion of "un-Americans" from eastern and southern Europe acted as a force in pulling that group considered to be the most "un-American" to take their places. The purpose of the 1924 Immigration Act was to "maintain the original streams of 'native' white stock in preference to later groups"(Newman, 1965). This drop in European immigration took place as the number of positions in and the output of manufacturing increased.

The cutting off of European immigration by World War I created a labor vacuum in the North that served as an invitation to the black man. Blacks had made some progress in the North since emancipation, but despite those achievements they were so handicapped by race prejudice and proscribed by trade unions that the uplift of the race by economic methods was nearly impossible. In addition the European immigrants had contributed to the exclusion of Blacks even from the menial positions. In the midst of the drudgery left for them, Blacks had frequently been debased to the status of dependents and paupers. Scattered through the North in such small numbers, they were unable to unite for social betterment and mutual improvement and naturally were too weak to force the community to respect their wishes as could be done by a large group with some political or economic power. With the advent of the war, there was an immediate change. Women of color formerly excluded from domestic service by foreign maids were in demand. Many mills and factories which prohibited Blacks from entering a few years before began to bid for their labor. Railroads could not find white help to keep their property in repair; contractors fell short of their schedules by failing to hold mechanics drawn into the industrial boom; and the United States government had to advertise for men to hasten the preparation for war.

An important point should be made here: there is a difference between white European and black southern immigrants to the North. It is from a superficial recognition that both groups arrived poor to the cities that one hears, "Well, my (white) ancestors made it, why haven't the Blacks?" It is true that white "nativism" excluded some Europeans as well as Blacks. But for the Europeans it was only temporary, and the ideology of exclusion was not developed; nor were European immigrants subject to slavery. Furthermore, Blacks were not wanted by northern society, only by the manufacturers, who needed cheap labor. As Osofosky points out, for example, "At no period in the history of New York City were Negroes accepted as full American citizens" (Osofosky, 1968). They were temporary substitutes.

BLACK ATTACHMENT TO THE LAND

There was an additional factor that distinguished this black migration from previous ones. There was a difference between slave and post-slave generations. These migrants were the first descendants of slaves, and although the conditions in the South were a type of neoslavery, they had known slavery, as such, only from stories. The difference was that this generation could conceive of reaching the goal of a new way of life as they were not as tied to the land. This, of course, does not mean that previous generations had not conceived of a new life outside of slavery. Obviously, many had not only conceived of such a chance but took it. The major point is that much greater numbers of the new generation could foresee a chance for change. The Blacks under slavery and immediately following the Civil War were systematically kept from knowing anything of the area outside of their immediate surroundings. The spatial realm of the new generation greatly increased.

The difference between the generations was, of course, seen by southern Whites. Many southern farmers expressed the feelings that the "before-the-war negroes" or the "old-time negroes" were the best farm hands; they were orderly, diligent, and faithful, but the younger ones "want to roam," they have a "migratory disposition," and are worthless, idle, and uppity. This raised a dichotomy in white southern racial ideology: Blacks were considered idle and worthless; yet they were needed as laborers.

ENCOURAGEMENT FROM FAMILY, FRIENDS, AND NEWSPAPERS IN THE NORTH

Once begun, migration caused further migration. Once a family member had moved North and established himself, he usually wrote back to his family and friends urging them to follow. The age-sex characteristics of the black population in the North indicated an excess of single adults, a lack of children and the elderly, an abundance of single men.

> My dear Sister: I was agreeably surprised to hear from you and to hear from home. I am well and thankful to say I am doing well. The weather and everything else was a surprise to me when I came. I got here in time to attend one of the greatest revivals in the history of my life—over 500 people joined the church. We had a Holy Ghost shower. You know I like to have run wild. It was snowing some nights and if you didn't hurry you could not get standing room. Please remember me kindly to any who ask of me. The people are rushing here by the thousands and I know if you come and rent a big house you can get all the roomers you want. You write me exactly when you are coming. I am not keeping house yet I am living with my brother and his wife. My son is in California but he will be home soon. He spends his winter in California. I can get a nice place for you to stop until you can look around and

see what you want. I am quite busy. I work in Swifts Packing Co. in the sausage department. My daughter and I work for the same company—We get $1.50 a day and we pack so many sausages we don't have much time to play but it is a matter of a dollar with me and I feel that God made the path and I am walking therein.

Tell your husband work is plentiful here and he won't have to loaf if he want to work. I know unless old man A—— changed it was awful with his shoulder and G—— also.

Well I am always glad to hear from my friends and if I can do anything to assist any of them to better their condition. Please remember me to Mr. C—— and his family I will write them all as soon as I can. Well I guess I have said about enough. I will be delighted to look into your face once more in life. Pray for me for I am heaven bound. I have made too many rounds to slip now. I know you will pray for prayer is the life of any sensible man or woman. Well goodbye from your sister in Christ.

P.S.   My brother moved the week after I came. When you fully decide to come write me and let me know what day you expect to leave and over what road and if I don't meet you I will have some one there to meet you and look after you. I will send you a paper as soon as one come along they send out extras two and three times a day (Scott, 1919).

These letters from migrants became the center of discussion in black churches, barbershops, and stores. The letters, however, were not the only source of information about the North. The *Chicago Defender* was important for several reasons. First, it printed numerous ads for job opportunities.

3,000 laborers to work on railroad. Factory hires all race help. More positions open than men for them (Scott, 1969).

The paper also served as a symbol of defiance against southern racism; something individual Blacks in the South were unable to do. The paper expanded the horizons of the isolated black farmer. It also printed letters and poems enticing Blacks to move North. Sparrell Scott's "When I Return to the Southland I Will Be" and William Crosse's "The Land of Hope" were printed in the paper. It even set specific dates, such as May 15, 1917, for large northward treks.

The *Defender* did entice many Blacks to leave the South and as such it was thought to be a menace by southern whites.   ·

He fished a creased newspaper clipping from his pocket and began to read:

"Some are coming on the passenger,
Some are coming on the freight,
Others will be found walking,
For none will have time to wait."

A deputy pushed through the crowd and laid his hand on the boy's shoulder.

"Reckon you'd better come with me, son," he said. "The sheriff wants to see you."

"What for? Ain't done nothing but read a little old poem."

"That's just it. Got orders to arrest all you colored boys I catch reading poetry out of that *Chicago Defender*. Been a lot of that stuff read and it's raising hell all over the South. Hands leaving the plow right in the field and running away from their honest debts to traipse North. You'll likely be charged with 'inciting to riot in the city, county and throughout the state of Georgia.' Yes sir, son, looks like you're bound for the prison farm" (Bontemps and Conroy, 1966).

Letters and the *Defender* functioned as surrogate labor agents. They were supplemented by those who returned South to bring their families back to the North with them. The established family member or friend acted as a cushion against the unknown urban world, providing a place to sleep and perhaps a job opportunity. Friends and relatives have a great impact on the location of the new homes of the black migrants. In the Fort Greene neighborhood of New York City, for example, there is a saying that "if you stand on a street corner long enough, you will see somebody you know from South Carolina." In Rochester, New York, the influence of friends and relatives through the years has brought some 8,000 Blacks from Williamsburg County, South Carolina.

Many northern companies sent agents to the South to recruit Blacks for the factories and the mills. Some companies even sent trains through the South upon which Blacks could hop and ride North to work. On the coast, it was the steamship that acted as a cheap form of transportation northward. The agents worked throughout the South but seem to have been more active in the large cities. There they were less conspicuous and less likely to be put in jail.

Southern Whites who became alarmed at the immensity of this movement tried hard to check it. To frighten Blacks about the North, southern newspapers were carefully circulating reports that many Blacks were returning to their native land because of unexpected hardships. When this failed, southerners compelled employment agents to cease operations, arrested suspected employers, prevented the departure of Blacks, and imprisoned those who appeared at stations to leave for the North.

Black social, business, and religious leaders acted both as leaders and as followers in this northward migration. In some cases they lost all of their clients, so they followed them. In other instances they led their congregations or groups to the North.

EMPLOYMENT OPPORTUNITIES

If there has been one factor singled out to be the major cause of the continued black migration to the North, it has been the expanded economic opportunities and the hope for better jobs in the North. There were two types of policy with regard to the hiring of Blacks: one was to hire Blacks in menial positions, the other was to employ no Blacks at all. The vast majority of black men worked as porters, janitors, teamsters, chauffeurs, elevator operators, longshoremen,

Year	Nonwhite male (%)	White male (%)	Nonwhite female (%)	White female (%)
1957	7.5	3.2	6.3	3.8
1960	9.6	4.2	8.3	4.6
1965	6.0	2.9	7.4	4.0
1969	3.7	1.9	5.8	3.4
1970	5.6	3.2	6.9	4.4
1971	7.2	4.0	8.7	5.3

Table 4.10   Unemployment Rates by Color and Sex for Selected Years, 1957 to 1971.*

* For ages 20 and over.

Sources: *The Social and Economic Status of the Black Population in the United States, 1971–1972,* p. 53; *The Negro in the U.S.: Their Economic and Social Situation,* 1966, pp. 83–84.

waiters, and in other service and general laborer jobs. Black women continued as domestics.

Northern Whites upheld nondiscrimination in jobs as a general principle, but their actions contradicted their words. Unless they were needed for some menial task, Blacks were thought of as undesirable. Where there were no typical "Negro jobs," Blacks were just excluded altogether, either by the employer or by other employees. Much of the employment gains for Blacks from 1910 to 1940 was a result of their use as substitutes during labor shortages, as strikebreakers, and as substitutes for the temporarily excluded foreign immigrants. But with the passage of time these conditions changed.

The "Negro jobs" in the North were marginal and subject to replacement by machines or abolishment altogether. It is ironic that the intervention of the federal government to improve bad labor conditions in factories—those conditions under which most Blacks worked—was a factor in increasing black unemployment. As exploitative working conditions changed, so did the race of the workers in the lower positions. Blacks gained only if they were allowed to keep their improved jobs, and that was unlikely.

Another federal policy that was seemingly developed to help people but had certain detrimental effects on black employment was public assistance, a part of the New Deal. The reason is that benefits from public assistance programs were sometimes higher than the wages paid to Blacks in many jobs. Although there was an absolute increase in black employment, Blacks did not participate in the increased employment after World War II as they had after World War I. There were no new marginal jobs; they had already made all the gains they were going to make in those industries that would have them. In fact, black unemployment was higher in 1942 than it had been 2 years earlier.

A number of other factors worked to lessen the opportunities for Blacks during this period. There was a high degree of white unemployment. Industry no longer needed Blacks as strikebreakers. The need for unskilled labor had declined relative to that of World War I, coupled with only slight gains in the area of skilled labor. Finally, northern industry had, over the years, learned how to more effectively organize its resistance to the hiring of Blacks. In effect, by the end of World War II Blacks had gained no better occupational positions than they had at the end of World War I. It should be noted that the low economic positions of Blacks have not been the result of low aspirations, but of high aspirations confronting limited and declining opportunities.

Table 4.10 indicates that Blacks have consistently had the highest rate of unemployment. During the 1960s the ratio of the jobless rate for non-whites averaged 2.1:1; this figure had declined slightly to 1.8:1 for the years 1970 to 1971. It is important to remember that the so-called black revolution of the 1960s did not significantly alter the relationship between black and white employment rates.

SELECTED BIBLIOGRAPHY

1. "Action Report of the National Council on Hunger and Malnutrition in the U.S.," Washington, D.C., 1970.
2. *Afro-American*, New York, 1932.
3. Bardolph, Richard: "The Civil Rights Record: Black Americans and the Law, 1849–1970," Thomas Y. Crowell Company, New York, 1970.
4. Berry, Mary F.: "Black Resistance and White Law: A History of Constitutional Racism in America," Appleton-Century-Crofts, New York, 1971.
5. Bonnen, James T.: The Distribution of Benefits from Selected U.S. Farm Programs, *Rural Poverty in the United States*, National Advisory Commission on Rural Poverty, 1968.
6. Bontemps, Arna and Conroy, Jack: "Anyplace but Here," Hill and Wang, New York, 1966.
7. Bracey, John H., Jr., Meier August, and Rudwick Elliot (eds.): "The Rise of the Ghetto," Wadsworth, Belmont, Calif., 1971.
8. Chilman, Catherine S.: "Growing Up Poor," U.S. Department of HEW, Washington, D.C., 1966.
9. Cox, Oliver C.: "Caste, Class and Race," Modern Reader, New York, 1948.
10. Delta Prisons: Punishment for Profit: Special Report, Southern Regional Council, March, 1968.
11. Dillingham, Harry C. and David F. Sly: "The Mechanical Cotton Picker, Negro Migration, and the Integration Movement," *Human Organization*, vol. 25, winter, 1966, pp. 344–351.
12. Franklin, John Hope and Isidore Starr: "The Negro in Twentieth Century America," Random House, New York, 1967.
13. Ginsberg, Ralph: "100 Years of Lynchings," Lancer Books, New York, 1969.
14. Good, Paul: "The American Serfs: A Report on Poverty in the Rural South," Ballantine Books, New York, 1968a.
15. ———: "Cycle to Nowhere," U.S. Commission on Civil Rights, 1968.
16. Greenberg, Polly: "The Devil Has Slippery Shoes," MacMillan, New York, 1969.
17. Harrington, Michael: "Toward a Democratic Left," MacMillan, New York, 1968.

18. Henderson, Vivian W.: "The Economic Status of Negroes: In the Nation and in the South," The Southern Regional Council, 1963.
19. Henderson, William L. and Larry C. Ledebur: "Economic Disparity," The Free Press, New York, 1970.
20. Holley, W. C., Ellen Winston, and T. J. Woofter: "The Plantation South, 1934–1937," DeCapo Press, New York, 1940.
21. Howard and Schoby vs. Adams County Board of Supervisors, Race Relations Law Reporter, vol. 3, March, 1972.
22. "Hunger U.S.A. Revisited," Atlanta: Southern Regional Council and National Council on Hunger and Malnutrition, 1973.
23. Irelan, Lola M.: "Low-Income Life Styles," U.S. Department of HEW, Washington, D.C., 1968.
24. Johnson, Charles S.: "Patterns of Negro Segregation," Harper and Brothers, New York, 1934.
25. Katz, William L.: "Eyewitness: The Negro in American History," Pittman, New York, 1969.
26. Kennedy, Louise: "The Negro Peasant Turned Cityward," Columbia University Press, New York, 1930.
27. Kester, Howard: "Revolt Among Sharecroppers," Arno Press, New York, 1969.
28. Kiser, Clyde Vernon: "Sea Island to City," Atheneum, New York, 1969.
29. Knowles, Louis L. and Kenneth Prewitt: "Institutional Racism in America," Prentice-Hall, Englewood Cliffs, N.J., 1969.
30. Kotz, Nick: "Let Them Eat Promises: The Politics of Hunger in America," New Jersey: Prentice-Hall, Englewood Cliffs, N.J., 1969.
31. Krumdick, Carlos L.: The Rural-to-Urban Malnutrition Gradient, Journal of American Medical Association, vol. 215, March 8, 1971.
32. Lester, Anthony: "Justice in the American South," Amnesty International, London, 1965.
33. Lewis, Hylan: "Blackways of Kent," United Printing Services, Inc., Connecticut, 1955.
34. "Majority Black School Districts in the 11 Southern States," Race Relations Information Center, Nashville, Tenn., 1970.
35. Mills, 1935.
36. Myrdal, Gunnar: "An American Dilemma," McGraw-Hill, New York, 1944.
37. Nelson, Jack: County Work Camps: Rehabilitation or Recrimination? New South, vol. 24, p. 55 (spring, 1969).
38. Newman, Dorothy K.: The Negro's Journey to the City—Part 2, Monthly Labor Review, vol. 88, 1965.
39. One of Four Thousand, Civil Rights Digest, vol. 2, p. 26, spring, 1969.
40. Osofosky, Gilbert: "Harlem: The Making of a Ghetto," Torch Books, New York, 1968.
41. Payne, William: There is a Hunger Here, Civil Rights Digest, vol. 2, winter, 1969.
42. Powdermaker, Hortense: "After Freedom," Atheneum Publishers, New York, 1968.

43. Price, Margaret: "The Negro Voter in the South," Southern Regional Council, Atlanta, 1957.

44. Raper, Arthur F.: "Preface to Peasantry," University of North Carolina Press, Chapel Hill, 1936.

45. Ray, Marshall F.: Racial Factors Influencing Entry into the Skilled Trades, in Mark Perlman (ed.), "Human Resources in the Urban Economy," Johns Hopkins Press, Baltimore, 1963.

46. "Report of the U.S. Commission on Civil Rights," U.S. Government Printing Office, Washington, D.C., 1959.

47. Rodgers, Harrell R., Jr. and Charles S. Bullock III: "Law and Social Change," McGraw-Hill, New York, 1972.

48. Rubins, Morton: Migration Patterns of Negroes from a Rural Northeastern Mississippi Community, Social Forces, vol. 39, pp. 59–66, October, 1960.

49. Scott, Emmett: "Negro Migration During the War," Arno Press, New York, 1969.

50. ——: More Letters of Negro Migrants of 1916 to 1918, Journal of Negro History, vol. 4, no. 3, pp. 457–458, October, 1919.

51. Sherman, Richard B. (ed.): "The Negro and the City," Prentice-Hall, Englewood Cliffs, N.J., 1970.

52. Spero, Sterling D. and A. L. Harris: "The Black Worker: The Negro and the Labor Movement," Columbia University Press, New York, 1968.

53. Spivak, John L.: "Georgia Nigger," Patterson Smith, Montclair, N.J., 1969.

54. Sugg, Redding: Poor Hungry Babies, New South, vol. 26, pp. 17–23, fall, 1971.

55. U.S. Census Bureau, Current Population Reports: Series P-23, no. 42, 1972.

56. United States Department of Agriculture, Cotton Contract AAA, Washington, D.C.

57. Vandiver, Joseph S.: The Changing Realm of King Cotton, Trans-action, vol. 4, pp. 24–30, 1966.

58. Walls, Dwayne E.: "The Chickenbone Special," Harcourt Brace Jovanovich, Inc., New York, 1971.

59. Wasserman, Miriam: White Power in the Black Belt, New South, Southern Regional Council, vol. 22, no. 1, winter, 1967.

60. Watters, Pat: CDGM: Who Really Won, New South, vol. 22, pp. 49–64, spring, 1967.

61. Williams, James: Bellamy, Alabama: Company Town Revisited, Civil Rights Digest, vol. 2, pp. 12–20, fall, 1969.

62. Woodson, Carter G.: "The Rural Negro," Association for the Study of Negro Life and History, Washington, D.C., 1930.

63. Wooten, James T.: Prison Road Gangs Are Fading Fast in the South, The San Francisco Chronicle, p. 24, Nov. 7, 1971.

64. Wright, Richard R., Jr.: The Negroes of Xenia, Ohio: A Social Study, Bulletin of the Bureau of Labor, no. 48, vol. 8, pp. 1006–1044, September, 1903.

Leonard Freed/Magnum Photos, Inc.

5   Migrant Labor

THE GRIM PICTURE

For the Blacks who move with the migrant labor stream, status has been an outgrowth of not only their "place" in American society but also the changing character of American agriculture. After the First World War the geography of perishable fruits and vegetables began to change. Farms were once restricted to those areas immediately surrounding the towns and cities which they served, but with more rapid truck and rail transportation and improved methods of refrigeration, the crops could be grown further from their markets. Thus the zone of truck farming moved further out into the countryside in particular, forested areas. These newer, larger, specialized farms needed large numbers of laborers to plant, pick, and pack the crops.

But for the black worker there was an added factor—his "place" in American society. With the decline of the plantation economy, many Blacks became perpetual wanderers in the eastern migrant stream. Their bleak existence is a result of being poor, black, and migratory in a society that respects none of these characteristics. The black migrants are marginal people, not allowed into the dominant society which surrounds them, yet expected to share its values and to cope with its legal, social, and economic institutions. "They are not accepted as belonging to a distinct and viable subculture, nor are they fully accepted as a part of the larger society" (Nelkins, 1972).

The East Coast migrant labor stream is made up primarily of Blacks, although Whites, Puerto Ricans, Indians, and Chicanos are also included. Their numbers are estimated at from 50,000 to 100,000 or 200,000. New York migrants, for example, are 75 percent black, with the remainder made up of Puerto Ricans, Indians, Chicanos, and Whites.

These migrants move up and down the eastern seaboard in a yearly cycle that begins with the harvest of citrus fruits, vegetables, and sugar cane in January in Florida, then moves northward with the ripening of the spring crops of berries, melons, tobacco, tomatoes, orchard and grove fruit. Summer finds them harvesting the cherries and apples of Michigan and New York and

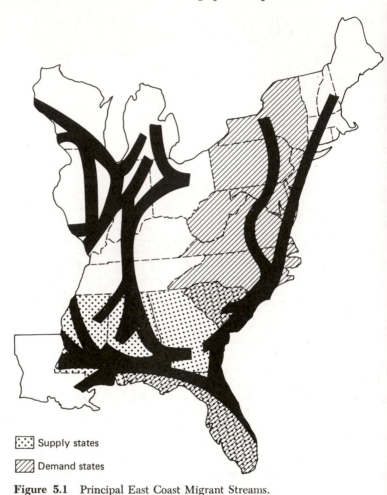

Figure 5.1   Principal East Coast Migrant Streams.

(*From U.S. Department of Labor, "Farm Labor Fact Book," 1959, p. 114.*)

the New England states. There has been, since World War II, a concentrated effort by federal and state employment services, crew leaders, and growers and their associations to get the workers to the right place at the right time.

The principal East Coast migrant streams are shown on Figure 5.1. This map also depicts the supply and demand states for the East Coast stream of migrants. Supply states are those which have a surplus of labor and thus supply migrants to demand states which have labor shortages. South Carolina and Florida function as both supply and demand states.

A more detailed breakdown of the East Coast migrant stream is presented in Figure 5.2. Of the 57,000 migrants making up the 675 crews moving north in 1968, the states of New York and Virginia received together more than 60 percent of the migrants (see Table 5.1).

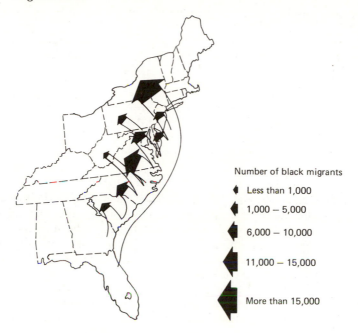

Figure 5.2   Dispersion of East Coast Migrants, from 675 Crews, 1958.
(*From U.S. Department of Labor, "Farm Labor Fact Book," 1959, p. 126.*)

Another detailed view of the East Coast migrant pattern is given from the data available at the Farm Labor Office at Little Creek, Virginia, which is located at the ferry slip on the Norfolk side of the entrance to Chesapeake Bay. The ferry is on a major route to the North, and is about halfway between Florida and Maine. During the 1958 harvest season, 21,000 workers used the ferry; one-third were women, nine-tenths were Blacks, about one-third were in families or crews, and almost 90 percent were destined for jobs in Maryland and the eastern shore of Virginia.

Movement has been generally thought of as a means to improve one's lot in America. But this has not been the case for Blacks, even less so for migrant blacks, whose promise of freedom and acceptance has gone unfulfilled. Black migrants know their "place," where they can stop, where they can stay, what roads they can take. The fact that Blacks have had a "place" apart from the rest of American society has not changed. Migrant labor differs not in its offering greater opportunities to Blacks, but in its forcing a larger cycle of movement upon them than was allowed under slavery and sharecropping. It is significant to note that, even with the greater spatial mobility inherent in migrant labor, the place of the Black in the restricted social and geographic space in America has remained very limited.

By early childhood, space and movement have come to have very special meanings to migrant children. They soon learn that people, things, and places

State	Migrants	State	Migrants
New York	15,600	New Jersey	3,700
Virginia	11,600	S. Carolina	3,300
N. Carolina	7,900	Delaware	3,200
Maryland	6,300	W. Virginia	900
Pennsylvania	4,200	Other states	400

Table 5.1 Dispersion of 675 Migrant Labor Crews in the East Coast Migrant Labor Stream, 1958.

Source: *Farm Labor Fact Book, U.S. Department of Labor, 1959, p. 126.*

are tentative and will soon disappear. They do not make the mistake of becoming attached to a lot of places and possessions. The migrant child has no space of his own and "he does not gain a feeling of his own space." As one 8-year-old migrant commented, " 'I love the yo-yo,' she told me, 'because it keeps going up and down, and that's what I do.' What did she mean? 'Well, we don't stay in one camp too long. When the crops are in you have to move' " (Coles, 1971). Movement and place simply come to mean different things to migrants than to settled people. The movement of the migrant is not like that of other people. This contrast in movement is brought out starkly by Peter.

> The teacher said you can fold up a lot of things and just carry them with you, so there's no excuse for us not having a lot of things, even if we're moving a lot, that's what she said, and one of the kids, he said his father was a salesman and traveled all over the country, and he said his father had a suitcase full of things you could fold up and unfold and they were all very light and you could hold the suitcase up with one finger if you wanted, that's how light. My daddy said it wasn't the same, the traveling we do, and going around selling a lot of things. He said you could make big money that way, but you couldn't do it unless you were a big shot in the first place, and with us, it's no use but to do what you know to do, and try to get by the best you can, and that's very hard he says (Coles, 1971).

The migrant is caught in a social and spatial trap. He is isolated from the communities that he serves. The camps are generally located far from towns and cities. They are not wanted by the townspeople. Poverty and blackness are traits that add to their isolation from the surrounding communities. Finally, those social services, police, health care, etc., that are seen by the dominant culture as helpful are seen by migrants as dangerous; and migrants are in turn treated by the agencies as problems. Migrants are denied access to services that many others take for granted. These services which are withheld become even more inaccessible because the migrants are constantly moving.

Being Black and in constant movement makes schooling a virtual impossibility. The children are not in any one place long enough to have a continual learning experience. As a result they are consistently behind their settled age mates. This problem has been put very well in Shotwell's novel:

> Roosevelt knew all about "taking away from"; he had learned that kind of arithmetic maybe three or four times in the last few schools he had been to. That was the trouble with always moving, following the crops; you never got a chance to find out anything new (Shotwell, 1963).

If the migrant child makes it as far as junior high school, the chances are that he will be 2 or 3 years behind the average child.

There do appear to be some programs under way to help combat illiteracy among migrants, both children and adults. Most of them seem to be federally funded pilot projects. A major problem with these types of programs is that they are consistently kept at the pilot stage or are terminated. This country, despite its avowed interest in quality education, simply is not willing to face the task of financing such an education for Blacks, much less migrant Blacks.

One such pilot program in Florida provides sixty-one specially designed house trailers near migrant housing for the education of migrant children. The New York Center for Migrant Studies is working with the concept of "individualized instruction" to try to improve the educational opportunities of migrant children. Although an education may be useful, its ability to help migrant children escape the system is extremely limited.

Migrant labor is one area in which the child labor laws of the country are ignored. The added income, though scant, that the children's labor provides is incentive to keep them out of school and in the fields. This practice is condoned and encouraged by crew leaders, growers, and inspection officials. While still young, children learn that they are to "get lost" when an inspector is sighted; they know that any trouble they cause is followed by sanctions against their parents. Also, in many states the compulsory school attendance laws permit children under 14 to be excused from school work to work in agriculture. In addition, school laws often do not apply to migrant children.

Education is an area of ambivalence for migrant families, much the same as it has been for nonmigrant, poor black families. An education is a prized possession and is looked upon as a way out of the system of poverty. Yet, the aspiration often conflicts with the financial needs of the family. Not only can children provide extra income, but their attendance in school puts added pressure on the parents to remain in one place, which the migrant worker finds hard to do:

> Then I was getting ready to say we shouldn't go at all, and my daddy told me to shut up, because it's hard enough to keep going without us talking about this friend and the school and the teacher and how we want to stay; so he said if I said another word I'd be sorry, and I didn't (Coles, 1971).

Another important aspect to this problem of ambivalence toward education is the conflict and inconsistency between those values presented in school and the reality of the children's lives. Added to this is the past experience of the adults that school is not realistic for the children as an avenue of escape. Pat,

The "culture of poverty": a sharecropper's child in 1938. The plight of migrant children today is not much better.

From the Picture Collection of the Library of Congress.

for example, wants to leave the migrant life, continue school, and eventually go to college. "But when she was talking about this in the fields, someone put her down, saying, 'You'll always be in the fields, so don't even think about it'" (Friedland and Nelkins, 1972). Migrant farm children "see schools as ultimately irrelevant to their future." Lorrie, for example, at 10 when asked to draw her school, drew "an isolated box essentially irrelevant to the carefully drawn landscape." She could draw certain natural features such as woods, fields, birds, and a nearby lake, but not a school (Coles, 1971).

Another aspect of migrant life that is different from nonmigrant is the legal aspects of movement. Migrants are not desired as neighbors by settled Whites, and thus to be law-abiding they must move on. This amounts to a modern adaptation of white law to control black movement. Like other aspects of of migrant living, the law is learned very early in life. The following comments of young children clearly indicate that they recognize that being a migrant has its legal rules that must be internalized. From Peter, age about 9:

> Once a policeman asked me if I like school and I said sometimes I did and then he said I was wasting my time there, because you don't need a lot of reading and writing to pick the crops, and if you get too much of schooling, he said, you start getting too big for your

> shoes, and cause a lot of trouble, and then you'll end up in jail pretty fast and never get out if you don't watch your step—never get out (Coles, 1971).

and from Tom, age 7:

> My daddy, he says you can get into a lot of trouble that way, because the police are always looking to see if we're not keeping moving, and if they catch you sitting by the road, they'll take you to jail and they won't let you out so easy either (Coles, 1971).

Constant movement brings about other problems. "From the migrant's perspective, the government and the law are neither supportive nor protective institutions; they are threatening and must be avoided at all cost" (Friedland and Nelkins, 1972). The American court system is based on at least semi-permanent residence, which makes it difficult for a migrant to obtain help from a bondsman or to remain in a place long enough for a court date. It is common for the government-sponsored legal aid services that are supposed to aid migrants to be actually run by growers and their interests to maintain the status quo.

As is the case with their relationships with other social institutions, migrants do not trust conventional medicine and often rely on home remedies and "root medicine." The latter types of health care are more easily transferable from place to place. Medical aid that is tied to the government is often hampered by bureaucracy and under the influence and control of local growers.

Dr. Wheeler and Mr. Davis concur with respect to the nature of the health care available to the migrants and the reasons behind the lack of care. Dr. Wheeler testified before the Senate Subcommittee of Migratory Labor that:

> Every effort is directed toward isolating the farm worker from the rest of society, maintaining him at the lowest level of subsistence which he will tolerate, then making certain that he has no means of escape from a system that holds him in virtual peonage. And to that end, the grower has the full cooperation of the federal government, the state and the local community.

The Field Director of the Florida NAACP, Marvin Davis, adds:

> I have reached the conclusion, based upon my work and direct involvement, that the 100,000 seasonal agricultural workers in the state of Florida are the victims of the most extreme abuse and exploitation to be found anywhere in the United States. In fact, it is my opinion that farm labor conditions in this state constitute a national disgrace, if not a deliberate conspiracy involving the U.S. Congress, U.S. government agencies, state, county and local business and public officials (Select Senate Subcommittee on Nutrition and Human Needs, 1969).

The migrants' relationship with the grower and crew leader is much like that with the social institutions of the outside society. That is, he has no word in the structure or has no decision-making power other than to continue in the migrant stream or leave. But for most migrants, leaving is really not seen as an alternative. They tend to perceive moving out of the system as nearly impossible. The migrant, for example, has no voice in the process that establishes the conditions under which he will work. These conditions are determined by agents of the Farm Labor Service of the U.S. Employment Service, growers, and crew leaders. The migrant has no decision-making power relative to the conditions of the camps in which he must live.

Camps vary in size and character; they are owned by growers on their cooperatives. The range of quality, however, is from bad to worse. Small, bare rooms, lack of adequate ventilation and bathroom facilities, crowding, no privacy, and impersonality characterize the camps. The concurrence of the growers and public officials maintain the unhealthy conditions. In Belle Glade, for example, housing that was condemned for 10 years remained occupied and paid for by migrants. It was pointed out by Reverend Paul Wilson that if you want to be a successful county sanitarian you work with the growers. Local building codes and sanitation rules are just ignored when it comes to migrant housing. For the migrant, "law and order" come to mean "lawlessness and disorder."

The crew leader is the middleman between the white grower and the outside world which wants no contact with the migrant and the migrant who is apprehensive and fearful of the outside world. The crew leader arranges the transportation, the time of movement, the destinations. He provides for the services found in towns. He supervises the work. Because he controls so much of the migrant's life, the crew leader becomes a very powerful figure. As Mr. Juarez of the Organized Migrants in Community Action commented before the Select Senate Subcommittee on Nutrition and Human Needs:

> Senator Javits: Does the crew leader take the crew from place to place throughout the United States?
> Mr. Juarez: Sometimes, yes, most of the time.
> Senator Javits: But there is no feeling that you can work for anybody else?
> Mr. Juarez: How? You go up North and I try to get work directly through the farmer, and he says, "No, go speak to so and so, he is the one in charge."
> Senator Javits: And that is always a crew leader or a contractor?
> Mr. Juarez: That is right, sir.
> Senator Javits: So the worker can't get out of it.
> Mr. Juarez: He can't get out of it (Select Senate Subcommittee on Nutrition and Human Needs, 1969).

Here again is the cruel ambivalence of the migrant's life. On the one hand, he is trapped and controlled by the crew leader and knows it. Yet the latter is his only hope in the only way of life that he knows. As one migrant mother put it, "Without him there would be nothing for us to do" (Coles, 1973).

We have stressed that the migrant has virtually no voice in those matters that affect his education, health, housing, travel, food, or income. He is de-

Figure 5.3 Origin and Destination of Migrant Workers. 1 = Memphis, Tennessee; 2 = Knoxville, Tennessee; 3 = Nashville, Tennessee; 4 = Hopkinsville, Kentucky; 5 = Bowling Green, Kentucky; 6 = Frankfort, Kentucky; 7 = Bluefield, West Virginia; 8 = Raleigh, North Carolina; 9 = Elizabeth City, North Carolina; 10 = Bergen, New York; 11 = Puerto Rico.

pendent for his basic needs upon others who, to say the least, do not place his needs very high. The organized nature of middle-class life allows for the planning of one's future and the expectation of at least a certain amount of control over one's life. But this is not the case for the migrant. The migrant's response to this disorganized life has been described as apathetic, but apathy is a middle-class term used to describe the inability of the poor to get out of the stark trap in which they are kept.

When one has little or no control over one's life, it may well be harmful to try to plan ahead. The adaptation to migrant circumstances is a self-perpetuating trap, as the social patterns needed to survive in the migrant camps are opposite those necessary to be successful in the outside world.

THE CAMP: A FORMER MIGRANT LABORER'S RECOLLECTIONS

This is a case study of the experiences of a young man who spent part of the summer in a migrant labor camp. This migrant labor camp was located in upstate New York between Buffalo and Rochester. It was large and complicated and was connected to canning and frozen food operations. The camp was open from late spring until late summer for 100 or 110 days. It had three primary sources of labor. It recruited black college students from predominantly black schools in the South, high school seniors in the same areas, and Puerto Ricans from sugar plantations. The contractors understood well that any young black male who was committed to acquiring a higher education would find it virtually impossible to find work; therefore they had a captive labor market. In the case of Arliss, who had completed his sophomore year at Kentucky State College, he had gone home looking for work. During the two previous summers he had worked as a custodian, a red-cap, a porter, a dishwasher, and a busboy. But that summer there was absolutely nothing available to him. Therefore, in frustration, he returned to the campus and discovered that one of his classmates had received a one-way nonredeemable Greyhound bus ticket to Bergen, New York, to work at the migrant labor camp. Having no idea what was ahead, but filled with desperation because of his need and desire to return to school the following autumn, he eagerly accepted the challenge. The rest of the story is told in Arliss' own words.

> I was given a one-way Greyhound bus ticket to Bergen, New York. This would be the longest bus ride that I had ever taken, from Frankfort, Kentucky, to Bergen, New York. But the long 19 hours would be worth it, if I could earn the money to return to school in the fall.
>
> The ride was long, hot, unexciting, and extremely tiring. Even though a half-dozen of my schoolmates accompanied me, it was a total bore. Upon arriving in Bergen, we were met at the bus stop by the black man who was used as a recruiting agent and by a driver with an open-bed truck. We piled into the back of the truck and made our way several miles to the camp. The camp was composed of a number of one-story buildings with one two-story building. Upon debarking from the truck, we discovered that the three smaller buildings were to be used as dormitories. The other buildings were related to various aspects of good processing, with one building each for a kitchen, dining hall, and an office building.
>
> Soon after reaching camp, we were assigned bunks and told to pick up bedding. For some strange reason, among the pieces of bedding there were no sheets. I was issued one pillow case, one

mattress cover, and one G.I. blanket. I remained at the camp for 4 weeks, during which time I slept on the same mattress cover with the same blanket without sheets. After making up my bunk and storing my gear, I looked about the area and began to meet my fellow workers.

On the next day, much to my amazement, practically everyone I met was in a situation similar to mine. That is, all of the other young men were enrolled in all-black colleges or were high school students who intended to enroll in college, and had taken this summer job for it represented their only opportunity to earn their way to school the following September. There were high school students from: Bowling Green, Kentucky; Frankfort, Kentucky; Hopkinsville, Kentucky; and Memphis, Tennessee. The college students came from: Bluefield State College, Bluefield, West Virginia; Elizabeth City State College, Elizabeth City, North Carolina; Kentucky State College, Frankfort, Kentucky; Knoxville College, Knoxville, Tennessee; Saint Augustine College, Raleigh, North Carolina; Tennessee State College, Nashville, Tennessee; and West Virginia State College, Institute, West Virginia. I learned that some of the college students were juniors and seniors and had been working at camp since senior high school.

In late afternoon of my second day there was a meeting. A meeting called by the black "contact man." The meeting was called for the purpose of spelling out the groundrules. Even though, by this time, I had noticed a number of Puerto Ricans around, none of them was present at this meeting. However, I didn't think much about it at the time. We were told that we would receive 90 cents an hour for a 56-hour week, and that we would receive time and a half for over 56 hours. We were told that a work day consisted of 12 hours (11½ hours with pay and a half hour off for lunch). We learned that we could expect to work 5 days a week and from time to time we would be requested, but not obligated, to work more.

I discovered that in order to earn any take home pay it was necessary to work 18 hours a day for at least 6 days a week. For, on a 56-hour-week there was only about $22 take-home. After paying state, federal, and local taxes along with Social Security and $17 for room and board, approximately $22 was left. Even working 12 weeks it is conceivable that my net would have been less than $300. But generally, there were opportunities to work overtime. Therefore, some of the guys earned enough to return to college. I remained at the camp for 4 weeks and only once earned a decent take-home pay. During that week, I worked in excess of 120 hours. Five days I was on the job for 18 hours each, and once I was on the job for 36 hours in succession.

The plight of the Blacks was obviously bad, but I soon discovered that things were even worse for the Puerto Ricans and the black families from Florida. The Puerto Ricans were there during the interim between the sugar cane harvest and planting. From Jorge, Miguel, and other Puerto Ricans, I learned that they received only 75¢ an hour and were not permitted to work in excess of 56 hours during pea season. Later I heard from others (non–Puerto Ricans) that Jorge, Miguel, and their friends were incorrect about their working conditions and during bean season they did very well. However, I choose to believe their version of their work arrangements.

Except for a few of the young men who had been there before and worked in "straw boss" positions, our work was long, hard, and back-breaking. The black students and the Puerto Ricans shared similar work experiences. They varied from working in the field, to harvesting, to thrashing or separating the peas from the vines and pods, to using pitchforks for 11½ hours a day, to working in the plant shoveling peas, green beans, or other vegetables, to pushing harpers, to working in the frozen food plant (going from a very hot un-air conditioned plant into the freezing room with the temperature variation of 80° or more). The Puerto Ricans were not sent air line tickets. They managed their transportation as best they could, with less opportunity to end up with profit than the black college students.

The saddest plight of all was that of the permanent migrant laborers, according to their own words. These were families who came from southern Florida, and their transportation consisted of a ride from the citrus groves of Florida to Bergen, New York, in closed vans. This was a trip which exceeded 1,300 miles in distance. The trucks were of the "moving van" variety, and to accommodate the passengers, they nailed two-by-fours around the walls and placed two-by-fours under the horizontal two-by-fours, for these were their seats. Thirteen hundred miles riding in the back of a van under slightly better conditions than cattle being shipped to slaughter. Entire families made the jaunt and everyone was expected to share in the labor. From family to family the wages often differed, but the consensus was that under no conditions did this group receive more than an average of 50 cents an hour.

These things I saw, heard and lived with for 4 weeks. As inhumane as the conditions were, I personally did not feel that I was as bad off as others, for I had an alternative. My alternative was not to return to school in the fall and enter the army, which I elected to do. Unfortunately most of the others had no such alternative. Since, I have often wondered where law and justice were at this labor camp (private interview).

The above narrative is as correct and as factual as Arliss could remember. It is included not to alarm, but to inform the many about the plight of a few who are forced to become migrant laborers.

SELECTED BIBLIOGRAPHY

1. Coles, Robert: "Migrants, Sharecroppers, Mountaineers," vol. II, "Children of Crisis," Atlantic-Little Brown, Boston, 1973.
2. ———: "Uprooted Children: The Early Lives of Migrant Farm Workers," Harper and Row, New York, 1971.
3. "Farm Labor Fact Book," Washington, D.C.: U.S. Department of Labor, 1959.
4. Friedland, William and Dorothy Nelkins: "Migrant," Holt, Rinehart, and Winston, New York, 1972.
5. Nelkins, Dorothy: Invisible Migrant Workers, *Society*, April, 1972, vol. 9.
6. Select Senate Subcommittee on Nutrition and Human Needs, Washington, D.C.: U.S. Government Printing Office, 1969.
7. O'Connell, Michael: Migrant Farmers in New York, *Civil Rights Digest*, vol. 5, pp. 11–16, winter, 1972.
8. Shotwell, Louise Rossiter: "Roosevelt Grady," World, New York, 1963.

Brown Brothers

6 Residential Segregation

ORIGINS

Segregation has been a commonplace practice in the United States, in the North as well as in the South, in rural and in urban areas. The social institutions in American life reflect in their locational patterns the geography of race relations. One of the important points in this sociospatial order is that there is not merely a white ruling class but a white population over Blacks. Many Whites have cared nothing one way or another about Blacks except that they be kept separate. Cox has called the United States a bipartite society and has found that "explicit segregation is at the foundation of all the racial discrimination and exploitative practices of whites."

> In fact, segregation is here absolutely necessary to maintain white ruling-class dominance. The colored zones, belts, and camps are fundamental restrictions upon the colored people. They restrict the latter's freedom of physical movement, the *sine qua non* of a normal life under capitalism. What segregation really amounts to is a sort of perennial imprisonment of the colored people by the whites (Cox, 1948).

Segregation is a process of differentiation and distinction in which an individual and/or group acquires positions in both the social and spatial orders of society. There can be segregation, supported by the sense and conventions of social distance, without physical separation. Segregation is not only spatial, but includes all conventions and social ritual designed to enforce social isolation and social distance, and those racial traditions not specifically or directly spatial are supported by and in turn support spatial segregation practices.

The sociospatial relationship between Blacks and Whites in the United States may be expressed on a graph (p. 110). As the Whites' perception of their need for social distance between themselves and Blacks increases, their need for geographic distance from Blacks decreases. At those times and places when Whites have been able to maintain great social distance, they have seen little need for great spatial distance. "The problem of segregation arises only when white families of approximately the same economic class are introduced"

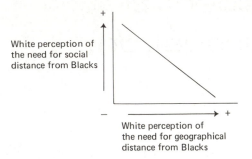

White perception of the need for social and geographic distance from
Blacks.

(Johnson, 1934). In the case of the plantation, master and slave were able to
live together so long as the proper social distance was maintained.

But once ambiguity begins to characterize the social distance between the
two groups, there has been a tendency for an increase in the need for spatial
distance.

> The taboo against social equality and intimate association ap-
> parently takes care of the problem of residential propinquity in
> southern communities, where there have always been Negroes and
> their place is so well defined in social space that their location in
> ecological space does not loom as a great issue. In the North, how-
> ever, where their social status is more anomalous and where they
> have no customary place in the community, the residential location
> of Negroes becomes an issue (Johnson, 1934).

The white reaction to the presence of Blacks has depended largely on the
spatial context in which the interaction occurred. White Americans have
seemingly needed to have either superior social or spatial positioning in relation to Blacks. Race relations, as they developed under the southern plantation system, were of the former type. That is, social distance as expressed in
interpersonal relations and positions was maximized.

> This great degree of social distance allows close symbiosis and
> even intimacy without any threat to status inequalities. Conse-
> quently, physical segregation is not prominently used as a mecha-
> nism of social control and may, in fact, be totally absent between
> masters and servants living together in a state of "distant intimacy"
> (Van den Berghe, 1967).

The competitive type of race relations seems to have been more character-istic of the early North and increasingly of the whole country, as efforts are made to equalize the social position of Blacks with that of Whites. "To the extent the social distance diminishes, physical segregation is introduced as a second line of defense for the preservation of the dominant group's position" (Van den Berghe, 1967). The sociospatial functioning of these two types of race relations is expressed in an old black saying: "In the South the white man doesn't care how close a black man gets so long as he doesn't get too high. In the North the white man doesn't care how high he gets so long as he doesn't get too close."

The spatial organization of American society has in many ways reflected its social organization. This has meant that the institutional caste-like social patterns have had correlates in spatial positioning. When differences in physical traits are considered a determinant of social behavior to the point that they are used as rationalizations for the discriminatory use and access to society's institutions, then we have a caste system.

But rather than digress into the problem of caste, race, and class as social structuring phenomena, we will develop the idea of caste as a spatial structur-ing mechanism. And here we seemingly find agreement between the views of Cox and Van den Berghe. The important point is that a person's caste affilia-tion can be determined by knowing where the person resides. In the slavery situation, slaves had neither social nor geographic mobility like a caste, and in the bipartite situation of post–Civil War America, the restrictions on move-ment and location of Blacks were basic to white supremacy. The attachment of the slave in space is also basic to Van den Berghe's paternalistic or slavery type of race relations in the United States. The competitive type of race rela-tion, Cox's bipartite situation, is characterized by increasing spatial gaps be-tween Blacks and Whites.

In his use of the concept of the total institution, Bryce-LaPorte has added an important dimension to the spatial structuring of black America. The total institution in Goffman's concept is defined as "a place of residence and work where a large number of like situated individuals cut off from the wider society for an appreciable period of time, together lead an enclosed, formally admin-istered life" (Goffman, 1961). Goffman has made spatial structure explicit in his definition. The functions of total institutions as set forth by Goffman in-clude the protection of the community against those who constitute threats to its welfare and the accomplishment of some worklike or instrumental task. Both the plantation and the ghetto are such total institutions. The slave plantation had two functions, one being commercial agriculture, the other the custody of a specific group of people. It is the latter function that corresponds to the denial of geographic mobility as well as to restrictions on residential location inherent in the spatial caste concept. Removal from such a system was escape, either physical or psychological. Also, like caste systems, inmate status in total institutions is ascriptive. The pervasiveness of the custodial function of the plantation was felt by Blacks, regardless of status—runaway, slave, or free—or location—South, North, West, countryside, or city.

Patterns of residential and educational land use are the most common examples of the spatial caste system in the country. It seems to be difficult to pin down the origins of segregation as a spatial process in the United States. There has been segregation in various aspects of life, housing, schooling, transportation, etc.; segregation in each varying with time and place. It seems, for example, that local, legal segregation with respect to schools began in the mid-nineteenth century while legally sanctioned residential segregation did not occur until the beginning of the twentieth century. It is important to stress that the structuring of space has been a mechanism at the disposal of white society to be used whether subtly or forcefully, sanctioned by law and/or custom. Obviously the character of black-white relations varied with the changes in background and organization of economic and social life, the methods to regulate these relations, and the nature of the popular sanctions and philosophies giving meaning and form to the relations dominant in each region. Segregation is not only a spatial process, but includes all conventions and social ritual designed to enforce isolation, and those racial traditions not specifically or directly spatial are supported by and in turn support spatial segregation practices.

Another issue is the fact that segregation can be both de jure and de facto. It is probable that segregation in fact was commonplace much earlier and in many more places than segregation by law. Some authors place the beginnings of segregation in the 1890s. Others maintain that de facto segregation was widespread and rigid soon after emancipation. Still others push the origins of segregation back to before the Civil War.

EARLY PATTERNS OF SEGREGATION UP NORTH

In colonial times, whether in the North or South, the severity of proscriptive legislation against Blacks was largely determined by the density and location of the black population. The growth of the black population and the white fear of uprisings produced a body of laws intended to control both the social and spatial movement and location of the black population. "Thus, in the early days of the Republic and in the place where the Republic was founded, Negroes had a definite 'place' in which they were expected at all times to remain" (Franklin, 1967).

The concerns of white society seemed to center on three geographic aspects of the racial situation: (1) relative numbers of Blacks as compared to Whites; (2) location of the black population;   (3) movement and communication capabilities of the black population.

Large numbers of Blacks in a given locality have always been a threat to the dominance of the white master class. For example, the control of slaves in New York City was more difficult than in the rural areas where the slave population was more dispersed.

The ratio of Blacks to Whites in cities, towns, and rural areas was an important determinant of the nature of local race relations. Racial tolerance has tended to be inversely proportional to the number of Blacks a community has been able to tolerate. As the number of Blacks increased in Cincinnati from 1800 to 1850, for example, the racial attitudes of Whites changed from toleration to persecution. Early Cleveland was like Cincinnati in that racial harmony was due, at least in part, to the relatively small number of Blacks in the city. In many colonies an increase in the black population caused the enactment of slave codes. After the slave revolt in New York City in 1712, white hysteria reached the point where they were worried about black congregation at slave funerals. As a result the city required in 1722 that all dead slaves had to be buried before sunset, and in 1731 the number of slaves at a burial was restricted to twelve.

Slave codes were the legal embodiment of the white wish for a segregated society. One of the consequences of this sociospatial caste system in the urban context was the restriction of Blacks to certain parts of the city. The black ghetto had an early beginning in the scheme of the American city. The exact origin of the "black ghetto" is debated. Some authors have suggested that the black ghettos of American cities have been of relatively recent origin, primarily of the twentieth century. These writers point out, however, that the twentieth-century black ghettos had their roots in the urban patterns of the nineteenth century. It is our belief that the roots of segregation, as reflected in the existence of urban black ghettos, are evident as early as the eighteenth century in both the North and the South. In colonial New England, for example, Blacks generally lived near the docks, riverfronts, or alleys. In Connecticut free Blacks were prohibited from residing in any town or colony in 1717. Blacks and Whites in pre–Civil War Cleveland inhabited different worlds. Litwack clearly indicates that the black ghetto was a reality in northern cities such as Boston, Cincinnati, New York, and Philadelphia at an early date. In Boston, for example, those Blacks who were not servants living in or near the houses of their masters congregated along the wharves in an area called "New Guinea." The establishment of the first black church, the African Meeting House, in 1805 in the West End accelerated the movement of Blacks from the older areas in the East End. From 1830 to 1890 the West End remained the predominant black section of Boston; but was thereafter to decline steadily in its percentage of the total black population. The black area of the city had by 1900 moved to the Roxbury area. By at least 1820, Blacks were concentrated in New York City in the Five Points area. This area was popularly called "Stagg Town" or "Negro Plantations" and was the first place of major settlement for New York's freed slaves.

In the 1870s the black population of Cincinnati was scattered in clusters throughout the city. The "mixed" neighborhoods were concentrated in certain areas, and in these areas black and white segregation existed on a smaller scale, either by block or by building. But the overwhelming majority of the black population lived in the older, deteriorating sections of the city, which bordered the river and downtown, called "Bucktown."

The cities of New Haven and New Salem had their black areas too. In

"Nigger Lane": An early black ghetto in Louisiana.

Louisiana State Museum.

New Haven, for example, by 1829 a black part of town was common knowledge. It was called "New Liberia." Other areas of black settlement were "Negro Lane," "Sodom Hill," and "Poverty Square." By 1864 the process of urban population redistribution had resulted in the consolidation of the black population near the area called Poverty Square, which became the principal black area from 1870 to the 1940s. All the black regions were, for one reason or another, unsatisfactory for habitation, either because of poor soil, poorly constructed dwellings, lack of sanitary facilities, roving animals, or disease.

By the twentieth century, Cleveland was touted as the Negro's Paradise, yet Blacks and Whites still inhabited different worlds. In the mid-nineteenth century Cleveland had two black areas, one being composed of more respectable artisans, the other of nameless drifters in shanties by the riverfront. The apparent racial harmony was partly attributed to the small number of Blacks in the city. In Philadelphia early patterns of racial residential dispersion, while not preventing the development of a Black Belt, did afford many centers where black people could reside. In Chicago, like Philadelphia, Blacks resided in well-scattered clusters prior to 1900; they usually settled, however, at the edge of areas inhabited by wealthy whites or in the poor areas of the city.

The northern slave codes seem to have been harshest in those areas like Boston and Narragansett County where large numbers of Blacks were concentrated. The Boston codes, for example, restricted the movements of Blacks on Sundays, while in the Narragansett area black slaves were not allowed to visit free Blacks.

Spatial concentration, however, was not the only urban residential pattern of Blacks. In early Washington, D.C., for example, the black population was scattered from the Navy Yard to Rock Creek.

There is some indication that the racial caste system was also a part of the rural landscape. Brown, Jefferson, Lawrence, Mercer, and Shelby Counties in Ohio, for example, were the location of rural black colonies in the early nineteenth century. From 1815 to 1860 the Quakers established rural, small, black towns in Howard, Wayne, Randolph, Vigo, Gibson, Grant, Rush, Tipton, and Hamilton Counties in Indiana. Other black settlements were located in Cass County, Michigan, and Greene County, Ohio. Movement to farms and small towns did not work in all cases. An attempt to establish Blacks in upstate New York on 40- to 60-acre plots failed partly because of the poor condition of much of the land and because of the expense. Frederick Douglass noted that, in 1853, Blacks would endure the hardships and cruelties of the crowded cities rather than live isolated in the rural areas.

EARLY PATTERNS OF SEGREGATION DOWN SOUTH

The social order of the pre–Civil War South had its concomitant spatial order. Segregation by custom and statute was common. The "place" of the black person in the South was both socially and spatially prescribed. The spatial proximity evident in early urban and rural residential patterns indicated on the part of Whites great social distance accompanied by a feeling of absolute control of the situation. A number of descriptive nouns—serf, sharecropper, tenant, peon, peasant—have been used to describe the position of the black person in rural southern society following the formal abolition of slavery. This position can be examined in both a social and a spatial sense.

Socially, the place of the "freed" black slave did not significantly change with emancipation. Only the form of slavery was changed. This, of course, is not surprising considering the weight of custom, morality, and legal sanction supporting the plantation system. The dependency relationship between planter and field hand remained virtually the same. Sharecropping and tenantry assured the planter of his needed labor supply, while "promising" the cropper his food and shelter. "For the most part, the plantation system and the relation of tenant to planter remained basically the same from its beginnings until the late 1950's" (Dunbar, 1969).

Spatially, two problems arose with the freeing of the slaves; these were mobility and segregation. Southern society had now to develop new and alter old ways of keeping blacks "in their place." With the development of these mechanisms the institution of slavery went through various stages from private to public, that is, from individual to community control of Blacks. Local sheriffs, black codes, the convict lease system, debt-peonage, and vagrancy laws provided the legal sanction for the arrest and holding of Blacks after 1865 much as the fugitive slave laws had done prior to that date. Like the slave's, "the sharecropper's freedom consisted almost entirely of freedom to move from place to place within the plantation network" (Vandiver, 1966). As put by an elderly black farmer in Macon County, Alabama, in the 1930s, "You know we'se jus' ingn'rint down heah we do'n see much dif'rence 'tween freedom an' slavery, 'cep' den we wuz workin' fer de marster an' now we'se workin' fer oursel's" (Johnson, 1934).

There were three general types of rural segregation expressed in the residential patterns of the South: (1) rural South, which is the plantation pattern in which the tenant's cabins are grouped either near the planter's house or adjacent to the fields that are their responsibility; (2) small town, which is the black residential areas that are usually clustered at the edge of town; (3) isolated community, which is small groups of cabins hidden on back roads or in the hills.

In the small towns the black areas are not usually "inherited" from previous white groups but develop as black quarters. In Kent, Ohio, for example, the majority of the Blacks live in well-defined areas that rim white neighborhoods. There may be more than one such black area, usually separated by white residential areas which have the water, sewer, light, and power facilities lacking in the adjacent black areas. In Kent, the presence of paved streets help distinguish the white from the black neighborhoods.

After the Civil War slaves found immediate restrictions on the possible locations for their homes, and they moved to districts already occupied by Blacks. Such "quarters" seemed to be the destination of Blacks searching for residential sites in Charlottesville and Albermarle County, Virginia. The three black neighborhoods of "Possum Hollow," "The 400," and "Stump Town" are such areas in Laurens, South Carolina. Blacks moved into similar segregated areas in Sandy Spring, Maryland.

The isolation of the type-three segregation pattern may be fairly complete, as in a cluster of cabins on a back road, or it can be a man-made boundary within towns. For example, in "Cottonville" the black and white communities are separated by a railroad track. This track provides the most striking feature of the community, the segregation of black and white dwellings. As in "Cottonville" the economic lives of the Blacks of Farmville, Virginia, touch those of Whites but the rest of their lives are separate. "The Negroes of Farmville, Isrial Hill, and the neighboring country districts form a closed and, in many aspects, an independent group life" (DuBois, 1898). Many small black settlements are isolated in the fields, hills, and woods. The spatial patterns of rural black-white separation along the oyster-bearing coastline and affluents of Maryland and Virginia have been likened to a layer of black between two layers of white. The rich river bottoms and coastal areas are owned and inhabited by Whites. These lands are not, as a rule, available to Blacks for purchase. Behind this waterfront belt is the less valuable land inhabited by Blacks, which is, in turn, backed by the large interior estates of more Whites.

In some cases, "Since the towns are so largely built for the convenience of the white folks and there is so little advantage to the Negro farming population in living in the town, these locations are scarcely more than post-office addresses and occasional market places for Negroes" (Johnson, 1934). The occupancy patterns of plantations, small towns, and isolated communities have at times and places resulted in separate spatial networks for black and white society.

A bird's-eye view of areas in the rural South, for example, may reveal two distinct yet interconnecting networks of transportation and communication. One, made up of roads and public highways, connects the planters' homes and towns. The other is a set of footpaths, unplanned and unofficial, connecting the cabins of black farmers. The two systems intersect, connect, and supplement but do not compete.

> Paths lead from the tenant's house to the commissary, to the crossroads store, to the school and church, neighbor's cabin, and to the midwife's house. Roads lead from the plantation owner's house to the cotton warehouse close by the railroad station, to the department store, to the high school and college, to the county seat, to the church, to the state convention of his lodge, to the hospital, to the home of his distant friends, to the rest of the world (Raper, 1936).

The southern plantations, especially the larger ones, were largely self-sufficient operations, somewhat isolated from their neighbors. Even though the white owner and the black slave lived on the same plantation, they inhabited different worlds. The plantation was a totalitarian factory, village, and police precinct. The plantation has been called a "total socio-cultural system located in ecological space" (Rubin, 1960). It was a self-contained unit, with a distinctive settlement pattern. Even though the residences of the slaves and owners were, many times, close to each other in space, the social distinctions were strong enough that different neighborhoods existed on the plantation. Typically the cabins of the slaves were compactly grouped in rows or in clusters near the home of the owner. The slave cabins, however, were sometimes found somewhat removed from the plantation house, or clustered together over several miles from the owner's residence. Figure 6.1 shows the spatial diffusion of the black quarters on a typical plantation from 1860 to 1881.

To a certain extent the "house" slave was more trusted to remain in his "place" than the "field" slave. Thus, "house slaves were encouraged to remain apart from the other slaves and to identify themselves with the interests of the masters" (Bennett, 1966).

Yet the change from slave to tenant, although doing virtually nothing to the socioeconomic relationship between owner and worker on the plantation, did in many cases seem to alter the spatial arrangement of this rural form of socio-spatial organization. With "freedom" the planter still had his land but no "hands." As a consequence of a multitude of factors associated with the decline of slavery, there has been a change in sequent occupancy in the rural landscape. Basically the change was from the clustering of slave quarters near the owner's house to placing them near the fields which they were to cultivate. This reflected the change from gang labor on large fields to more individual labor on smaller fields. In the newer pattern, whether the inhabitant was

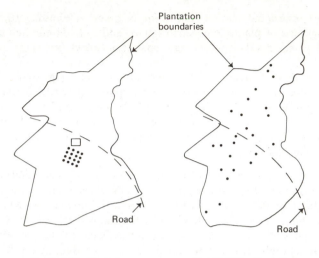

Pre-Civil War Plantation   Post Civil-War Plantation

Figure 6.1   The Spatial Diffusion of Black Quarters on a Typical Plantation from 1860 to 1881 (after Prunty, 1955.) *a* Slave Plantation, 1860. *b* Sharecropper Plantation, 1881.

cropper or tenant, the compact residential unit of the ante-bellum plantation was fragmented and the cabins dispersed (see Figure 6.1). This change did not occur throughout the South, however. In the sugar cane areas the nucleated plantation village remained the dominant settlement pattern.

A new plantation occupancy form has come about since World War II; it has been called the neoplantation. Its settlement pattern more closely approximates that of the traditional plantation than the dispersed cropper-tenant pattern. Dunbar describes the plantation housing patterns as being much like those of the neoplantation in that the tenant cabins are clustered in small neighborhoods along dirt roads. Johnson (1934), however, finds the plantation layout of the 1930s to be the same as it has always been.

There are a number of significant factors associated with this sociospatial change from clustered slaves to dispersed tenants, including control of the means of cultivation, mobility, and the complex social relationship between Whites and Blacks.

One of the problems following the emancipation of the slaves was the degree of mobility of the "freed" Blacks. One author asserts that slaves received unrestricted mobility with emancipation. Although it appears to be generally true that many Blacks did exercise their freedom by moving about, this newfound mobility was short-lived as white society could not tolerate such black mobility. What appeared to be a mass migration to town was not only smaller than imagined, but temporary. What mobility there was existed within an extremely narrow range; slaves who exercised real "freedom" as Whites know it were in the minority. Pre–Civil War mores asserted their power with force and vigor. The plantation aristocracy retained their vast acreage as well as their ideas as to how society should be organized and run. "The four and one-half million Negroes had a kind of 'freedom' and that was about all. They had been 'emancipated' and left there" (Kester, 1969).

During 1865 most "freed" slaves probably remained on the plantations. For those, however, who went to town to test their freedom, some found what they had feared—they had not been freed:

> The Marshall of Columbus has just returned from tearing down a negro shanty town near Muscogee. They tore down the houses in order to drive the negroes into the country to work (Wilson, 1965).

A second even more complex point is the relative power and control Blacks and Whites had over each other after 1865. One author asserts, for example, that the desire for amenities by former slaves when coupled with the economic situation following the war found the planters, if they wanted labor, forced to cater to the wishes of their former slaves. Some planters who were in the line of march of the Union Army, for example, found it necessary to institute some form of wage labor in order to keep hands. There was, also, the stereotype held by the planters of the Blacks that they would not work if given freedom. This idea was, of course, at the heart of slavery. Also, the planters found that if they could retain their former slaves as sharecroppers, they did not need as much cash as they would have if they used wage labor.

Social traditions had developed to the point that emancipation was not uniformly a ticket to independence. On the one hand, there was a great disbelief on the part of Blacks that they were really free. As a result they kept up the habits of earlier associations when "assured" by Whites that the controls were no longer in operation. On the other hand, there was also the habit of dependence which kept the Blacks tied to the old socioeconomic patterns of the plantation. It should be remembered, also, that Whites had become accustomed to the dependent status of Blacks and were not easily detached from the expectations of such relations. The following description of the dependency relations between tenant and planter differs very little from that under slavery.

> The status of tenancy demands complete dependence; it requires no education and demands no initiative, since the landlord assumes the prerogative of direction in the choice of crop, the method by which it shall be sold. He keeps the records and determines the earnings. Through the commissary or credit merchant, even the choice of diet is determined. The landlord can determine the kind and amount of schooling for the children, the extent to which they may share benefits intended for all the people. He may even determine the relief they receive in the extremity of their distress. He controls the courts, the agencies of law enforcement (Kester, 1969).

A black sharecropper put it more succinctly, "You got to be loyal, 'cause you know this is a white man's country" (Johnson, 1934).

Another problem was the nature of the debt relationship between the planters and the freed men. On the one hand, there were numerous difficulties in

"A cabin in the cotton": A South Carolina cotton picker's home.

The Bettmann Archive, Inc.

having the planter enforce verbal or written contracts made with his laborers. To stress these difficulties, however, ignores the exploitative nature of the debt relationship between planter and tenant. One result of debts was to spatially restrict Blacks. The cooperative functioning of the local law official, local vagrancy laws, the planter, and the debt system all worked together to keep the black person tied spatially and socially to the same "place" that he had occupied under slavery.

> I will give you the peonage system as it is practiced here in the name of the law.
> If a colored man is arrested here and hasn't any money, whether he is guilty or not, he has to pay just the same. . . . I will give you an illustration of how it is done:
> I was brought in a prisoner, to go through the farce of being tried. The whole of my fine may be fifty dollars. A kindly appearing man will come up and pay my fine and take me to his farm to allow me to work it out. At the end of the month I find that I owe him more than I did when I went there. The debt is increased year in and year out. You would ask, "How is that?" It is simply that he is charging you more for your board, lodging, and washing than they allow you for your work, and you can't help yourself either . . . because you are still a prisoner (Katz, 1967).

The tenant and sharecropper finds himself at the bottom of a system of short- and long-term indebtedness which engulfs the whole Cotton Belt.

Federal government attempts to intervene in the cotton regime have not trickled down to the bottom levels of the system. The plow-up program of 1933 and the crop reduction program of 1934 forced the sharecropper and tenant off the land with no compensation in Mississippi, Arkansas, and Tennessee. Although Section 10 of the current Cotton Acreage Reduction Contracts guarantees to the tenants and croppers a share of the benefit payments, the planter received the money while the laborers lost not only the benefits but their agricultural livelihood.

Another problem has been the size of the residential area of the tenant of the plantation. The residential area surrounding the tenant cabin is described as expanding at the expense of the cropped lands. But this is not the only pattern. As a rule, tenants in cotton country rarely have gardens; they reside, literally, in a "cabin in the cotton." There are three possible reasons for this. First, gardens take land out of cotton production. Second, there is very little time during growing season to work one's own garden. Finally, the planter's profits from the commissary would decline if the tenants produced their own food. As a Georgia planter put it:

> There is only one way for a planter or farmer to make money with the use of hired labor, and that is to have a grab or commissary and keep books—always careful that no laborer exceeds his account, and making sure that at the end of the year he has gotten it all, and his labor has just lived, as one would say (Kester, 1969).

In the Louise-Midnight area of the Mississippi delta the tenants were, until recently, allowed a small truck garden. This, however, has changed rapidly in the press for more land by the planters.

A major factor in the spatial change in the plantation pattern is the control of cultivating power. In the ante-bellum plantation this control was centralized in the hands of the owners. In the subsequent tenant-cropper pattern, partial control of the means of production was dispersed with the residences of the laborers. In the third pattern, the "neoplantation," there is no centralized control of the agricultural power that necessitated the return to the nucleated settlement pattern. Of course, the decentralization of the control of agricultural power that we are speaking of must be placed in perspective. That is, in the tenant-cropper pattern the laborer may either own his own mule or stable the planter's mule near his cabin rather than in a central barn. There is no question, however, about where the real decision power resides; that always remains in the hands of the planter.

The landlord-tenant relationship has undergone many changes since its inception. Table 6.1 indicates the basic types of landlord-tenant relationship as they were in 1936. There are many variations and combinations based on these major ones. The major differences among the types are who provides the work stock and agricultural implements and the type and division of income at the end of the year.

Wage labor and displaced tenants are two other subtypes of labor relation-

	Sharecropping (croppers)	Share-renting (share tenants)	Cash-renting (cash or standing tenants)
Landlord furnishes	Land, cabin, fuel, ½ fertilizer, tools, seed, work stock, and feed	Land, cabin fuel, ¼ to ⅓ fertilizer	Land, cabin, fuel
Tenant furnishes	Labor, ½ fertilizer	Labor, ⅔ to ¾ fertilizer, tools, seed, work stock, and feed	Labor, fertilizer, tools, seed, work stock, and feed
Landlord receives	½ crop	½ to ⅓ crop	Fixed amount of crop or lint cotton
Tenant receives	½ crop	½ to ⅔ crop	Entire crop less fixed amount

Table 6.1   Planter-Tenant Relationships

Source: *After Woofter, 1969, p. 10.*

ships between planters and laborers. Displaced tenants are allowed to live on the planter's land but no longer work for him nor are they financed by him. This type is increasing as machines replace men in agriculture. The other type is wage labor, in which the relationship is based on the payment of a specified wage and may or may not include provisions for living space. Many of these people are old and sick or single women who can find no work. In some cases nothing is done to evict them, yet nothing is done to keep them alive. Others in this situation find themselves told one afternoon to leave by the next morning, so that the house can be burned and the land planted over in cotton. Many of the tenants remaining on the land in the Louise-Midnight area of Mississippi are in this type of situation. The following brief profiles give some insight into the hardships of households who are left on the plantation with no work.

> A woman alone, unemployed. She will sometimes cook a meal for a white family and earn a little money. She missed buying food stamps because she had doctor's bills. She eats mostly what her neighbors contribute. Her income might be as high as $260 a year.

> The husband has been laid off on the plantation. He is unskilled and had been tending the few cows, but they were being sold, and his job is gone. They can no longer buy food stamps. The children sleep four in one bed, three in another. The family income is $1,300 a year.

Both husband and wife are too sick to work. They keep two children and four grandchildren. The mother was hospitalized after a heart attack and they owe $180 for her bills. She has raised 10 children and had 16 miscarriages. Their whole house is collapsing; they cook over an open fire. Social Security and ADC checks provide $948 a year (Dunbar, 1969).

There has been some change in the planter-tenant relationships as set forth in Table 6.1. The introduction of the tractor has added new jobs but at the same time has caused a decline in the cropping and tenant jobs. Table 6.2 illustrates that, like the tenants and croppers of the 1930s, the Blacks left on the plantation in the 1960s are very poor and retain the dependency relationship with the planter.

The grouping of slaves in an urban setting was not the same as that developed on the plantation. On the plantation, even when the omnipresent overseer was not near, the slaves all belonged to one owner and shared the same events, whereas the social experiences in a city would allow for the meeting of Blacks from a more varied background and with a more extensive information spread.

If linear distance could not be maintained as in the southern city, then the two groups had to be placed in such a way that social distance between the races was maintained. Isolation of Blacks in the urban environment was difficult. Even so the basic objective of urban slave housing was to seal off Blacks from outside contact.

The urban slave's residential complex was transformed into a compound, surrounded by high brick walls, with no windows and the only entrance and exit through or next to the master's house. This compound became the urban equivalent of the rural plantation. As a result of this pattern, black housing in the southern cities was not generally spatially segregated from that of Whites before the Civil War.

The purpose of this residential mixture was not, of course, to integrate the community but rather to prevent the growth of a cohesive Negro society. Local authorities used every available weapon to keep the blacks divided, housing was simply the physical expression of this racial policy (Wade, 1964).

Many processes worked to change this residential pattern. In some cases, Blacks were allowed to "live out" or "work out." That is, they did not have to live and work in the same place. Also with passage of time and growth of population, small, black, residential sections appeared on the edges of towns and cities. By 1880 "ghettos were built up in nearly all southern cities, not always sharply defined but pretty definite, and in these, Negroes must live" (DuBois, 1899). A South Carolinian described conditions in Charleston in 1865 as follows: "I know little of the upper portion of the town but below the burnt district, you see almost a Negro settlement. They occupy abandoned dwellings of which there are many and it is a matter of wonderment how they support themselves"(Wilson, 1965). According to Wade, controlling bondsmen

Employment categories	Number of people in family	Yearly income	Income source
A. Have own farm			
1. 120 acres	14	$950	Farming
2. 120 acres	4	2,400 to 2,900	Farming, wife's job
3. 80 acres	3	1,084	Farming, ADC,° APTD†
4. 40 acres	4	600	Farming
5. 80 acres	2	1,300 to 1,900	Farming, wife's job
6. 80 acres	14	2,550	Farming
7. 40 acres	4	480	Farming, "furnish"‡
8. 100 acres	6	1,140	Farming
9. 37 acres	7	1,342	Farming, rent out land
10. 180 acres	5	600	Farming
11. 4 acres	8	432	Farming, "furnish," veterans' check
12. 120 acres	4	2,240	Rent out land
13. 72 acres	5	892 to 2,192	Farming, rent out land, social security
B. Work on plantation			
1. Tenants			
a.	10	1,635	Tenant relationship
b.	8	1,920	Tenant relationship
c.	9	1,820	Tenant relationship
d.	8	900	Tenant relationship
e.	11	1,960	Tenant relationship
f.	11	2,584	Tenant relationship, ADC
g.	4	1,680	Tenant relationship
2. Sharecropping			
a. 6 acres	7	1,224	Sharecrops
b. 15 acres	16	775	Sharecrops
c.	4	2,240	Sharecrops, social security, daughter's job
3. Rent land			
a. 40 acres	2	440	Crops, "furnish"
b. 27 acres	10	2,456	Crops, wife's job
c. 17 acres	2	1,008	Crops, social security

Table 6.2 Employment, Yearly Income, and Source of Income of Families in Louise-Midnight Community, Mississippi, 1969

° Aid to Dependent Children.
† Aid to Partially and Totally Disabled.
‡ Part of income or food provided by planter.

Source: *Anthony Dunbar,* The Will to Survive, *Atlanta, The Southern Regional Council, 1969, pp. 54–63.*

Employment categories	Number of people in family	Yearly income	Income source
4. Hand labor			
a.	2	846 to 976	Hand labor, social security
b.	5	700	Hand labor
c.	18	2,400	Hand labor
d.	10	2,412	Hand labor
e.	12	700	Hand labor, social security
f.	1	300	Odd jobs, welfare
g.	10	1,108	Hand labor
h.	7	700	Hand labor
i.	3	900	Hand labor
j.	3	1,700	Hand labor
5. Tractor drivers— skilled labor			
a.	9	2,008	Drives tractor, wife works
b.	10	1,000	Drives tractor
c.	7	1,632	Drives tractor
d.	13	1,081	Drives tractor
e.	8	2,924	Skilled labor
f.	8	3,580	Skilled labor, wife's job
g.	15	2,992	Drives tractor, APTD
h.	5	910	Drives tractor
i.	7	1,780	Drives tractor, wife's job
j.	4	1,800	Drives tractor
k.	10	900	Drives tractor
l.	5	1,170	Drives tractor
m.	10	1,612	Drives tractor
n.	14	2,160	Drives tractor
o.	12	1,260	Drives tractor
p.	6	1,930	Drives tractor
q.	12	2,320	General work
r.	15	3,472	General work
s.	3	1,200	Machine operator
t.	4	2,810	Machine operator
u.	4	832	Skilled work
v.	7	1,540	Drives tractor, wife's job
w.	4	1,764	Drives tractor, social security
x.	3	1,550	Drives tractor, wife's job, rent out land
y.	15	2,992	Drive tractor, APTD
C. Other kinds of work			
1.	3	1,928	Odd jobs
2.	2	334	Odd jobs
3.	9	1,129	Teacher

Table 6.2   (continued)

Employment categories	Number of people in family	Yearly income	Income source
4.	10	3,512	Gas service man
5.	11	936	Maid
6.	5	1,753	Maid, welfare
7.	6	334	Cotton gin
8.	8	1,860	Cotton gin
9.	8	3,380	Saw operator
10.	3	360	Auto repair
11.	2	600	Vocational school, wife's job
12.	4	1,380	Maid, ADC, APTD
13.	10	2,900	Maid, social security
D. Unable to work			
1.	5	648	ADC
2.	3	300	ADC
3.	4	492	ADC
4.	4	516	ADC
5.	8	804	ADC
6.	7	732	ADC
7.	2	888	Social security
8.	2	720	Social security
9.	8	1,668	Social security
10.	8	948	Social security, ADC
11.	10	1,104	Social security, ADC
12.	13	1,540	Welfare, social security
13.	3	1,104	Welfare, social security
14.	10	1,708	ADC, children's jobs
15.	6	1,292	ADC, APTD
16.	4	1,795	Welfare, social security
17.	7	1,702	School
18.	9	1,300	Tending cows
19.	9	1,690	Son's job

off the job was the primary problem associated with urban slavery. Increasingly Blacks received their pay directly from their employer and were put on their own to find food and housing. This created a tendency for uncontrolled movement on the part of Blacks.

In the urban setting, systems of racial deference became more apparent, whereas traditional controls had obscured the importance of these forms in the rural setting. The development of more overt forms of social and spatial segregation and discrimination in the southern city was a reflection of the replacement of private control of slaves with public control.

They came to the city: black children in a Harlem public housing development.

Bruce Davidson/Magnum Photos, Inc.

THE PATTERNS HARDEN: THE GROWTH OF THE CITY WITHIN A CITY

To the extent that one can say the American city is largely a product of the twentieth century, it is also true that the black ghetto is predominantly a function of population growth and associated social, economic, and political processes formulated to deal with the increased black population in the urban context. Prior to the twentieth century, however, the spatial context of urban Blacks had been established. The point is that because numbers were relatively small, in general, there had not yet developed the necessity as perceived by Whites for social, political, and economic restrictions that were to develop more strongly in the twentieth century. Before 1900, there was both scattering and clustering of the urban black population. In those places where Blacks were used as domestics, they lived more scattered among Whites and adjacent to their white employers. If and where the black population was large enough, there was more likely to be a clustered pattern within racially mixed neighborhoods. Again as a consequence of small numbers these spatial clusters were seldom found throughout the city.

Residential segregation was not as early a concern of Whites as was segregation in schools and transportation. The first prescribed housing segregation in the United States seems to have been aimed at the Chinese in San Francisco in 1890.

> The significance of this development for other colored minority groups was not to become apparent until World War II, when the Whites on the Pacific Coast pointed to the precedent of the "successful" residential segregation of Orientals as basis for a similar program to meet the housing needs of the latest migrant—the Negro (Weaver, 1948).

State-prescribed segregation aimed at Blacks was soon to follow. In Virginia, for example, the state act of 1912 required each city and town in the state to be divided into segregated and clearly demarcated districts; it was unlawful for Whites and Blacks to move into one another's districts.

The process of segregation was progressing at different rates in various cities. Before the passing of the second decade of the twentieth century, residential concentrations of Blacks were established in the large urban centers. In Chicago, for example, there were by 1912 four relatively well-defined black areas: the South Side, the Near West Side, Englewood, and Lake Avenue in Hyde Park. Harlem was rapidly becoming a city within a city. Detroit, also, had well-defined black areas. Although Pittsburgh's residential pattern was not absolutely segregated, the black districts had become distinct. A pattern of scattered clustering was also present in Minneapolis, Minnesota, and Columbus, Ohio.

As was pointed out in the introduction, the number of Blacks relative to the number of Whites has been a significant aspect of race relations. This was the case in the North with the influx of Blacks during the period of the "Great Migration" of 1915 to 1918.

White racism in the North seems to have been absent or, more accurately, dormant when there were no Blacks around. Racism was subtle when there were only a few Blacks and they "stayed in their place." Race relations were seen as improving in the North up to 1915, but the increase of black population altered this relationship, rekindling social antagonism. Such was the case in Chicago, New York City, and the North in general. The white reaction to the black migration to northern cities was to increase racism not only against the newcomers, but against all Blacks. This generalized reaction indicates that white society had not been able to adjust to the presence of black people as a group but only as isolated individuals. As long as their numbers remain small and they do not assert their claim for a better place, they are "accepted." This generalized white reaction also intensified antagonism between the older black residents and the new migrants. The new migrants to the northern industrial cities were considered "lazy," "dirty," and undesirable by the older black residents.

The influx of black population and the increase of white fear, coincident with the virtual stoppage of building construction, created an increased black demand for housing within a decreasing or static market. According to Forman the modern black ghetto began with the Great Migration. Segregation practices put forth quietly for years were now brought out in the open. The informal means of maintaining black spatial confinement were made increasingly formal and institutionalized. Scattered clusters of black homes were to become less scattered and more clustered. The means used to develop and maintain residential segregation became more complex and varied.

The black-white residential pattern was fairly well set by 1920. In the large, northern urban centers, large numbers of Blacks moved into districts that were retaining a racial as well as an economic stigma. The existence of black ghettos became justifications, in and of themselves, for continuing segregation; just as 40 years earlier the segregation of Orientals had been used to justify the same process for the confinement of Blacks. Residential segregation increased through the third and fourth decades of the century. Two of Woofter's four patterns of segregation are descriptive of the northern cities at this time. In some cities black concentration was great, and Blacks were confined to small areas of the cities. Such was the case, for example, in Chicago and New York City. In the early twentieth century, Chicago black neighborhoods were becoming more, not less, segregated. The same was true of Harlem. The second pattern is characterized by smaller numbers of Blacks located in a small area of the city, yet scattered within this area. Gary, Indiana, was such a city.

Residential segregation of Blacks steadily increased. In Chicago, for example, "The same restrictions that had limited Negro opportunities in the early twentieth century still operated in 1966" (Spear, 1967). There has been and is a very high degree of residential segregation in American cities regardless of their size or location.

It is very difficult to unravel cause and effect in the process in which residential segregation reinforces and is itself reinforced by other forms of discrimination. Yet there is no doubt that residential segregation is a major force in the formation and maintenance of black ghettos. The process of diffusion of black population in the urban environment has been and is being fought vigorously by the white segment of the population. "To be sure, we can be reasonably certain that there is discrimination against Negroes in almost all American communities" (Blalock, 1967).

There are three basic components essential to the process of ghetto formation. These are population groups, space, and value positions or mores defining what is good and bad for people and space. The formation of black ghettos involves the implicit or explicit categorization on the part of one group, Whites, of another group, Blacks, as "bad" and the association of the latter with a particular location in space. Then, the space allotted to Blacks becomes undesirable to Whites. The placement of negative values by Whites on Blacks and the space allotted to them has existed for a long time in the United States. The black ghetto is a subcommunity within the confines of the larger community. It has boundaries which are as real as a brick wall, limiting and channeling social and economic relations between Whites and Blacks. The formation and maintenance of the black ghetto is both an individual and a group process. The movers are individuals and must undergo the hardships of moving, but the absorbing group views them not as individuals looking for homes but as invading group members who must be repulsed.

The number of variables involved in the process of residential segregation is probably as diverse and as myriad as the people involved. These variables can be classed, however, as either socioeconomic or ecologic.

Ecological Variables

The physical characteristics of a city can play an important role in the formation, maintenance, and growth of black ghettos. The characteristics, amount, location, cost, and ease of access of suitable land for residential expansion influence the degree of housing competition between Blacks and Whites. Blumberg and Pittman and Holland agree that ecological variables are important in the segregation process. Frazier found that black population predominated in areas with a majority of nonresidential structures. Black residential areas in Miami were zoned commercial and industrial.

Physical landmarks and topography are also important elements of the environment that may act as barriers to residential movement. Train yards, highways, and rivers form boundaries for black ghettos, "man providing where God has not wrought" (Carter, 1960). "Physical boundaries, whether they are simple natural obstacles to movement or socially contrived barriers designated by custom, are something of a guarantee of the racial status quo" (Clark, 1962). The Harlem and Cuyahoga Rivers, for example, separated black and white residential areas in New York City and Cleveland. In Washington, D.C., the Anacostia River is an effective barrier between communities—making social and other meaningful contact almost impossible. Mountain slopes threading through Los Angeles act as barriers to black residential movement and have become known to Blacks as "the white highlands." In San Francisco and Seattle hilly terrain serves as a barrier to black residential movement as the vertical rise in topography is often positively associated with a high socioeconomic position. In Richmond in the 1920s the worst section of the city was in a deep valley and along steep hillsides. The use of the term "bottom" as a place name for many black residential areas is economically as well as ecologically descriptive. Salem Street in Lynchburg, Virginia; Davis Bottom in Lexington, Kentucky; and Willow Street in Knoxville, Tennessee have been black bottoms. "In Washington, D.C., the most important factor in describing the location of the Negro population is low elevation" (Anderson, 1962). In Detroit, one such area is called "Blackbottom."

Frequently major streets, railroads, and industrial or other nonresidential land define and confine black areas. In Atlanta from the 1930s to the 1950s housing segregation was buttressed by the use of "buffer strips" which were major streets strip zoned for commercial uses for long distances on both sides as a planned barrier to population movement. These buffer strips in Atlanta have included street closures, the planning of thoroughfares that hinder travel between black and white residential areas, and the placement of cemeteries, public housing projects, and open spaces to inhibit any spillover of Blacks at the edges of the ghetto (Georgia State Advisory Committee to U.S. Commission on Civil Rights, 1968, p. 17). The largest black residential area in Durham, North Carolina is bounded on its southwest side by a railroad. Black communities in Xenia, Ohio; "Cottonville," Chicago; and New Haven, Connecticut are also cut off by railroads. The black ghettos of Detroit, San Francisco, and Chicago are at least in part hemmed in by major streets. The Los Angeles transportation system that served Watts before the rebellion was a flagrant example of a bus system that locked in residents.

In both Atlanta and Philadelphia, commercial and industrial land use has been important in determining black residential location. In Branford, Connecticut, railroads and industrial land use define the location of the black section of town. Suttles has indicated that "no-man's lands" (expressways, industrial areas, razed areas, and railroads) and "impersonal domains" (nonresidential areas controlled by impersonal authorities—police, medical centers, business centers) are important in determining residential behavior of inner-city people. The amount of space in the city for residential expansion may also be important. If the total area of settlement expands rapidly, the sharpness of ethnic group competition may be reduced.

In summary, it seems that white attitudes toward and manipulation of the many ecologic aspects of a city are a reflection of the fact that Blacks tend to be negatively valued people in American society and are thus located on marginal or negatively valued land and confined by physical barriers.

Socioeconomic Variables

There are innumerable socioeconomic variables that are involved in the diffusion of black households in American cities. Basically the process involves space, time, living quarters, and people—white and black. There are some basic assumptions that should be stated at the outset. There must be a decision to move, an actual transfer, and assimilation into the new environment. This means that there must be a desire and demand among Blacks to move into white areas. Also, the means for making the actual move must be available. There must be vacancies in white areas in which there is some hope on the part of the black movers for acceptance and/or protection. In a more general vein, in any given situation there is both group and individual sensitivity to segregation-integration. Most importantly, spatiotemporal proximity alone does not produce social integration or assimilation. For the sake of clarity the socioeconomic variables will be classified into three subgroups: demographic, social, and economic. The demographic factors include such population characteristics as size, age-sex structure, ethnicity, and distribution. Social variables include government (local and national) programs, social institutions (religious and educational), and violence. Housing type, income, journey to work, and real-estate activities are examples of economic factors.

DEMOGRAPHIC VARIABLES

The white residents of a racially changing neighborhood develop an acute sensitivity as to the direction and rate of change in their area. One of the major determinants of this sensitization is the number of Blacks moving into a given white area. This is commonly known as the "tipping-point mechanisms," or that point at which a white residential area becomes a black residential area. This "point" cannot be precisely fixed, but evidence indicates that one exists. Clark indicates that the "tip-point" is usually defined as below one-third minority occupancy. Fishman writes that the turning point varies as to numerical definition. McEntire places the range of white tolerance from 10 to 60 percent black. Whatever the percentage, the tipping-point may be defined as the tolerance level of a given white area for interracial living.

Stephan found the black-white population ratio to be the principal factor associated with residential desegregation. Where the ratio of black to white is high, segregation is more common; and where the proportion is reversed, desegregation is in progress. In neighborhoods that are termed racially mixed, the white buyer tends to be in the minority. This pattern is not universal, however; Northwood and Barth's data do not show a tendency for white disinterest in racially mixed neighborhoods.

This concern with the percentage of Blacks in an area may be called the "racial numbers game." To Whites, an integrated neighborhood tends to have only a few Blacks.

> For integration to be acceptable, the incidence of Negro ownership must remain so low in most middle class areas that it does not precipitate the flight of white persons. Hence middle-income Negroes in Lakeview and Long Island, New York discouraged other Negroes from buying homes in their racially mixed community by displaying signs proclaiming: "Negroes: Your purchase of a home in this neighborhood is your contribution to segregation." While the number of Negroes in a community is small, the situation may remain stable. But when more Negroes move in, the critical point is approached and the white population flees (Hill, 1967).

Interviews with South Shore, Chicago Whites indicated that the difference between "integrated" and "high-quality" neighborhoods is based on the maintenance of the area as middle class and the retention of as many white people as possible.

While it can be argued that there is no such thing as a uniform tipping-point, there is little doubt that white residential areas are aware of black "pioneers." A dormant neighborhood consciousness may become restive with the introduction of Blacks. The number of Blacks defined as crucial will vary in different circumstances.

Another factor which may be important in the process of black residential diffusion is urban population growth, both white and black, in relation to the city's capacity for housing. Population increase may be a result of natural increase and/or immigration. The diffusion of Blacks is a function of Negro population increase and the ability of the existing Negro residential areas to absorb the population increase. If the area cannot absorb the increase, then black residential diffusion will occur.

It is important to remember that the diffusion of Blacks is not particular evidence of residential racial integration. For example, as the black residential area expands, the Whites can leave and thus expand their residential area outward. The spatial extent of the black ghetto and the white suburbs is increased, but the spatial relationship between the two remains the same. This pattern is recognized as being rather common.

The stage of the life cycle also seems to be important in the black residential diffusion process. Clemence points out that, "White adults in their prime working years are leaving the city and being replaced by non-white children and by young adults who have not yet reached their most productive years" (Clemence, 1967). Clark adds that the residual white population in Negro areas includes those who cannot economically move, the isolated and the elderly. Typical family-cycle factors that create vacancies in the older white areas include: the move of adult offspring to their own homes, the move to larger quarters because of births and growth of children, and the death of parents.

As with the white population, it is the young among Blacks who tend to move or integrate. For families with children it is not only the age of the parents that influences the decision to move. The beginning teens may be a crucial age for residential change. This may present a cruel dilemma for the black family. This age may be crucial in terms of the importance of attending the "right" high school, but social integration at this age may be more difficult. Watts also indicates that this type of move may be harder if the teen-ager is a girl.

Another factor that seems to influence and channel black residential movement is the ethnicity of the white population. The social geography of American cities has been such that white ethnic groups and Blacks have competed for space and social position. The central city ghetto has been viewed as an adaptive mechanism allowing the immigrant the fellowship of those who are best able to help him adapt to the urban environment and assimilate into American life.

Because it has been "common knowledge" that nonwhite people occupy the least valued "place" (spatial and social) in American society, the white immigrant communities, partly because they are also trying desperately to move from their "place," are barriers to Negro residential mobility. The German, Polish, Jewish, and Italian areas which bordered the Negro district in St. Louis in the 1930s, Polish Hamtramick in Detroit, and the white ethnic ghettos along Franklin Street in North Philadelphia are examples of white ethnic areas restricting the residential diffusion of Negroes. The perception of these communities as barriers by Blacks may last longer than the passing of the first generation of white immigrants. There are at least two reasons for this. First, because of the effectiveness of most racial barriers in America, Blacks may not wish to continue subjecting themselves to rejection and violence and, as a result, may perceive barriers where they may have weakened. Second, and probably the more important reason, an area of even third- or fourth-generation moderate, diffuse, ethnic identification may be sparked to a strong affinity when it comes to the resistance to Negroes.

Social Variables

Because black residential segregation is a response to many socioeconomic factors, it is not surprising that the institutionalized forms of these variables (churches, schools, businesses) influence the pattern of housing. There has been a translation of the white dominant–black subordinate relationship from individual relations to the whole "design for living."

Schools seem to play a major role in the residential location plans of many families; this is heightened when black families move. In Seattle, middle-class black families who moved into white neighborhoods stressed that there were good schools nearby. Watts also found the schools to be an important consideration when middle-class black families with children moved.

The school many times is substituted for the residence as a barometer of racial change. White discontent grows in direct proportion not only to the increased number of black residents in the neighborhood but also to the gain in number of black students in the neighborhood school. People who have no reluctance to mixed neighborhoods may be pressed to leave an area with an influx of black children into the local school. Fishman points out that the number of transfer requests by teachers in local schools and evaluation of the school's excellence are also used to make a decision as to whether the neighborhood is "going Negro."

There is a basic conflict in both school and residential integration between white and black definitions of what constitutes an integrated school or neighborhood. What is integrated in the black view tends to be perceived as "Black" by Whites.

Churches may also be important factors in the location of black households in the city. Watts found that many black families wish to live close to their black church. Among those in old southwest Washington, D.C., forced to move by urban renewal, over 44 percent still identified with their old church after relocation. Clark indicates that the final stage of residential expansion, minority domination, is reflected in the growth of ethnic churches in the new areas. Drake found the religious behavior of Blacks to be class-stratified; and people, both black and white, make social mobility jumps by changing religious affiliations as they move. The move seems to be from Pentecostal and Baptist to Congregational and Episcopalian.

The church may also help, hinder, or remain neutral to the integration of a black "pioneer" into a new area. Fishman suggests that the clergy play only a minor role in this respect, but he identifies a differential response on the part of the "low churches" (Baptist, Methodist, Evangelical, Reformed, Jehovah's Witness) and the "high churches" (Episcopalian, Presbyterian, Lutheran). The former were less concerned with helping black movers than the latter.

Blumberg found, however, that friends and not churches were stronger in reinforcing the sense of community for black families integrating into white neighborhoods. When people were forced to move from the old southwest area of Washington, D.C., to new communities, only 10.3 percent of them went to a clergyman for help in adjusting to their new environment. In Blumberg's study, 9 percent of the black families that moved felt the church was important in becoming integrated into the new community.

The location of business concerns also seems to be involved in the segregation process. Location of business has seemed to be related to the racial and status group to which it catered. Certain types of service centers, barbershops, beauty shops, bars with dancing, are more sensitive to racial patterns than others. They change ownership from Whites to Blacks as the clientele becomes genuinely mixed. There is some indication that black families who are forced to move by urban renewal feel some attachment to the businesses in the old neighborhood. The presence of ethnic goods and services and the desire to support black business probably account for much of the ties with businesses in the former neighborhood.

Violence that affects black residential movement may be specifically aimed at black "pioneers," or it may be of a more general type not directly related to housing. The expectation of violence of some kind must have an important role in restricting the range of housing sought by Blacks. Specific violence aimed at discouraging Blacks from occupying property is perhaps the most obvious yet the least-studied factor in retarding their mobility in cities. "Aside from juvenile gang warfare, housing has been the steadiest source of urban racial violence in the North and West" (Clark, 1962). Except for major race riots, the location of most racial violence occurs in contested residential areas in northern cities. In a survey of forty-three Negro families living in predominantly white areas in Rochester, New York, and its suburbs, there were twenty-four cases of hostility compared to nineteen cases of no overt hostility. However, Northwood and Barth found no violence in nineteen cases of black pioneering in Seattle.

The effectiveness of this deterrent is based on the fact that it can be recurrent and wholly unpredictable. The antagonists have round-the-clock proximity. This type of violence, when it occurs, usually takes place upon the entry of a black family into a white neighborhood. In the Watts study, 50 percent of the black families that looked for housing in white areas reported trouble because of race.

Clark has defined three reactions to black moves based on white social class. The money-minded upper class uses bribery; the civic-minded middle class uses protest meetings and petitions; the lower class uses intimidation and violence. The suburbs of Deerfield, Illinois, Riverside, California, and Seattle, Washington, are examples of type two. Another common white reaction is passive resistance and "negative" neutrality.

There are a number of conditions that can produce or give impetus to violence. One is the length of the waiting period between the initial challenge of possible black entry and the actual move. Blacks may move in at night or not go through the normal buying process because of worry over the possible consequences of giving a white neighborhood time to organize. Indeed, it has been shown in a number of areas that the presence of a black family may create and consolidate neighborhood bonds that would not have existed without its presence.

Any heightening of racial consciousness that supports racial segregation is likely to increase the difficulty of black residential movement. Violence need not be specifically aimed at black "pioneers" to have an effect on the general residential pattern. The pattern can be affected by a growth in antiblack attitudes. Urban race rebellions, protests, and publicized crimes committed by Blacks all have a congealing effect on antiblack attitudes. These events may be local or not; their influence depends upon the degree to which the local white population perceives the action on the part of Blacks as threatening. There is a spatial aspect to this perception of threat and its influence on black residential diffusion. In contrast to long-distance moves to white suburbs, black movement at the edge of the ghetto is "expected" and may lack the shock element of entry. Short-distance movement provides the black family with a potentially large group of black allies; the realization of this possibility may act as a deterrent to hostile Whites. On the other hand, it may act as fuel for quick magnification and expansion of violence.

There are three criteria for the evaluation of the role of violence in residential diffusion. These are (1) kind of incident (overt assault, covert threats, general riot, etc.); (2) time of incident (school vacation, period of tense public opinion); (3) location of incident (ghetto or suburb). Although it cannot be measured, the psychological perception of racial violence may have a more significant effect on black residential diffusion than actual incidents. The threat of violence is the more insidious in its effects because the actual occurrence is so erratic.

The New Deal gave public housing its initial impetus. The emphasis was on creating jobs and bolstering the economy. During the 1940s, public housing was used for war workers; there was little if any intent to provide an adequate supply of housing for low-income people. Public housing was not seen as an instrument for desegregation; on the contrary, early policy decisions, which stated that it would not be permitted to alter the racial patterns of neighborhoods, caused the program to reinforce residential segregation. The public housing bureaucracy has been governed by the necessity of demonstrating to its critics that the housing being built is bare of any amenities which might be pleasing to the eye; public housing was to be for shelter only. The phrase "urban renewal as Negro removal" indicates that government policy has had a major effect on black residential diffusion.

A crucial factor in the role of the federal government in public housing programs is that, with few exceptions, it has not conferred its housing benefits directly on the ultimate recipients but operates instead in a helping role to private business and local public authorities. Thus critical decisions with regard to race and segregation are left to local real-estate boards and government officials. This has resulted in three trends. First, sites for public housing have been extremely restricted. Second, public housing has been filled up with Blacks and other poor and minority groups. Finally, the relocation process associated with urban renewal has furthered the process of segregation. In too many cases the result of relocation due to urban renewal has been ". . . the further-

Public Housing near Boston. Railroads frequently function as social and racial barriers between communities.

John Urban.

ance of segregation trends at the edge of the ghetto" (Clark, 1962). Urban renewal has tended to fill up public housing with minority groups. In many, if not most, cases, however, there is little reliable information as to where displaced families go after being ousted from their homes as a result of urban renewal.

Spatial movement as a result of urban renewal is not necessarily coincident with upward social mobility. In a study of relocated families (95 percent Negro) in seventeen cities of the Southeast, 19 percent were relocated in substandard housing. Thursz found that 52 percent of the Washington, D.C., households were not working before their removal, after relocation this figure rose to 61.9 percent. Also, urban renewal does not seem to "remove" Blacks very far. A study of urban renewal in Boston indicated that most of the displaced families looked for housing in the same or adjoining areas and only 4 percent chose to move to white areas. In San Francisco most displaced families moved into deteriorated neighborhoods on the fringe of the clearance project area. Twenty-five percent of the families removed from their homes in southwest Washington, D.C., remained in the same area in public housing units. The urban renewal program in Cleveland only increased the racial density of surrounding ghettos. Urban renewal projects in Savannah, Georgia, have set into motion a domino movement pattern. Uprooted black families moved into areas previously inhabited by low-income Whites and into areas once popular for middle-class Negroes who moved further out. Relocation of families displaced by urban renewal in Nashville has been found to be inadequate by the Tennessee State Advisory Committee to the U.S. Commission on Civil Rights. The same has been true of Atlanta's urban renewal program, in which, as of May, 1967, 4,715 black and 245 white families had been displaced; 5,753 dwellings were demolished and replaced by 1,066 houses.

Public housing has a great impact on the diffusion pattern of Blacks in cities, both because it is a prime source of housing for Negro families and because it is restricted in location. In Chicago, Cleveland, and Philadelphia there has been political and social pressure to "contain" public housing within existing racial and poverty concentrations in central cities. "Public housing . . . has historically conformed to and continues to reinforce racial segregation" (National Commission on Urban Problems, 1968). The result of this general residential policy has been that "the one type of housing generally open to Negroes is a quarantine system of low-rent compounds specializing in wrecked families" (Clark, 1962). The Boston Housing Authority, for example, has made the point that ". . . the non-white occupancy ratio in public housing generally exceeds the racial pattern in private housing in the neighborhood surrounding the development" (Mass. Advisory Committee to the U.S. Commission on Civil Rights, 1963). The National Commission on Urban Problems found that in six of the twelve case histories it studied, the policy was to locate public housing projects in such a manner so as to identify with the existing racial pattern of the area. "Public housing in Atlanta has served to guide and concentrate the distribution of Negro population" (Glazer and McEntire, 1960). The same is true for New Orleans and Dade County, Florida.

City	95 to 100% WHITE OCCUPANCY		95 to 100% BLACK OCCUPANCY		MIXED OCCUPANCY	
	Number of projects	Total number of units	Number of projects	Total number of units	Number of projects	Total number of units
Nashville	6	1,530	6	2,306	2	908
Atlanta	9	2,165	15	6,478	5	600
Newark (central ward)	1	No data	2	2,617	4	No data

Table 6.3   Occupancy of Public Housing in Nashville, Atlanta, and Newark's Central Ward, by Race, 1966

Sources: *Tennessee State Advisory Committee to U.S. Commission on Civil Rights. Housing and Urban Renewal in the Nashville-Davidson County Metropolitan Area, February, 1967, p. 10; Georgia State Advisory Committee to U.S. Commission on Civil Rights. Toward Equal Opportunity in Housing in Atlanta, Georgia, 1968, p. 64; New Jersey State Advisory Committee to U.S. Commission on Civil Rights. Public Housing in Newark's Central Ward, April, 1968, p. 21.*

In 1966 public housing projects in Atlanta, Nashville, and Newark were almost all segregated; this was a result of policy decisions of the public housing authorities in each city to concentrate low-cost housing in certain areas of the cities. There was a great deal of variation in the black-white ratio in the mixed occupancy public housing in these cities (see Table 6.3). In Newark, for example, two of the mixed projects were over 90 percent white, while the other two were in excess of 90 percent black. The mixed projects in Atlanta ranged from 44 percent white to 88 percent white. The two mixed projects in Nashville had 39 and 57 percent white occupancy.

According to the director of the Nashville Metropolitan Planning Commission, race was not used as a criterion in land-use decisions, but he added, "We consider economic levels and it happens that the economic level of Negroes is lower than that of whites" (Tenn. Advisory Committee to the U. S. Commission on Civil Rights, 1967). In Newark the director of the Housing Authority said that there was no segregation and that any separation of races in public housing was a result of people choosing where they wanted to live. In contrast to these two views, the Reverend Andrew Young has described the Perry Homes project in Atlanta as "a kind of relocation center on the outskirts of town, out of the way of public transportation and job opportunities and everything else, with a separate school system set up for the poor Negro" (Ga. Advisory Committee to the U. S. Commission on Civil Rights, 1968).

The U.S. Commission on Civil Rights found (in 1967) that of the quarter of a million low-rent housing units that have been built by city public housing authorities in the nation's 24 largest metropolitan areas, in only one—Cincinnati—has the city housing authority been permitted to build outside the central city. There, the authority has provided low rent units in a Negro enclave in the suburbs (Sloane, 1968).

Public housing in many of the larger cities has become a program for low-income black families. "In proportion to their numbers among low-income families, more non-whites than whites live in public housing units" (National Commission on Urban Problems, 1968).

Local governments rarely allow public housing projects to be located outside the central city. Besides the suburban veto there are a variety of apparently neutral activities that are used to maintain this exclusive policy. These include building code decisions and inspection standards, location of water and sewer facilities, and zoning policies. Glendale, California, and Deerfield, Illinois, are examples of places in which building permits and inspections have been used to keep the community white. Dearborn, Michigan, on the other hand, uses the termination of public facilities such as gas supply and garbage collection to try to force out black families. The Chicago city council has instituted a containment policy to keep public housing in black areas. Oklahoma City unsuccessfully attempted to exclude Blacks from within the city by retracing the city boundaries. In Atlanta 75 percent of the public housing projects are in areas that are 70 to 100 percent black; not a single low-rent unit has been built outside of the incorporated city. Fulton County (in which Atlanta is located) refused building permits because the houses were for low-income Blacks. The same kind of restrictive zoning has been used in the towns of Berlin and Simsbury, Connecticut. Through 1970, 100 percent of the public housing in Baltimore, San Diego, and San Antonio was built within the city boundaries.

During the 1960s the executive, legislative, and judicial branches of the national government have acted to remove the legal basis for continued racial discrimination in housing. President Kennedy issued Executive Order No. 11063 in 1962 prohibiting discrimination in federally assisted housing. Six years later Congress passed a Federal Fair Housing law which prohibited discrimination in about 80 percent of the nation's housing. Also in 1968, the Supreme Court upheld an 1866 civil rights law prohibiting racial discrimination in private as well as in public housing. These laws form part of an elaborate structure of protection, but they still have yet to be effectively enforced.

Most of the federal housing programs are concerned with the provision of rental housing to the poor. The Housing and Urban Development Act of 1968, however, established a program of home ownership for low-income families. This program is called Section 235. This is not the first program to try to provide home ownership for poor families, but it is the largest in scope. There are also some other differences which make Section 235 potentially better than previous housing legislation. The income limits for housing under Section 235 are sufficiently flexible to avoid the problems of concentrating only poor people in the houses. The program also makes extensive use of existing houses as well as building new units. Another important difference is that Section 235 is free to operate without the interference of the veto power of suburban communities, but it is still restricted by local zoning and land-use requirements.

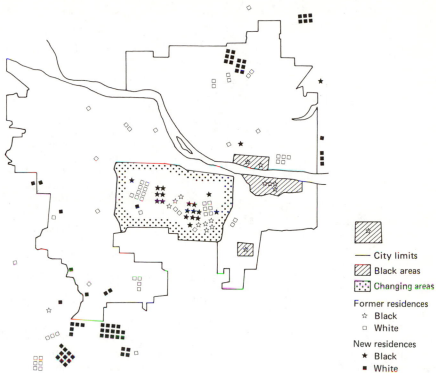

Figure 6.2   Little Rock: New and Former Residences of Buyers of Section 235 Homes, 1970.
(From U.S. Commission on Civil Rights, "Home Ownership for Lower Income Families," June, 1971, pp. 27–28.)

In terms of volume, the 235 program has increased the amount of housing available to low-income people. In 1970, for example, 30 percent of all the new houses selling for less than $25,000 were bought using Section 235. The impact of the program has been far stronger in the South and in the border states than in the North; only 6 percent of the Section 235 units by 1970 were in the Northeast, while the former areas accounted for almost half of the units.

But for all its potential benefits, Section 235 housing has conformed to the pattern of racial segregation so common in the nation. Restrictive zoning and land-use policies have restricted the sites available for new building. The dual housing market—separate and unequal—is also present in the 235 housing program. Whites buying Section 235 housing are buying new units in the suburbs, while Blacks receive the existing housing in ghetto areas; and where they do get new units, the housing is in subdivisions serving exclusively Blacks. This pattern of explicit racial "separate but equal" housing patterns has been found in Denver, Philadelphia, Little Rock, St. Louis, Louisville, Lexington, New Orleans, and Phoenix City, Alabama. Figures 6.2 and 6.3 indicate this pattern for the cities of Little Rock and Denver. In both cities Whites are buying houses throughout the city except in the black or racially

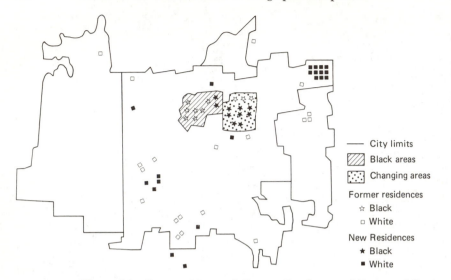

Figure 6.3   Denver: New and Former Residences of Buyers of Section 235 Houses, 1970.
(From U.S. Commission on Civil Rights, "Home Ownership for Lower Income Families," June, 1971, pp. 18–20.)

changing areas. Blacks, on the other hand, are moving only within the black and racially changing areas. These are typical of the nationwide buying pattern for Section 235 houses. Up to 1971 "all new 235 homes constructed in 'blighted' areas are being purchased by black families, while 70 percent of new 235 homes constructed outside 'blighted' areas are being purchased by white non-minority families" (U. S. Commission on Civil Rights, 1971).

Section 235 housing is a good example of what can happen when a federal civil rights program is put under the control of local people. The primary responsibility for the implementation of the program has been in the hands of real-estate brokers, builders, and mortgage lenders—exactly those people who have maintained the dual housing market. Builders and brokers have marketed the 235 housing as they have housing in general. Discrimination has been common. Advertisements such as the following have been used.

ANYONE—4 BEDRMS

Completely remodeled inside and out on full corner lot. A bargain at $12,500. Only $400 down FHA. Walk to Central High (*Little Rock Gazette*, fall, 1970).

There are two signal words in the ad. First, "anyone" is a clue that the area is "racially changing" and open to Blacks. Second, Central High is one-third black. Builders are also involved in discrimination. In suburban St. Louis, for example, builders of Section 235 housing did not advertise it as such and discouraged applications from black families.

Another major problem has been that the federal agency under whose auspices the 235 program is run has not taken special steps to ensure that the civil rights guidelines are met. The FHA has, in fact, denied any responsibility for the dual housing market that it is involved in supporting.

ECONOMIC VARIABLES

Other factors that seem to be more economic are also involved in the diffusion of black households in the city. One of these variables is the type of housing. For example, racial change seems to occur faster in areas of high-density apartment house renters than single-family home owners. Renters do not have the economic investment in a location that owners have. Blacks are generally the last to enter the private housing market and therefore must accept what is made available by departing Whites. On the other hand, middle-class Blacks may find homes easier to purchase than to rent. This theory is probably directly related to the supply of homes and rentals in a given city. In the case of the Watts study there was no shortage of housing, but a shortage of apartments existed. "The supply of housing available to segregated groups is determined primarily not by their demand expressed in the market but by the interplay of forces determining their segregation pattern" (McEntire, 1960).

There is a cyclic pattern between housing and place of work that mitigates against Blacks moving at will in the city. Negroes live in segregated areas, with consequent barriers to information flows about jobs except those in which there are already Blacks, and they apply for jobs that they know that they can get. Access to transportation facilities also is a limiting factor in residential diffusion. For example, Tucker and Jacobs have described the public transit system in Los Angeles as one that locks the residents into the inner-city. This variable may be especially crucial if, as in Watts, car ownership is minimal. According to the McCone report only 14 percent of the families in Watts had cars. "Metropolitan transit systems often do not service slum areas adequately even though slum residents are almost entirely dependent on public transportation" (U.S. Civil Rights Commission, 1973). Another example comes from people relocated by urban renewal in Washington, D.C.: "When asked the extent to which the move from the old Southwest had affected their work and employment, the most frequent comment was that those employed had to cope with greater distances and more difficult transportation problems" (Thursz, 1966).

The actions of the real-estate profession seem to be the most important economic factor in limiting the residential diffusion of Blacks. Realtors are the keepers of the keys in a society that condones racial compounds. The real-estate system is one of the institutions whose antiblack policies are sanctioned by society. "Residential segregation is seen as a result of essential aspects of good business practice, and as reflecting the preferences of the general public who still view the possibility of Negro neighbors as threatening the welfare and stability of the neighborhood" (Taeuber and Taeuber, 1965).

After the 1896 *Plessy v. Ferguson*, "separate but equal" decision, southern and border cities began racial zoning. In Louisville, for example, in order to promote peace and the general welfare the races were to reside in separate blocks. This kind of restrictive zoning by race was struck down by the U.S.

Supreme Court in 1917 in the *Buchanan v. Warley* case. Following this ruling, efforts to achieve racial segregation concentrated on restrictive covenants. These were not struck down until the *Shelley v. Kramer* decision in 1948. The federal government was an important partner in the maintenance of residential segregation prior to 1948. The underwriting manual of the FHA prohibited occupancy of properties except by the race for which they were intended. This put the federal stamp of approval on racial covenants. The references to racial groups were deleted from the manual in 1947. An important point about the *Shelley v. Kramer* decision is that the restrictive covenants were interpreted as being private and, as such, not in violation of the Fourteenth Amendment; what seems to have been crucial is that their enforcement by state courts was state action and is therefore unconstitutional as a denial of equal protection.

Langendorf has written that a dual housing market exists for Blacks and Whites. Blumberg agrees that real-estate controls operate in the formation and maintenance of black and white segregation. Unlike Whites, Blacks do not function in a free market where it comes to housing choice. In a 1969 published report on civil disorders, the Seattle Urban League estimated that only 4.2 percent of Seattle's black population has been able to choose freely where they want to live. The demand for housing by middle-class Blacks has been concentrated in certain areas. Only 33 percent of the total rental vacancies in San Francisco in 1961 were open to Blacks, and these were almost all located in existing black areas. The problem is accentuated for low-income Blacks. "The mobility of the low-income Negro family . . . is not now nor will it be in the near future a matter of personal choice" (Handlin, 1959).

"Racial discrimination in real estate is much more than a practice of individual brokers and salesmen. It is one of the standards of the real estate business, to which businessmen are expected to conform and are liable to sanctions if they do not" (McEntire, 1960). In 1954 the National Association of Home Builders initiated a program with heavy emphasis on preserving segregation. In Rochester, New York, black families found agents mainly for low-status areas and hardly at all for higher-status areas.

> The multiplication of new suburban communities from which non-whites are absolutely excluded by decision of the builders has unquestionably contributed largely to the extension and intensification of racial segregation since the end of World War II, especially of the minority middle-class (McEntire, 1960).

Builders, real-estate brokers, and developers use many varied techniques in maintaining housing segregation. These include outright refusal, convenient rentals and sales, ostensibly nondiscriminatory rejection, and delaying and discouraging an applicant.

Blockbusting is another common practice among realtors. It is a device whereby realtors generate panic sales in white homeowners by telling them that black families are intending to move into their neighborhood and thereby lower the property values. Then they buy the houses from the panicked Whites at devalued prices and resell them to Blacks at inflated prices. In 1969 at least twelve real-estate concerns and salesmen were indicted for blockbusting in the Brooklyn and Queens sections of New York City. Six firms in Atlanta were enjoined from practicing blockbusting in 1971. The following plea from Detroit expresses a humorous reversal of idea implicit in blockbusting.

> I'm Black and just moved into an all-white block on the east side. The people next door just won't keep up their property. There are high weeds in the front and rubbish in the back. It's a beautiful neighborhood but if it goes down, you know who'll be blamed (*Detroit News*, 1970).

Realty boards may act independently of the wishes of the white client in matters of race. For example the following bulletin was sent to all active members of the St. Louis Real Estate Board on June 1, 1955: "No member of our board may, directly or indirectly, sell to Negroes or be a party to a sale to Negroes, or finance property for sale to or purchase by Negroes, in any block, unless there are at least three separate and distinct buildings in such block already occupied by Negroes" (Litwack, 1961). In Seattle, Washington, the Urban League has indicated that only 4 percent of the realtors have offered equal treatment to Negro people. The same problems are evident in Cleveland, Nashville, and Newark. According to the Urban League in Chicago, the real estate industry is the major institutional bulwark of residential segregation. Most realtors in Riverside, California, flatly and explicitly refuse to show Negroes housing not located in the ghetto.

One of the methods used to maintain segregated neighborhoods has been the inclusion of restrictive covenants in property title insurance. A policyholder from Montgomery County, Maryland, brought a complaint to the attention of the Justice Department because he had a policy which stated, "for the purposes of sanitation and health, this property cannot be sold, transferred, or rented . . . to a member of the Negro race" (*Consumer Reports*, 1970). It was not until 1968 that the Justice Department negotiated with one of the largest property title insurers, Lawyer's Title Insurance Company of Richmond, to drop all racial restrictions from future policies.

SPATIAL MOBILITY

Intraurban spatial mobility is the elementary behavior being studied, and the individual's perception of a response to urban space must be considered in urban, black residential diffusion.

Space has connotative as well as denotative meanings; "the same real object can have vastly different connotations to different people" (Sommer, 1965). The meanings attached to spatial symbols by different groups depend on their interests, expectations, and experiences in that or a similar space. People consistently use and organize sensory clues from the environment, relying on a selection process that forms a simplified model of the real situation so that the latter can be dealt with. Prokop and Webber have found that space, distance,

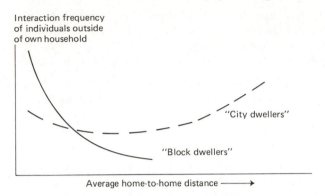

Figure 6.4   Frequency of Individual Interaction Outside of Household.

and place have different meanings to middle-class and lower-class people. Hall has written that the differences between Blacks and the dominant culture in America ". . . are basic and have to do with such core values as the use and structuring of space, time, materials, all of which are learned early in life" (Hall, 1969).

"Space seems to end where the social interactions of an individual or of a group end" (Prokop, 1967). The inhabitants of Farnam Courts in New Haven, for example, have a very restricted sense of community and neighborhood: "neighborhood" is "my building," "community" is "the whole project"; outside of the project is the outer world, a place to which most will not journey. Very little movement occurs outside racially homogeneous areas of cities compared to that inside of the area. Some residents of Harlem and Pruitt-Igoe do not feel free to move in their respective environments. Fried and Gleichner found that people in an urban slum feel that they belong to specific spatial regions and not to others. Also in a Chicago slum, "Life in the Addams area is extremely provincial and what goes on a few blocks away may hardly affect the daily routine of commercial transactions, social engagements, and family life" (Suttles, 1968). The restrictive impact of the physical world on the lower class has also been pointed out by Rainwater and Montgomery. This spatial restrictedness in an urban environment will at least limit the kinds and availability of information on housing to the inhabitants. Whether or not the fact of spatially limited behavior within the ghetto is correlated with a corresponding lack of movement out of the ghetto is debatable, but at least, the suggestion of such a relationship may be made.

The local community is spatially organized with reference to the daily movements of the population. Some people (the middle and upper classes) seem to be "city dwellers" while the lower classes may be more of "block" or "neighborhood dwellers." If this is true the graph relating interaction and distance may be redrawn as shown in Figure 6.4. "Block dwellers" make many close contacts in their immediate areas, but their rate of interaction declines rapidly outward from their neighborhoods. "City dwellers," on the other hand, do not seem to have as high a rate of interaction in their immediate neighborhoods but have more extensive interactions at greater distances. The dotted line on the graph indicates the spatial mobility of the middle and upper classes; the distance covered by them is probably greater, and their knowledge of widespread parts of the city is probably greater. The line for lower-class and minority groups is shorter and drops off more rapidly. At shorter distances there is probably more interaction among lower-class and minority groups than among the middle and upper classes.

There are also indications that distinctions exist between working-class slums and black ghettos with respect to the inhabitants' spatial mobility. "And the primary difference lies in the degree of freedom of choice, the inner conflict, and the external opportunity to select the housing and a residential area in which to live" (Fried and Gleichner, 1968). This has two serious implications for the diffusion of black households. First, discrimination against Blacks is stronger than against the working class in general; and second, goal-oriented communal activities may be relatively more absent in black ghettos than in working-class slums. Cohen found that among poverty groups "there is greater emphasis on seeking a personal rather than a collective escape" (Cohen, 1968). There is little evidence that poverty unites racial groups. "The evidence is strong, however, that lower class people, again like most Americans tend to think of the most direct route to a decent life as one that is pursued along highly individual lines" (Rainwater, 1966). This point is substantiated by Austin who writes that, "Also the cultural attitudes and patterns of behavior generally found among a low income population that is discriminated against do not support a pattern of systematic, consistent, and persistent collective action on environmental problems" (Austin, 1968).

This restricted perception of and action in space may result in either of two types of action. On the one hand, people may tend to keep within the confines of the area in which they feel comfortable. Rainwater has called this a state in which people settle down seeking greater stability. On the other hand, people may use spatial mobility as a problem-solving device. Geismar and Krisberg found that lower-class families in New Haven took the geographic way out of their problems, only to find themselves relocated in a new problem area.

Contrary to popular opinion it seems that slum dwellers are less mobile than most people. This is substantiated by a study of displaced families in Washington, D.C.; they were less transient than other Americans. Ethnic groups are limited as to where they can move. But within these limited environments, slum dwellers are very mobile.

For those who do use spatial mobility to improve their housing situations, a restricted view of their environment and the tendency for a limited amount of information may severely hamper their ability to make successful moves out of the ghetto. This may be part of the reason that those who do move long distances out of the ghetto tend to be upwardly mobile and rapidly assimilating families. Rossi found that "families moving up the occupational ladder are particularly sensitive to the social aspects of location and use residential mobility to bring their residences into line with their prestige needs" (Rossi, 1955).

SELECTED BIBLIOGRAPHY

1. Action Line: *The Detroit News*, 1970.
2. Anderson, Theodore R.: Social & Economic Factors Affecting the Location of Residential Neighborhoods, *Papers and Proceedings of Regional Science Association*, vol. 9, pp. 161–170, 1962.
3. Austin, David M.: Influence of Community Setting on Neighborhood Action, in John B. Turner (ed.), "Neighborhood Organization for Community Action." New York, National Association of Social Welfare, 1968.
4. Bardolph, Richard: "The Civil Rights Record: The Black American and the Law, 1849–1970." New York, Thomas Y. Crowell Company, 1970.
5. Bennett, Lerone, Jr.: "Before the Mayflower: A History of the Negro in America, 1619–1964," (rev. ed.). Baltimore, Penguin Publishing Co., 1966.
6. Blalock, Hubert M.: "Toward a Theory of Minority Group Relations," New York, John Wiley and Sons, 1967.
7. Blumberg, Leonard: Segregated Housing, Marginal Location and the Crisis of Confidence, *Phylon*, vol. 25, pp. 321–330, winter 1964.
8. Bracey, John H., Jr., August Meier, and Elliot Rudwick (eds.): "The Rise of the Ghetto," Belmont, Calif., Wadsworth Publishing Co., 1971.
9. Bryce-LaPorte, R. Simon: The Slave Plantation: Background to Present Conditions of Urban Blacks, in Peter Orleans and William Russell, Jr. (eds.), *Race Changes and Urban Society*, Urban Affairs Annual Review, vol. 5, Beverly Hills, Calif., Sage Publishing Co., 1971.
10. Carter, Wilmoth A.: Negro Main Street as a Symbol of Discrimination, *Phylon*, vol. 21, pp. 234–239, fall 1960.
11. Clark, Dennis: "The Ghetto Game," New York, Sheed and Ward, 1962.
12. Clemence, Theodore G.: Residential Segregation in the Mid-Sixties, *Demography*, vol. 4, pp. 562–568, 1967.
13. Cohen, Nathan E.: Building a Social Movement among the Poor, in John B. Turner (ed.), *Neighborhood Organization for Community Action*, New York, National Association of Social Welfare, 1968.
14. Property Title Insurer Drops Anti-Negro Clause, *Consumer Reports*, vol. 35, February 1970, p. 113.
15. Cox, Oliver C.: "Caste, Class and Race," New York, Modern Reader, 1948.
16. Drake, St. Clair: Should We Expect Newcomers to Conform, in *Welcoming Newcomers to Cities*, Chicago, National Federation of Settlements and Neighborhood Centers, 1961.
17. Drake, St. Clair, and Horace R. Cayton: "Black Metropolis: A Study of Negro Life in a Northern City," New York, Harper and Row, 1962.
18. DuBois, W. E. B.: "The Philadelphia Negro," Philadelphia, University of Pennsylvania Press, 1899.
19. ————: "The Negro of Farmville Virginia: A Social Study," U.S. Labor Bulletin, vol. 3, January 1898, pp. 1–37.

20. Dunbar, Anthony: "The Will to Survive," Atlanta, The Southern Regional Council, 1969.
21. Duster, Troy: Silence and Civic Responsibility: Combination of Fear and Right, in Raymond Mack (ed.), "Our Children's Burden," New York, Vintage Press, 1968.
22. Fishman, Joshua A.: Some Social and Psychological Determinants of Intergroup Relations in Changing Neighborhoods, in Alfred Avins (ed.), "Open Occupancy vs. Forced Housing Under the Fourteenth Amendment: A Symposium," New York, Bookmailer, 1963.
23. Forman, R.: "Black Ghettoes, White Ghettoes, and Slums," Englewood Cliffs, N.J., Prentice-Hall, 1971.
24. Franklin, John Hope: "From Slavery to Freedom," New York, Alfred Knopf, 1967.
25. Frazier, E. Franklin: Negro Harlem: An Ecological Study, *American Journal of Sociology,* vol. 43, pp. 72–88, July 1937.
26. Fried, Marc, and Peggy Gleichner: Some Sources of Residential Satisfaction in an Urban Slum, in Bernard J. Friedes and Robert Morris (eds.), "Urban Planning and Social Policy," New York, Basic Books, 1968.
27. Fried, Marc, and Joan Levin: Some Social Functions of the Urban Slum, in Bernard Friedes and Robert Morris (eds.), "Urban Planning and Social Policy," New York, Basic Books, 1968.
28. Geismar, Ludwig, and Jane Krisberg: "The Forgotten Neighborhood," Metucker, N.Y., The Scarecrow Press, 1967.
29. Glazer, Nathan, and Davis McEntire (eds.): "Studies in Housing and Minority Groups," Berkeley, University of California Press, 1960.
30. Goffman, Erving: "Asylums," Garden City, N.Y., Doubleday, 1961.
31. ———: "Encounters: Two Studies in the Sociology of Interaction," Indianapolis, Bobbs-Merrill, 1961a.
32. Green, C. McLaughlin: "The Secret City," Princeton, N.J., Princeton University Press, 1967.
33. Greene, Lorenzo Johnson: "Negro in Colonial New England," New York, Atheneum, 1968.
34. Hall, Edward T.: "The Silent Language," Garden City, N.Y., Doubleday, 1969.
35. Handlin, Oscar: "The Newcomers," Cambridge, Mass., Harvard University Press, 1959.
36. *Hearings in Washington, D.C., June 14–17, 1971, U.S. Commission of Civil Rights,* Washington, D.C., U.S. Government Printing Office, 1971.
37. Hill, Herbert: America: Goals and Problems, *Hearing Before the Subcommittee on Urban Affairs of the Joint Economic Committee, September-October 1967,* Washington, D.C., U.S. Government Printing Office, 1967.
38. Housing and Urban Renewal in the Nashville-Davidson County Metropolitan Area, *Tennessee State Advisory Committee to U.S. Commission on Civil Rights,* 1967.

39. Irwin, Marjorie Felice: "The Negro in Charlottesville and Albermarle County," University of Virginia, Phelps-Stokes Fellowship Papers, no. 9, 1929.
40. Jacobs, Paul: "Prelude to Riot," New York, Random House, 1966.
41. Johnson, Charles S.: "Shadow of the Plantation," Chicago, University of Chicago Press, 1934.
42. ———: "Patterns of Negro Segregation," New York, Harper and Brothers, 1943.
43. Documents, *Journal of Negro History*, vol. 1, pp. 302–308, July 1916.
44. Katz, William L.: "Eyewitness: The Negro in American History," New York, Pittman Publishing Corporation, 1967.
45. Kennedy, Louise Venable: "The Negro Peasant Turns Cityward," New York, Columbia University Press, 1930.
46. Kester, Howard: "Revolt among Sharecroppers," New York, Arno Press, 1969.
47. Koestler, Frances A.: Pruitt-Igoe: Survival in a Concrete Ghetto, *Journal of Social Work*, Vol. 12, October 1967, pp. 3–13.
48. Koponen, Niilo E.: The Myth of a Tipping Point, *Integrated Education*, vol. 4, pp. 10–14, August-September 1966.
49. Langendorf, Richard: Residential Desegregation Potential, *Journal of the American Institute of Planners*, vol. 35, pp. 90–95, March 1969.
50. Lee, Frank F.: The Race Relations Patterns by Areas of Behavior in a Small New England Town, *American Sociological Review*, vol. 19, pp. 138–143, 1954.
51. Lewis, Hylan: "Blackways of Kent," Chapel Hill, N. C., University of North Carolina Press, 1955.
52. *Little Rock Gazette*, fall 1970.
53. Litwack, Leon F.: "North of Slavery," Chicago, University of Chicago Press, 1961.
54. McCone, John A.: "Violence in the City—An End or a Beginning?" *Report by the Governor's Commission on the Los Angeles Riots*, Dec. 2, 1965.
55. McEntire, Davis: "Residence and Race," Berkeley, Calif., University of California Press, 1960.
56. McManus, Edgar J.: "History of Negro Slavery in New York," Syracuse, N.Y., Syracuse University Press, 1966.
57. Maslen, Sidney: Relocation in the Southeastern Region During the Process of Renewal, *Phylon*, vol. 19, pp. 70–71, spring 1958.
58. Massachusetts Advisory Committee to the U.S. Commission on Civil Rights, *Report on Housing in Boston*, Boston, 1963.
59. Million, Ebner M.: Racial Restrictive Covenants Revisited, in Alfred Avins (ed.), "Open Occupancy vs. Forced Housing under the Fourteenth Amendment: A Symposium," New York, Bookmailer, 1972.
60. Molotch, Harvey: Toward a More Human Ecology: An Urban Research Strategy, *Land Economics*, vol. 43, August 1967, pp. 336–341.
61. Montgomery, Roger: Comment on Fear and House-as-Haven in the Lower

Class, *Journal of American Institute of Planners,* vol. 32, pp. 31–37, January 1966.

62. Morrill, Richard L.: The Negro Ghetto: Problems and Alternatives, *The Geographical Review,* vol. 55, July 1965, pp. 339–361.

63. More Than Shelter: Social Needs in Low and Middle Income Housing Period, National Commission on Urban Problems. Research report no. 8, Washington, D.C., U.S. Government Printing Office, 1968.

64. Northwood, L. K., and Ernest A. T. Barth: "Urban Desegregation: Negro Pioneers and Their White Neighbors," Seattle, Wash., University of Washington Press, 1965.

65. Osofsky, Gilbert (ed.): "Puttin' on Ole Massa," New York, Harper Torch Books, 1966.

66. Peskin, Allan (ed.): "North into Freedom," Cleveland, The Press of Case Western Reserve University, 1966.

67. Pittman, David, and William L. Holland: Isolated Negro Penetration of White Residential Areas in a Metropolitan Community, in Melvin M. Tumin, "Segregation and Desegregation: A Digest of Recent Research," Princeton, N.J., Princeton University Press, 1958.

68. Powdermaker, Hortense: "After Freedom," New York, Atheneum, 1968.

69. Prokop, Dieter: Image and Function of the City, in "Urban Core & Inner City," Leiden, E.J. Brill, 1967.

70. Prunty, Merle, Jr.: The Renaissance of the Southern Plantation, *Geographical Review,* vol. 45, October 1955, pp. 459–491.

71. Public Housing in Newark's Central Ward, New Jersey State Advisory Committee to U.S. Commission on Civil Rights, 1968.

72. *Race Relations Law Survey,* vol. 3, March 1972, p. 230.

73. Rainwater, Lee: Fear and the House-as-Haven in the Lower Class, *Journal of the American Institute of Planners,* vol. 32, pp. 23–31, January 1966.

74. ———: Neighborhood Action and Lower Class Life Style, in John B. Turner (ed.), "Neighborhood Organization for Community Action," New York, Association of Social Welfare, 1968.

75. Raper, Arthur F.: "Preface to Peasantry," Chapel Hill, N.C., University of North Carolina Press, 1936.

76. Record, Wilson: "Minority Groups and Intergroup Relations in the San Francisco Bay Area," Berkeley, Calif., Institute of Governmental Studies, 1963.

77. Rosen, Harry M., and David H. Rosen: "But Not Next Door," New York, Juan Obolensky, 1962.

78. Rossi, Peter H.: "Why Families Move," Glencoe, Ill., Free Press, 1955.

79. Rubin, Morton: Migration Patterns of Negroes From a Rural Northeastern Mississippi Community, *Social Forces,* vol. 39, pp. 435–444, October 1960.

80. Sikorsky, Igor I., Jr.: A-95: Deterrent to Discriminatory Zoning, *Civil Rights Digest,* vol. 5, pp. 16–19, August 1972.

81. Sloane, Martin: The 1968 Housing Act: Best Yet, but is it Enough? *Civil Rights Digest*, vol. 1, fall 1968, pp. 1–8.

82. Sommer, Robert: "Personal Space," Englewood Cliffs, N.J., Prentice-Hall, 1965.

83. Spear, Alan L.: "Black Chicago: The Making of a Negro Ghetto, 1890–1920," Chicago, University of Chicago Press, 1967.

84. Stafford, Walter W., and Joyce Ladner: Comprehensive Planning and Racism, *Journal of American Institute of Planning*, vol. 35, pp. 68–69, March 1969.

85. Stephan, A. Stephan: Population in Ratios, Racial Attitudes, and Desegregation, in Melvin M. Tumin (ed.), "Segregation and Desegregation: A Digest of Recent Research," Princeton, N.J., Princeton University Press, 1958.

86. Suttles, Gerald D.: "The Social Order of the Slum," Chicago, University of Chicago Press, 1968.

87. Taeuber, Karl, and Alma Taeuber: "Negroes in Cities," Chicago, Aldye, 1965.

88. Thom, William T.: The Negroes of Sandy Spring, Maryland: A Social Study, *U.S. Labor Bulletin*, vol. 6, January 1901, pp. 43–101.

89. ———: The Negroes of Litwalton, Virginia: A Social Study of the Oyster Negro, *U.S. Labor Bulletin*, no. 37, vol. 6, pp. 1115–1170, November 1901.

90. Thursz, Daniel: "Where Are They Now?", Health and Welfare Council of the National Capitol Area, Washington, D.C., November 1966.

91. "Toward Equal Opportunity in Housing in Atlanta," Georgia State Advisory Commission to U.S. Commission on Civil Rights, 1968.

92. Tucker, Sterling: "Beyond the Burning," New York, Association Press, 1968.

93. U.S. Commission on Civil Rights, "Understanding Fair Housing," Washington, D.C., 1973.

94. Van den Berghe, Pierre L.: "Race and Racism," New York, John Wiley & Sons, Inc., 1967.

95. Vandiver, Joseph S.: The Changing Realm of King Cotton, *Trans-action*, vol. 4, pp. 24–30, November 1966.

96. Virrick, Elizabeth L.: New Housing for Negroes in Dade County, Florida, in Nathan Glazer and Davis McEntire (eds.), "Studies in Housing and Minority Groups," Berkeley, Calif., University of California Press, 1960.

97. Wade, Richard C.: "Slavery in the Cities: The South 1820–1860," New York, Oxford University Press, 1964.

98. Wakin, Edward: "At the Edge of Harlem," New York, William Morrow & Co., 1965.

99. Watts, Lewis, Howard E. Freeman, Helen M. Hughes, Robert Morris, and Thomas F. Pettigrew: "The Middle-Income Negro Family Faces Urban Renewal," Waltham, Mass., Brandeis University Press, 1964.

100. Weaver, Robert C.: "The Negro Ghetto," New York, Harcourt Brace & Co., 1948.
101. Webber, Melvin M.: Culture, Territoriality and the Elastic Mile, *Papers of the Regional Science Association,* vol. 13, pp. 59–69, 1964.
102. Weissbourd, Bernard: "Segregation subsidies and Megalopolis," Santa Barbara, Calif., Center for the Study of Democratic Institutions, 1964.
103. Wheeler, James O., and Stanley D. Brunn: Negro Migration into Rural Southwest Michigan, *The Geographical Review,* vol. 58, April 1968, pp. 214–230.
104. Whorton, Vernon Lane: Jim Crow Laws and Miscegenation, in Joel Williamson, "The Origins of Segregation," Lexington, Mass., D.C. Heath, 1968.
105. Williamson, Joel: "The Origins of Segregation," Lexington, Mass., D.C. Heath, 1968.
106. Wilson, Theodore B.: "The Black Codes of the South," University, Ala., University of Alabama Press, 1965.
107. Wolf, Eleanor P., and Charles N. Lebeaux: Class and Race in the changing city, in Leo S. Schnore and Henry Fagin (eds.), "Urban Research and Policy Planning," vol. 1. Beverly Hills, Calif.: Sage Publishing Co., 1967.
108. Woodson, Carter G.: The Negroes of Cincinnati: Prior to the Civil War, *Journal of Negro History,* vol. 1, pp. 1–23, January 1916.
109. ———: "A Century of Negro Migration," Washington, D.C., The Association for the Study of Negro Life and History, 1918.
110. Woodward, C. Vann: "The Strange Career of Jim Crow," New York, Oxford University Press, 1955.
111. Woofter, T. J., Jr.: "Landlord and Tenant on the Cotton Plantation," New York, New American Library and Negro Universities Press, 1969.
112. ———: "Negro Problems in Cities," New York, Doubleday and Co., 1928.
113. Wright, Richard R., Jr.: The Negroes of Xenia, Ohio: A Social Study, Bulletin of the Bureau of Labor, vol. 8, September 1903, pp. 1006–1044.
114. Wynes, Charles E.: Social Acceptance and Unacceptance, in Joel Williamson, "The Origins of Segregation," Lexington, Mass., D.C. Heath, 1968.

7   School Segregation

The historical geography of school segregation is a clear example of the use of space as an instrument of social control. School segregation is much more than the placing of boundaries in space; it is apportioning children to schools according to discriminatory criteria. As in other forms of segregation, school segregation is buttressed by general white attitudes that relegate Blacks to an inferior position relative to Whites. As far as education is concerned, Whites have had very definite ideas about the "educability" of Blacks and the capabilities of their minds. The ideology behind and the spatial structuring of education in America has been and continues to be to exclude and separate Blacks. "Place . . . is in fact the main avenue for unequal educational opportunities" (Weinberg, 1967). This discrimination by place has the appearance, with the passage of time, of looking natural and "built in," thus facilitating the appearance of the separation as the "right" way of handling race and schools. As the white president of the Hempstead, New York, school board commented, "De facto segregation develops naturally. It's not that things are done politically. It just grew up naturally as people moved." The previous school board president adds, "It's a case of congregation, not segregation!" (Dworkin, 1968). The exceptions to this segregated pattern, although perhaps of great significance to the individuals involved, have done little or nothing to alter the basic racist structuring of the dominant educational pattern in America.

Because of the difference in the geography of racial segregation throughout the country, the arguments surrounding school segregation have changed with time and location. In those places and at those times when residential segregation has been strong, Whites have argued for neighborhood schools. This, in effect, maintains separate schools. However, in those locations and at those times when Blacks have resided among Whites, the latter have fought against the neighborhood school and sought to establish separate schools. In both cases the geography of schools has been used to isolate black children.

Both the dominant ideology and the spatial structuring of American education have been that, when Blacks are allowed an education, it is separate.

RACIST IDEOLOGY AND EDUCATION OF BLACKS

Although the pronouncement of ideas by people in positions of social and political importance does not directly affect the spatial patterns of education, the weight of their opinions when added to an established tradition increases the probability that the common man will follow and not take the initiative if it would contradict the position of a leader. The weight of the expressed opinion of American presidents, for example, has been that Blacks are inferior and that segregation is a natural action in which one does not interfere.

Thomas Jefferson, for example, in 1785 wrote that, "In general their [blacks'] existence appears to participate more of sensation than reflection. . . . It appears to me that in memory they are equal to the Whites; in reason much the inferior . . . and that in imagination they are dull, tasteless, and anomalous" (Bardolph, 1970).

Much the same position was taken by President Andrew Johnson as he maintained that Blacks should be held as an illiterate work force. Taft was more explicit in making the same point.

> The hope of the Southern Negro is in teaching him how to be a good farmer, how to be a good mechanic; in teaching him how to make his home attractive and how to live more comfortably and according to the rules of health and morality (Bardolph, 1970).

Theodore Roosevelt had the same idea about the education of Blacks, that is, the best type of training for them was to be industrial.

Other presidents simply remained quiet or virtually so with regard to the education of Blacks. These included Warren Harding, Herbert Hoover, and Franklin D. Roosevelt. The negligence of Eisenhower and the actions of Nixon were more racist. The inaction of President Eisenhower increased the effectiveness of mob rule, violence, and intimidation in the white stoppage of school integration in the South and border states. The Nixon administration has been the most guilty of weakness, inconsistency, and vacillation with respect to the issue of school integration. In his policy statement of July 4, 1969, for example, despite being "unequivocally committed to the goal of finally ending racial discrimination in schools," Nixon relaxed the desegregation effort of the federal government. Six civil rights organizations reached the conclusion in May, 1972, that "the illusion of 'progress,' the inactivity and even opposition of federal civil rights enforcement agencies, and the negative leadership of the President of the United States now place the movement toward equality of educational opportunity in serious jeopardy" (Nixon, 1971). Nixon's proposals must be rejected according to Kenneth Clark for the following reasons:

1. They reflect the fact that the President of the United States is using the power of his office in a racial controversy on the side of those who have been consistently opposed to equality of educational opportunity for racially rejected minorities.
2. They represent the first attempts since Reconstruction to have the legislative branch of the federal government enact legislation which would constrict or qualify the rights of minorities.

3. They represent an attempt of the part of the President of the United States not only to slow the pace of public schools de-segregation, but to return the civil rights movement to a point at or before the Plessy "separate-but-equal" stage.

4. The President's proposal would seek to restrain the federal courts as an independent protector of the rights of minorities against the oppression, passions, and prejudices of the majority (Clark, 1972).

We have included the full text of President Nixon's speech "Education and Busing" because it is a good example of racial propaganda. It is important to recognize that Whites are continually telling Blacks that "progress takes time," and then when real progress seems to be imminent, these same Whites are anxious to slow down or cancel the programs that might be responsible for the progress. This is the case with Nixon's speech as he urges quick action to halt the "runaway courts." He argues that Whites must not wait for a constitutional amendment because it has a fatal flaw—"it takes too long." His assertions and proposals simply play on the fear and racism of Whites. He proposes, for example, putting more money into inner-city schools, knowing full well that such aid never reaches the children. When he asserts that busing is a bad means of ending segregation, he is ignoring the wide variety of experience throughout the country in which busing has achieved integration. He continues by attacking those in favor of busing as using social policy to drag children from their neighborhood schools at the cost of a better education. It should be noted that busing is only one alternative among many social policies, one of which is to do nothing.

EDUCATION AND BUSING;
NEIGHBORHOOD SCHOOLS*

by Richard M. Nixon
President of the United States
delivered on television March 16, 1972

Good evening. Tonight I want to talk to you about one of the most difficult issues of our time—the issue of busing. Across this nation—in the North, East, West and South—states, cities and local school districts have been torn apart in debate over this issue.

My own position is well known: I am opposed to busing for the purpose of achieving racial balance in our schools. I have spoken out against busing scores of times over many years. And I believe most Americans—white and black—share that view. But what we need now is not just speaking out against more busing, we need action to stop it.

Above all, we need to stop it in the right way, in a way that will provide better education for every child in America in a desegregated school system.

* *Vital Speeches of the Day,* City News Publishing Co., Inc., Southold, New York, 1971.

The reason action is so urgent is because of a number of recent decisions of the lower Federal courts. Those courts have gone too far; in some cases, beyond the requirements laid down by the Supreme Court in ordering massive busing to achieve racial balance.

The decisions have left in their wake confusion and contradiction in the law; anger, fear and turmoil in local communities, and worst of all, agonized concern among hundreds of thousands of parents for the education and safety of their children who have been forced by court order to be bused miles away from their neighborhood schools.

What is the answer? There are many who believe that a constitutional amendment is the only way to deal with this problem. The constitutional amendment proposal deserves a thorough consideration by the Congress on its merits.

But as an answer to the immediate problem we face of stopping more busing now, the constitutional amendment approach has a fatal flaw—it takes too long. A constitutional amendment would take between a year and 18 months at the very least to become effective.

This means that hundreds of thousands of schoolchildren will be ordered by the courts to be bused away from their neighborhood schools in the next school year with no hope for relief.

What we need is action now. Not action two, three or four years from now. And there's only one effective way to deal with the problem now. That is for the Congress to act. That is why I am sending a special message to the Congress tomorrow urging immediate consideration and action on two measures.

First, I shall propose legislation that would call an immediate halt to all new busing. And, next, I shall propose a companion measure —the Equal Educational Opportunities Act of 1972.

This act would require that every state or locality grant equal educational opportunities to every person regardless of race, color or national origin. For the first time in our history, the cherished American ideal of equality of educational opportunity would be affirmed in the law of the land by the elected representatives of the people in Congress.

The act would further establish an educational bill of rights for Mexican-Americans, Puerto Ricans, Indians and others who start their education under language handicaps to make certain that they, too, will have equal opportunity.

The act I propose would concentrate Federal school aid funds on the areas of greatest educational need. That would mean directing over two and a half billion dollars in the next year mainly towards improving the education of children from poor families.

This proposal deals directly with the problem that has been too often overlooked. We all know that within the central cities of our nation there are schools so inferior that it is hypocritical even to suggest that the poor children who go there are getting a decent education, let alone an education comparable to that of children who go to schools in the suburbs.

Even the most extreme proponents of busing admit that it would be years before programs could be set up and financed which would bus a majority of these children out of the central-city areas to better schools in the suburbs.

That means that putting primary emphasis on more busing rather than on better education inevitably will leave a lost generation of poor children in the central cities doomed to inferior eduction.

It is time for us to make a national commitment to see that the schools in the central cities are upgraded so that the children who go there will have just as good a chance to get quality education as do the children who go to school in the suburbs.

What I am proposing is that at the same time we stop more busing we move forward to guarantee that the children currently attending the poorest schools in our cities and rural areas be provided with education equal to that of good schools in their communities.

Taken together, two elements of my proposal—the moratorium on new busing and the Equal Educational Opportunities Act—would focus our efforts where they really belong, on better education for all of our children, rather than on more busing for some of our children.

In addition, I am directing all agencies and departments of the Federal Government at every level to carry out the spirit as well as the letter of the message in all of their actions.

I am directing the Justice Department to intervene in selected cases where the lower courts have gone beyond the Supreme Court requirements in ordering busing.

These are the highlights of the new approach I propose.

Let me now go to the heart of the problem that confronts us. I want to tell you why I feel that busing for the purpose of achieving racial balance in our schools is wrong, and why the great majority of Americans are right in wanting to bring it to an end.

The purpose of such busing is to help end segregation; but experience in case after case has shown that busing is a bad means to a good end. The frank recognition of that fact does not reduce our commitments to desegregation. It simply tells us that we have to come up with a better means to that good end.

The great majority of Americans—white and black—feel strongly that the busing of school children away from their own neighborhoods for the purpose of achieving racial balance is wrong. But the great majority—black and white—also are determined that the process of desegregation must go forward until the goal of genuinely equal educational opportunity is achieved.

The question then is how can we end segregation in a way that does not result in more busing? The proposals I am sending to the Congress provide an answer to that question.

One emotional undercurrent that has done much to make this issue so difficult is the feeling that some people have that to oppose busing is to be antiblack. This is dangerous nonsense.

There's no escaping the fact that some people do oppose busing because of racial prejudice. But to go on from this to conclude that antibusing is simply a code word for prejudice is a vicious libel on millions of concerned parents who oppose busing—not because they are against desegregation, but because they are for better education for their children. They want their children educated in their own neighborhoods.

Many have invested their life savings in a home in a neighborhood they chose because it had good schools. They do not want their children bused across the city to an inferior school just to meet some social planner's concept of what is considered to be the correct racial balance or what is called progressive social policy.

There are right reasons for opposing busing and there are wrong reasons. And most people, including a large and increasing number of blacks, oppose it for reasons that have little or nothing to do with race.

It would compound an injustice to persist in massive busing simply because some people oppose it for the wrong reasons. There's another element to consider, and this is the most important one of all. That is the human element, which I see reflected in thousands of letters I have received in my mail from worried parents all over the country—North, East, West, and South.

Let me give you some examples:

I believe it is wrong when an 8-year-old child who was once able to walk to a neighborhood school is now forced to travel two hours a day on a bus.

I believe it is wrong when a working mother is suddenly faced with three different bus schedules for her children and that makes it impossible for her to continue to work.

I believe it is wrong when parents are burdened with new worries about their children's safety on the road and in the neighborhoods far from home.

I believe it is wrong when a child in a poor neighborhood is denied the extra personal attention and financial support in his school that we know can make all the difference.

All these individual human wrongs add up to a deeply felt and growing frustration. These wrongs can be and must be set right. And that is the purpose of the legislation I am sending to Congress tomorrow.

I submit these proposals to the Congress and I commend them to all of you listening tonight mindful of the profound import and the special complexity of the issues they address. The key is action and action now. And Congress holds that key.

Deep in the heart of Dixie: Alabama highway patrolmen inform black children in a Macon County school bus that they will be denied entry at the Tuskegee High School (1963).

United Press International.

If you agree with the goals I have described tonight to stop more busing now and provide equality of education for all of our children, I urge you to let your Congressmen and Senators know your views so that Congress will act promptly to deal with this problem.

Let me close with a personal note. This is a deeply emotional divisive issue. I have done my very best to undertake to weigh and respect the conflicting interest, to strike a balance which is thoughtful and just, to search for answers that will best serve all of our nation's children.

I realize the program I have recommended will not satisfy the extremists on the one side who oppose busing for the wrong reasons and I realize that my program will not satisfy the extreme social planners on the other side who insist on more busing even at the cost of better education.

But while what I have said tonight will not appeal to either extreme, I believe that the majority of Americans of all races want more busing stopped and better education started.

Let us recognize that the issue of busing divides many Americans but let us also recognize that the commitment to equal opportunity in education unites all Americans.

The proposals I am submitting to Congress will allow us to turn away from what divides us and to turn toward what unites us.

The way we handle this difficult issue is a supreme test of the character, responsibility and the decency of the American people. Let us handle it in a way we can be proud, by uniting behind a program which will make it possible for all the children in this great and good country of ours to receive a better education and to enjoy a better life.

Thank you. Good night.

SPATIAL STRUCTURING OF AMERICAN EDUCATION

Early Patterns: South

Prior to 1865, the issue of school segregation was largely a matter of state and local policy. Public school segregation by race was common both in the North and in the South.

Under the southern plantation regime it was unlawful to teach Blacks to read and write. Every southern state except Maryland and Kentucky had stringent laws forbidding anyone to teach slaves reading and writing, and in some states the penalties applied to the education of free blacks and mulattos as well. This resulted in the "stealing" of educations by Blacks.

> I was born under the slave law in Georgia, in 1848, and was brought up by my grandmother in Savannah. There was three of us with her, me, my younger sister and brother. My brother and I being the two eldest, we were sent to a friend of my grandmother, Mrs. Woodhouse, a widow, to learn to read and write. She was a free woman and lived on Bay Lane, between Habersham and Price streets, about half mile from my house. We went every day about nine o'clock, with our books wrapped in paper to prevent police or white persons from seeing them. We went in, one at a time,

through the gate, into the yard to the kitchen, which was the school room. She had twenty-five or thirty children who she taught, assisted by her daughter, Mary Jane. The neighbors would see us going in sometimes, but they supposed we were there learning trades, as it was the custom to give children a trade of some kind. After school, we left the same way we entered, one by one, when we would go to a square, about a block from the school and wait for each other (Katz, 1968).

Rather than provide for the education of slaves, the plantation was meant to be a "school" for the mass training of Blacks in the ways of slavery.

Considering the weight of tradition, work, and white force, it is remarkable that "public education for all at public expense was in the South, a Negro idea. . . . The public school systems in most southern states began with the enfranchisement of the Negro" (DuBois, 1969).

Scattered public and private schools for Blacks could be found in the South during and following the Civil War. The first day school for Blacks was begun in Hampton, Virginia, on September 17, 1861. In 1867, twenty-three schools were started in various parts of the South. Efforts by the Union Army and philanthropists before and during the war were taken over by the Freedman's Bureau which reported that in "former slave states and the District of Columbia, there were 90,589 Negro pupils and 1,314 teachers in 740 schools" (DuBois, 1969). But after Reconstruction, with the return to power of the white southerners, the public schools which had started to flourish were greatly curtailed. Blacks seemed to want, at this time, mixed schools for two reasons. First, mixed schools were thought to be of better quality. Second, mixed schools were seen as proof of their newly acquired equality. From the time of the Civil War to the turn of the century, racial separation in the schools became an established part of the regime of segregation.

In the 1930s nearly half of the states still either required, as did all southern states, or expressly permitted segregation in the schools. The white attitude toward black education lasted long after slavery; sharecroppers and tenants, like slaves, were not encouraged to get an education. During the 1930s the most complete educational facilities existing for Blacks were, as a matter of course, segregated.

Not only were schools for Blacks separate, they were in poorer physical shape; transportation was meager or nonexistent; and in some cases, schools were simply not provided. Many southern counties had no schools for Blacks. In 1934 in Bolivar and Coohoman Counties in Mississippi only fifty-one of 226 black schools were actual school buildings, the remainder were makeshift; this contrasted with the consolidated, well-constructed schools for Whites in these counties. Woodson and Powdermaker also point out the contrast between poor black schools and better white schools. The lack of transportation to schools is a notable example of the denial of equal opportunity to blacks. For example, in the states of Arkansas, Alabama, Georgia, Maryland, North and South Carolina, and Florida, the expenditures for the transportation of black students were very low during the 1930s. Johnson found that in Mississippi

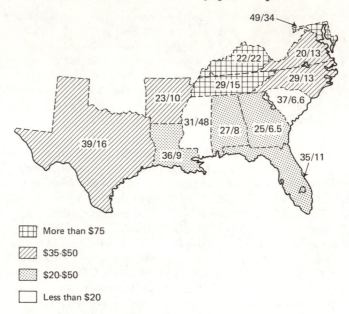

Figure 7.1 Expenditures per Pupil for Black and White Students under "Separate but Equal," 1930.

transportation was not provided for black children. A decade earlier, Irwin found the same situation in Charlottesville and Albermarle Counties, Virginia.

Figure 7.1 indicates that expenditures under "separate but equal" were hardly that, except for the state of Kentucky. In ten of the southern states the expenditures for black students in 1930 was less than half that for white students.

Early Patterns: North

The "separate but equal" doctrine originated not in the South but in the North, prior to the Civil War. Until the end of the Civil War that doctrine was prevalent in the section of the country in which Blacks were theoretically free. In New England the place of residence was not the determinant of the place of schooling for black children, as they were assigned to separate schools regardless of the district in which they lived. By the 1830s public policy, statute, or custom placed black children in separate schools in nearly every northern community. In 1859 Frederick Douglass wrote that "The point which we must aim at . . . is to obtain admission for our children to the nearest school house in our respective neighorhoods" (Litwack, 1961).

In the North it appeared to be the number of Blacks in an area that provided the impetus for school segregation. In an 1867 case (*Westchester and Philadelphia Railroad Co. v. Miles*), the Court acknowledged that even the common school law provides for separate schools when their [blacks'] numbers are adequate. The states of New York (1850), Pennsylvania (1854), Ohio (1838), Indiana (1850), Illinois (1857), Iowa (1846), Michigan (1841), and

State	SCHOOL DISTRICTS		% Black Majority	Number schools in Black Majority
	Total	Black Majority		
Alabama	118	14	12.0	140
Arkansas	388	37	9.5	97
Florida	67	3	4.5	67
Georgia	192	53	27.5	434
Louisiana	67	17	25.4	323
Mississippi	150	56	37.3	345
N. Carolina	155	27	17.5	238
S. Carolina	92	36	39.2	290
Tennessee	151	4	3.8	171
Texas	1265	24	1.9	68
Virginia	135	25	18.5	185

Table 7.1 Number and Percentage of Majority Black School Districts in Eleven Southern States, 1970

Source: *Race Relations Information Center, Majority Black School Districts in the 11 Southern States, July, 1970, p. 1 and Table II.*

California (1855) had statutes providing for separate schools for Blacks and Whites. Blacks migrating to the Midwest generally had to wait until after the Civil War for free public education. By the 1870s, if black children were educated at all, they were attending separate schools in the North.

Thus by the Civil War both the ideology and the geographic pattern of school segregation were established throughout the country. Separate schools were the rule, that is, where education at all was available for Blacks. The ideology of separation and the spatial pattern itself, once set in motion, have never been seriously questioned by Whites.

Modern Patterns

The result of these early patterns has been the development of a dual system of education in America. The pattern is evident in the North as well as in the South, in the country as well as in the cities. Thirteen years after the 1954 Brown decision, for example, segregation increased in schools. Of the 1.6 million black children enrolled in schools in seventy-five cities studied by the Civil Rights Commission, 75 percent attended schools that were over 90 percent black. In the same cities 83 percent of the 2.4 million white children were in schools over 90 percent white.

As of 1973, there has been undeniable progress toward desegregation and in some cases even integration of schools. But the dual school systems have not been dismantled as Moynihan and Nixon suggested in 1970. Within so-called unitary districts there remain many "black" and "white" schools. And within so-called desegregated schools, classrooms remain segregated. One study, for example, found that in 273 of 467 southern districts monitored in September, 1970, classroom segregation existed. As seen in Table 7.1 there is a great range in the extent of all-black school districts remaining in the South.

We will now examine briefly some examples of school desegregation around the country. These are not to be taken as typical of a state or region but rather as exhibiting the range of success, problems, and failure in the nationwide process of dismantling the dual public schools.

SOUTHERN CASES

Charlotte-Mecklenburg, North Carolina   The city of Charlotte became a symbol in 1970 in the outcry over school busing. On February 5, 1970, Judge McMillan issued an order calling for the complete desegregation of all schools in the Charlotte-Mecklenburg school district, which was upheld by the U.S. Supreme Court on August 20, 1971 (*Swann v. Charlotte-Mecklenburg Board of Education*).

The result of these decisions has been the implementation of a combination of geographic plans to achieve desegregation. At the high school level the city was divided into wedge-shaped attendance areas from the center of the city outward. The reason for the wedge shape was that the pattern of residential segregation in the city was like that typical of northern ghettos; that is, Blacks were contained in the center of the city. Rezoning and satellite schools were used to desegregate the junior highs. The elementary schools were altered with a combination of geographic zoning, pairing, and grouping procedures. Even with these plans thirty-three schools were left untouched, nine in the black inner-city and twenty-four in the white suburbs. These were then grouped, one black school to two or three white schools. Black first through fourth and White fifth and sixth graders were bused. It was this latter pairing and busing that caused the furor in Charlotte. In effect, 4,876 black and 4,998 white children were to be bused. Prior to the busing order 34 percent of the 84,500 pupils in the district were bused; this increased to almost 59 percent in November, 1971. Blacks were 42 percent of those bused.

Much of the opposition to the busing plan came from white parents living in the northwest part of the city and county whose children would be sent to black schools. It seems that they were not only concerned about their children in black schools but that, unless school boundaries were changed, they felt that their neighborhoods would also become all-black.

The human response to busing and school desegregation in the city ran the gamut from violence and mistrust to understanding and hope. Although significant problems remain to be solved, the school system seems to be attacking problems of education rather than being embattled over busing. Watters has suggested that if the children were allowed to work out the problems with no interference from adults, either parents or presidents, there would seem to be a majority will to work things out.

Athens, Georgia   In the 14 years from 1954 to 1968 the only step toward desegregation taken in Clarke County, Georgia, was the institution of a "free-

School	% Black	% White	% Indian
Hoke	49	36	15
Upchurch	50	30	20
South Hoke	45	34	21
Raeford	49	30	21
J. W. McLauchin	50	26	24
West Hoke	57	30	13
Scurlock	47	45	8
Total school population	50	35	15

Table 7.2 School Enrollment, Hoke County, North Carolina, by Race, October, 1971

Source: *U.S. Commission on Civil Rights, The Diminishing Barrier: A Report on School Desegregation in Nine Communities, December, 1972, pp. 29–31.*

dom-of-choice" plan. As in hundreds of other communities around the country, this did nothing to alter the pattern of segregated schools. In order not to lose federal funds the county developed a busing plan. As the superintendent of schools put it, "For a half century we have been busing students past white schools and vice versa to maintain segregation. Now we're busing to eliminate segregation" (Barker, 1971). The 1969 plan set a 20 to 40 percent black student body in eleven of the thirteen elementary schools and 50 percent in the other two. The two high schools were paired in 1970. The plan resulted in an increase of 200 in the number of children who were bused. As in Charlotte, a group of white parents who felt that the burden of desegregation was falling on them brought suit, but it was dropped. Overall, Clarke County seems to have taken the first steps, and the whites are becoming more attentive and responsive to the needs of black children.

Mobile, Alabama As in Athens, the white community sought to get by the desegregation order by implementing a freedom-of-choice plan, but the segregated pattern remained. The fifth Circuit Court insisted that the city use a different method to desegregate. The new plan was a geographic zone assignment. As of 1971 the Mobile case was still pending, while the schools remained segregated. The situation has not been as optimistic as in Athens. The major reason for the lack of progress in the city seems to be the weakness of the white leadership. Racism and intimidation have driven the white moderates underground, where they remain.

Hoke County, North Carolina Until 1964 Hoke County operated three separate school systems—black, Indian, and white. HEW had indicated that the freedom-of-choice plan was not satisfactory as an instrument to destroy the separate schools, but there were no court fights. The movement to change the schools was accomplished with little outside pressure. Consolidation, reorganization, and redistricting were necessary to desegregate the schools. Table 7.2 indicates that the county did a good job of desegregating the schools in accordance with the ethnic mixture in the total school populations.

NORTHERN CASES

Harrisburg, Pennsylvania   The geography of schools in Harrisburg was like that of most northern cities—black inner-city schools surrounded by white suburban schools. In 1968 the school district began submitting plans for desegregation. Their second plan was accepted in 1970 but was fought in the courts by white parents who feared the loss of their "neighborhood schools." In effect, the Pennsylvania Supreme Court drew on the Swann case and ruled that, if busing and pupil assignment were necessary to overcome de jure segregation, they were equally good means to dismantle a dual school system brought about through de facto segregation. This decision resulted in a complete reorganization on the schools along a 3-4-2-2-2-2 plan. White negative reaction was passive, with no boycotts, protests, or violence. Those who did not like it, moved.

Jefferson County, Ohio   Jefferson County school district is a majority black one, a rural-suburban community of Whites from Appalachia and Blacks, which is located adjacent to Dayton. School desegregation here was neither the result of court orders nor of voluntary plans; it was the indirect result of a consolidation plan. The scheme has integrated all the elementary schools in proportion to the black-white ratio in the school district at large. There was some opposition to the plan at first by both Blacks and Whites, but since its inception, parents seem to be either resigned to it or are actively supporting it.

Pasadena, California   The Pasadena case is one of only a few suits that the U.S. Justice Department pursued outside of the South. Prior to the 1970 to 1971 plan the city operated a neighborhood school system that was highly segregated, with some evidence that school attendance zones were drawn so as to maintain segregation. The city also tried, unsuccessfully, to get by with a freedom-of-choice plan.

To meet the court order the city redrew its school boundaries so that they would meet the following criteria: each school would have a population mix similar to that of the whole district; neighborhood schools would be maintained insofar as possible in keeping with the order to desegregate totally, optimum use would be made of all facilities, traveling distances would be minimized. The plan required large-scale busing. Even though the busing program was a great increase over that before desegregation, it seems to have been well-planned and has not received militant opposition.

Pontiac, Michigan   Pontiac has been another symbol—a northern Little Rock —of white resistance to desegregation. Bus burning, picketing, and school boycotting were common in 1971. The city and its schools have a history of racism and segregation, in some cases consciously maintained. The geography of school segregation in the city was a result of both de facto and de jure segregation. Boundaries were drawn so as to perpetuate neighborhood schools, and new schools were located in such a way as to intensify racial imbalance constituting de jure segregation.

A black child comforts her white classmate in this 1965 photo of integrated school lines in the Hyde Park section of Boston.
Wide World.

Whites in the city fought the order to desegregate all the way to the U.S. Supreme Court but lost. The high schools were desegregated by a change in the boundary line. Children in kindergarten still go to neighborhood schools. All the remaining grades must be from 20 to 40 percent black. The plan has required large-scale busing. Prior to "busing" 3,500 children were riding buses to school; this number increased to 9,619 after desegregation.

These few cases point out both the common problems and the range of solutions sought in the struggle to desegregate America's schools. The violence of Pontiac is in direct contrast to the compliance of Hoke County. Many cities try to maintain the status quo by implementing either a freedom-of-choice or a neighborhood school plan. There seems to be a tendency, shown in northern cities like Harrisburg and Pontiac, for Whites to move if they dislike the results of desegregation. Moving does not seem to be as common an alternative in the South. This could, eventually, result in greater school desegregation in the South than in the North.

Also the legacy of segregation has left behind a wide gulf in the perception of Blacks and Whites as to the crucial problems in the dismantling of dual school systems. Besides a general antibusing attitude, Whites stress discipline, bus schedules, and safety as their major concerns.

Problems seem much more varied from the black point of view. Blacks are more concerned with issues such as firing and placement of black teachers, unfair treatment of black students involved in fights with Whites, loss of identity, internal segregation within the school, and intergroup training for white teachers and counselors.

SOCIOSPATIAL STRUCTURING OF EDUCATION

To a large extent the quality of education any child in America receives depends on where he or she happens to reside. This fact is even more important for black children, because in their case the question is not where they "happen" to live but where they are forced to live. There are a number of spatial factors associated with residence and schools that have become important in the geography of American schools. These factors include distance, neighborhood, gerrymandering, busing, "white flight," and de facto–de jure segregation.

The argument for equal educational opportunity as a constitutional principle rests on different sets of cases. First, the school desegregation cases (*Brown v. Board of Education,* 1954) established that an education provided by the state cannot be discriminatory based on color. Second, in the reapportionment decisions it was decided that the state cannot use the accidents of geography and arbitrary boundary lines to discriminate among citizens. Finally, the indigent defendant case (*Griffin v. Illinois,* 1956) established the general principle that the state cannot discriminate amongst its citizens based on wealth.

But ultimately the question is not a constitutional one but a human one. The actions of the courts have not been translated into actions by citizens. The Court proposed dismantling America's dual school system but could not enforce that decision without the acquiescence of local communities. Thus, the problem with the Court's decisions with respect to schools has been that when they run counter to the wishes of the dominant white society the chances for their being carried out are few indeed. Alexander Hamilton's description of the Court is still quite accurate today.

> The judiciary . . . has no influence over either the sword or the purse; no direction either of the strength or of the wealth of society and can take no active resolution whatever. It may truly be said to have neither force nor will, but merely judgment, and must ultimately depend upon the aid of the executive arm even for the efficacy of its judgments (Hamilton, 1901).

Distance

Distance has been involved in numerous law suits from 1849 to the present dealing with school segregation. In those cases in which race and distance are involved, race has overridden distance as a criterion for the assignment of children to schools. In *Roberts v. Boston* (1849), *Lewis v. Board of Education of Cincinnati* (1876), *Dietz v. Easton* (1872), *King v. Gallagher* (1883), and *Lehew v. Brummell* (1890) black children were denied admittance to nearer white schools and forced to attend black schools that were further away.

The question of distance, children, location, and schools first came before the courts in the North, not in the South. Blacks were prohibited by the general school committee in Boston, Massachusetts, from attending school with Whites, even though a school board regulation stated that students "are especially entitled to enter the school nearest to their place of residence" (Weinberg, 1967).

Massachusetts state law, however, made no provision for separate schools for Blacks and Whites.

In the Boston case the argument of the black parents was that it was inconvenient to send their children to black schools that were further than white schools, because of the distance involved. But the argument of distance did not help. The court ruled in 1849 that "the good of both classes of schools will be best promoted, by maintaining the separate primary schools for colored and for white children" (Bardolph, 1970). This was the first enunciation of the "separate but equal" doctrine.

Much the same situation occurred in Albany in the Dietz case of 1872. The Albany school board required a black child to attend a more distant school than the one nearest to his or her home. The Court made the point that, "The school which is nearest to his residence is no more his than that which is most distant" (Weinberg, 1967).

The Court's attitude toward distance and race is also indicated in the following cases. In the Lewis case the black children had to walk 4 miles each way to attend the black school. In part the Court declared, "Somebody must walk further than the rest" (Weinberg, 1967). The Court in the Gallagher case rejected the contention that proximity created any right to attend a given school. "The fact that by this system of classification (separate black and white schools) one person is required to go further to reach his place of instruction than he otherwise would is a mere incident to any classification of the pupils in the public schools of a large city and affords no substantial grounds of complaint" (Weinberg, 1967). In the Lehew case the Court, in forcing Brummell's children to go 1.5 miles further than any white child in the district, said that "The law does not undertake to establish a school within a given distance of anyone, white or black" (Weinberg, 1967).

A similar problem arose in Rochester, New York, as Frederick Douglass sought to have his children allowed into public school after they were barred from P.S. 15. This must have reminded Douglass of what his former master had said about his own education, "Learning would spoil the best nigger in the world" (Bennett, 1965).

Even though *Plessy v. Ferguson,* 1896, specifically dealt with railroads, it reaffirmed what had long been common practice in schools. Perhaps the importance of the establishment of this "separate but equal" doctrine was that it said nothing about distance. The Court rulings cited above clearly indicate that the separation of black children was taken for granted. It was assumed that black children could travel further to school than white children. The logic does not recognize that distance was not a random variable, but one largely determined by race. "What was too far for a white child became reasonably near for a Negro child" (Weinberg, 1967).

Courts continued to rule against black parents in their efforts to have their children attend schools near their homes. In *Dameron v. Bayless,* 1912, the Arizona State Supreme Court ruled that "The matter of nearness or remoteness of a schoolhouse to the pupil's residence ordinarily should have no place as a factor in determining the adequacy and sufficiency of school facilities. . . . It is not possible to locate new buildings equidistant from all patrons. The law will not measure with a yardstick these distances" (Weinberg, 1967). In *McSwain v. County Board of Education*, 1952, location was used against black parents. In this Tennessee case black high school students bypassed a white high school on the 19-mile bus ride to the black school. The ruling judge said that, "Equality of opportunity cannot in practice be measured in terms of place, for opportunity rather than place is the heart of equal protection" (Weinberg, 1967). This judge certainly did not understand that place, indeed, has a great deal to do with "equality of opportunity." It is a central premise of this book that location or place has been an instrument of both conscious and unconscious oppression used by Whites against Blacks. "Whether North or South, Negro students generally lived farther from school than did whites. This was especially but not exclusively so in legally segregated school systems. . . . At the same time, Negro students had much less transportation available despite the greater need" (Weinberg, 1967). From 1865 to 1935 the legal principle of school segregation was not struck down.

From 1935 to 1954 the Court came closer and closer to considering the inherent inequality of separate educational facilities. But this did not come until 1954; in the preceding 20 years the Courts ruled primarily on whether equality existed in the separate facilities. In a number of cases during this period the abstract principle of separate schools was not questioned.

Finally, in *Brown v. Board of Education of Topeka*, 1954, it was ruled that segregated public schools were inherently unequal. There are two important points to remember here. First, the Brown decision was binding on only those school boards who were parties in the suit. The result has been 18 years of suits by schools trying to forestall desegregation. Second, the difference between a decision and its enactment and enforcement can in effect make the former meaningless. The importance of these points lies in the apparent contradiction in the position taken by the Court and its inability to carry out its judgment. The result has been that segregation, though struck down on paper, is maintained and condoned in actuality. In essence Brown II (1955) set local courts to rule on the good faith compliance with the law according to local circumstances. The Brown doctrine only forbade publicly enforced segregation. "It has not decided that the states must mix persons of different races in the schools. . . . What it has decided, and all that it has decided, is that a state may not deny to any person on account of race the right to attend any school that it maintains. The Constitution in other words does not require integration" (Bardolph, 1970). It seems also that Brown II sanctioned the manipulation of school boundaries as a way of delaying school integration. One of the factors listed for consideration in the decision for the timing of school integration was "revision of school district lines to accommodate the altered situation" (Rogers and Bullock, 1972).

From 1955 to 1958 the courts refused to face directly the fact that local and state governments and courts were deliberately evading or obstructing the carrying out of school integration. This was attacked in *Cooper v. Aaron*, 1958, in which the Court laid down the "with all deliberate speed" doctrine, which has since been side-stepped. Desegregation could be put off indefinitely by the multitude of slow actions, repeated postponements, and administrative red tape. What Davis wrote about education in Texas in 1917 has been and continues to be true of the country as a whole: "The Texas educational system has been a dual system in name only; the Texas system is essentially a white system with Negro education incidental to it" (Weinberg, 1967).

It was unfortunate that the courts were the instrument for school integration from 1954 to 1964. There are a number of factors that made the courts ineffectual as a source of improvement of the school systems of America. Basically the courts are a symbol, especially when it comes to race and schools. The power of the courts rests primarily on a respect for the law. It is blatantly apparent that when it comes to the education of black children white Americans from presidents on down do not respect law and order. Whether it is the quiet indifference of Eisenhower or the adamant disagreement of Nixon, or the disobedience of other elected officials and appointed judges, they all erode the respect and condone disrespect for the court's rulings. It is these same officials whose support is necessary for the implementation of the court's rulings. Also, the process of litigation does not move quickly, as do the lives of black children.

District courts, which had the charge of carrying out and enforcing the Supreme Court's rulings in Brown I and II, found themselves in a tight position. In many cases the district judges were simply products of the local environments and ruled with the biases of their local white constituents. Even when district judges tried to enforce the order of the Supreme Court, they received no backing from the federal government. It was blatant racism when "Eisenhower insisted that the refusal to obey the Federal courts could not be dealt with by law enforcement but only by moral conversion" (Rogers and Bullock, 1972). This was another example of two systems of law—one for Whites, another for Blacks—that have always existed in the country. The federal government simply ignored its laws and the Blacks, with the result that the safest stand for the district courts was to do nothing at all.

Another problem with the Brown decisions was that they were interpreted as applying only to de jure and not to de facto school segregation, thus it was an attack on southern and not northern school segregation patterns. This was to backfire in 1970 when Senator Ribicoff supported the Stennis Amendment, which, on the face of it, was to attack school segregation nationwide, whether de jure or de facto. But in reality the result was nationwide unenforcement.

Distance has also been a factor in more recent cases. Residential proximity was used unsuccessfully as a ground for claiming the right of a black child to attend a white school in *Thompson v. County School Board of Arlington County* (1958), *Shuttlesworth v. Birmingham Board of Education* (1958), and *Evans v. Buchanan* (1962).

Neighborhoods

The neighborhood as a sociospatial unit based on school attendance is another geographic concept that has been entangled in the issue of school segregation. The assignment of students to neighborhood schools arose principally as a result of population growth beyond what villages and small towns could handle.

It would seem that spatial assignments would be simply a matter of convenience, sending children to the nearest school. This may well have been the case had it not been for the fact of race. But even during the nineteenth century, proximity was not a legal principle.

It was the factor of race, long before Plessy, that changed the meaning of the common or neighborhood school. It has to be emphasized that racial segregation was an integral part of the sociospatial structure of American education. It was as much a part of the system as the three R's. It has, in fact, been the fourth R. Separate schools for blacks, or no schools at all, were part of the accepted white philosophy of education.

During the nineteenth century, the rural character of the population distribution in the South with its pattern of residential segregation facilitated separate schooling for Blacks and Whites. Thus in the rural South neighborhood schools were supported by Whites as these were separate.

In the North in the nineteenth century, rural and urban segregation, though prevalent, was not as pronounced as in some areas in the South, with the result that it was the black parents and not the Whites who argued for neighborhood schools, as they would be integrated schools. As we will see, with the hardening of racial boundaries and increased residential segregation, white parents are again supporting the neighborhood school, as it means separate black and white institutions.

There have been at least two Court rulings that have attacked the concept of the right to a neighborhood school as too "elastic and dependent on circumstances, it may be equally satisfied by areas measured by rods or by miles" (Weinberg, 1967). In 1964 the New York Supreme Court held that "Legal rights may not be founded on such nebulous geographic neighborhoods" (Weinberg, 1967).

The legal issue is not as clear as it might seem, however, as many cases have established a link between residence and constitutional right. Residential segregation has, in effect, legitimized school segregation. A court ruled, for example, in Pontiac, Michigan, in 1958, against a black family who wanted to send their daughter to a predominantly white school located further from her home than the local black school. The court ruled that "The plaintiff has no constitutionally guaranteed right to attend a public school outside of the attendance areas in which she resides" (Weinberg, 1967). The effect of these neighborhood cases seem to be that one has no constitutional right to attend any school, or put another way, the location of the school is not tied to the right to attend a school. This would seem to be no problem if the location of schools and their attendance boundaries were located only on the basis of safety of the children, distance, natural obstacles, and utilization of classroom space. But such is not the case; race is a dominant factor in the geography of schools.

Gerrymandering

The process of gerrymandering has also been prevalent as a way of segregating black children in school. Racial gerrymandering involves the manipulation of boundaries, in this case school attendance boundaries, by which Whites seek to isolate and segregate Blacks, with the result that white children have better access to the educational resources of a community. This manipulation of space can involve both the site of a school and the attendance boundaries of a particular school or district. These spatial decisions are social and political. The most common criteria for the drawing of school attendance areas are natural obstacles, safety, classroom space, distance, and, of course, race. The first four criteria are elements of school districting; gerrymandering occurs when the fifth element is included, whether conscious or not. "Prejudice cannot be separated from gerrymandering" (Weinberg, 1967). Districting and gerrymandering are not synonymous. Also, gerrymandering does not necessarily depend upon irregular spatial forms; an attendance area that has been gerrymandered for the purpose of racial segregation can be quite regular in shape.

Where a school is located may be the most important factor in a decision to segregate children. A school can be located, for example, in the center of a black residential area, or it can be put elsewhere with the children drawn to it. Indianapolis, Pontiac (Michigan), New Orleans, San Francisco, Cleveland, Sweetwater (Tennessee), Englewood (New Jersey), Mt. Vernon (New York), and Danville (Illinois) have been involved in court cases because of discriminatory school sites. The central issue in site location cases is that schools are built in the center of black residential areas and white children are then bused out. In these cases, it is interesting to note that white parents do not argue against busing. The building of schools within all-black residential areas put the black parents in a cruel dilemma. On the one hand, the school is close by and may be physically newer, yet it remains segregated, which has traditionally meant an inferior education.

An important issue not examined in the above cases involves the question of who decides where, using what criteria, the school site is to be located. In one case, the newest high school in Oakland, California, built in the 1960s, was located in the center of an all-white, affluent residential area. The NAACP and CORE argued that, if the school has been built nearer the center of Oakland, the student body would have been racially diverse. An extremely important key to an understanding of the sociospatial structuring of American society in general and education in particular is that "The kind of pluralistic decision typical of American school politics resulted in a racist decision" (Hayes, 1972).

In a San Francisco case, the building of the new Anza school in 1962 helped perpetuate school segregation. Even though the nearby (eight blocks away) Golden Gate School was overcrowded and its students were bused from the Fillmore District to Pacific Heights, none of these minority children were included within the attendance area of the nearly all-white Anza school.

> In Houston, almost every school constructed after 1955 was located in racially homogenous residential areas. Of the 56 Negro schools in Houston in 1965, for example, 49 were newly built or enlarged in Negro residential areas after 1955 (Rogers and Bullock, 1972).

Gerrymandering more often involves the placing of boundary lines according to race. Beliefs are critical for an understanding of people's actions. This is obvious in the geography of race. Segregation is the spatial manifestation of the white belief in the inferiority of Blacks.

The use and effects of spatial structuring are often viewed differently by Whites and Blacks. In Riverside, California, for example, the "Longfellow Corridor" was viewed by Blacks as deliberate gerrymandering to keep the Longfellow school segregated. Yet "what was for Negroes a blatant administrative policy was to whites non-existent" (Duster, 1968). This supports the contention that spatial structuring is taken for granted by the group that does that structuring, Whites, and only fully realized by the group adversely affected, Blacks. Powdermaker makes the same point in describing the differential sociospatial knowledge of Blacks and Whites in a small southern town.

> Across the tracks is a life but little known to the whites, who rarely go there. Everything that happens on the white side, however, is known to the Negroes, who have constant access to white homes and business places. This disparity of information is both a natural and a significant factor in the relations of the two groups (Raper, 1936).

There have been numerous attempts by Whites to control and alter school attendance boundaries in an attempt to maintain or initiate segregation. During the 2 years 1962 to 1963 the NAACP filed suits against sixty-nine communities ranging from large cities to small towns charging gerrymandering of interdistrict boundary lines. Gerrymandering of school district boundaries for racial reasons has occurred in Malverne, Baldwin, and Hempstead, New York; Chicago, Illinois; Durham, North Carolina; Johnson County, Kansas; New Rochelle, New York; Jackson and Memphis, Tennessee; Hillsboro, Ohio; Ramapo, New York; Savannah, Georgia; and Englewood, New Jersey.

In Johnson County, Kansas, the court found that the local school board segregated the schools, "by a process of gerrymandering up streets and alleys so that all of the Negro children would be within that district" (Weinberg, 1967). The result was that all the Blacks attended Walker School, while Whites, some even passing Walker, attended South Park School. Much the same actions took place in New Rochelle. A black school district, Lincoln, was gerrymandered in 1930, and as the black residential area expanded into the surrounding white areas, the school boundaries were altered to keep the black youths in Lincoln and allow white children to keep attending the white schools. This case was finally settled in court in 1961; in striking down this instance of racial gerrymandering, the Court stated that there was no difference between segregation as a result of a formal dual system and that resulting from gerrymandering.

In many cases geographic manipulation of school boundaries is a new tool used to support the established spatial pattern of racial segregation. Informal segregation of schools was the pattern in Hillsboro, Ohio, prior to the registration of seven black students at a white school in 1954. This occurred even though school segregation had been outlawed in Ohio since 1886. The school board promptly drew gerrymandered attendance areas to preserve school segregation. The spatial result was that "The attendance area for the black school,

Lincoln, consisted of two separate sections; the school itself was not located in its own attendance area. Several students had to walk by a white school on their way to Lincoln" (Weinberg, 1967).

Perhaps the most well-known instance of racial gerrymandering occurred in Tuskegee, Alabama, in 1957. Although this boundary case was not specifically one involving school boundaries, it is important. The reason that Whites redrew the boundary of the town was to convert it into a white town, thus taking away the voting power of the Blacks in municipal elections. In order to do this "The Alabama State legislature drew up an ingenious new city boundary, altering the shape of Tuskegee from a simple square to a curious 28 sided figure resembling a stylized sea horse" (Taper, 1962). The importance of the decision in *Gomillion v. Lightfoot* noted that the drawing of boundary lines has human effects aside from being exercises in geometry and geography, and these are aimed only at Blacks.

Busing

One of the methods available for the dismantling of America's dual school system has been and continues to be busing. In the early 1970s this issue has been the biggest controversy in the racial struggle. Busing has not been a sectional issue; virtually every section of the country, North, South, East, West, urban, suburban, and rural, has been involved in the controversy. All regions have seen some successes, more failures, some hope for change, more dismay at continued racism. Perhaps the greatest sidelight to the enormous amounts of energy and money being expended on this issue will be a real interest on the part of white Americans in the quality of education their children are receiving. We obviously do not have the space here to deal conclusively with the complex problem of busing, as the question is still being dealt with at both local and national levels. The assistant superintendent of the Riverside, California, schools has ten volumes of material just on his school system.

When busing is proposed, it usually draws a storm of protest. Convenience, cost, safety, neighborhoods are just a few of the issues involved in the debate. But busing of school children is nothing new in America. Rural and suburban children have had as a matter of course to ride buses to school. In the 42 years from 1920 to 1962 the rate of school bus usage by children increased from one out of fifty to one out of three. In all that time there was no national outcry against busing by white parents. One finds rather that there were sighs of relief that the kids were out of the house sooner in the morning and did not get back before mother had a chance to put up her feet for a while. Or as Ray Jenkins recollects about his bus ride to his white school in rural Alabama in the late 1930s and early 1940s:

> When I complained, my elders did not hesitate to remind me that only a few years earlier they enjoyed no such luxury; they got to school on foot—often walking five or six miles (Jenkins, 1971).

Mr. Jenkins' bus wandered 14 miles over country roads getting to the school 3 miles from his home. Students at the "other" school further down the road

Mothers protest school busing in this 1970 Miami scene.
Wide World.

still operated as did Mr. Jenkins' elders; "they" still went to school on foot.

Busing has also been used to maintain school segregation. For more than a century white and especially black children have been transported across town past schools to get to the schools assigned to their race. Again there was no national outcry from whites against this kind of busing. The same whites who insisted on busing to maintain segregated schools have altered their point of view when these buses have changed their mission and are used to integrate schools. "Busing" means more than children riding buses to school; it means racial mixing. It is the latter, not the former, that whites protest. In Wilcox County, Alabama, busing has been used to maintain segregated schools. But that is not busing. "We don't call what we've been doing busing. That's just carrying the children to school," comments a state senator. He continues, "If a kid's got to ride a bus 50 miles to get to school, I'm in favor of it. But I'm not in favor of carrying them one mile to achieve integration" (Maxwell, 1971). A white resident of Wilcox County agrees, "As long as we don't have niggers on there, it's not busing; busing is making the white children get on with the niggers" (Maxwell, 1971). Another resident adds that the court order to integrate through busing if necessary "destroyed the public school system in Wilcox County for white children" (Maxwell, 1971). These statements are excellent examples of the common black opinion that they prefer southern to northern racism because the former is more direct and honest about racial feelings. It is important to note that the last resident quoted equates public school with white schools. The result of the busing controversy in Wilcox County, Alabama, has been the continuation of segregated education; Blacks still go to their black schools, Whites attend private academies or stay home.

It is only when their children go to school with black children that white parents become concerned about "quality" education. In this context "quality" education has become another euphemism for segregated education. White parental concerns about health and safety are a ruse. "It seems clear that the feeling against busing is purely racial" (Maxwell, 1971). "When people talk about busing, they're talking about segregation" (Jenkins, 1971).

To a large extent the early attempts to desegregate schools meant the busing of black children to white schools. In the 1960s this pattern was a common practice in most cities (Crain, 1969). Initially there were white backlash reactions located at the schools to which the black children were bused. The author remembers the picketing white mothers who spat on and struck young black children as they entered Edgar A. Guest School in northwest Detroit in the 1950s. It has been common practice that white parents do not strongly oppose busing as long as their children are not bused, and it is the black children who are transferred. Crain found this to be a common aspect of busing in the cities of St. Louis, Newark, Buffalo, San Francisco, Pittsburgh, Baltimore, Fort Lauderdale, and Bay City.

Buses have been a part of American education for a long time. Tax money has been used for pupil transportation in Massachusetts since just 17 years after the inception of its compulsory attendance laws. By 1919 every state authorized public tax money for pupil transportation. Racial integration, of course, has not been the primary reason for busing. Busing has long been an integral part of rural schooling; consolidation of the old one- and two-room schools into larger unified schools has necessitated the use of school buses to get the children to these more distant schools. Buses have also had to serve the expanding suburbs surrounding American cities. In urban areas buses have been used for relief of overcrowding, for "special" needs such as transporting handicapped and "bright" children to special schools, and for transportation to special events and trips. In 1971 43.5 percent—almost 20 million—of the pupils enrolled in public schools in America were bused.

Busing for the purpose of desegregation has been of more recent origin. The National Highway Traffic Safety Administration estimated that as of March 24, 1972, less than 1 percent of the annual increase in busing can be attributed to desegregation. Most estimates put the number of children bused for desegregation purposes from 2 to 4 percent of the total number transported.

In fact, buses have been used more extensively to maintain segregation than to promote integration. In one case, black children are bused over 100 miles to school where they stay for the week, rather than make such a long trip twice daily. Also, the use of private academies not only increased the use of buses but also lengthened the rides, all in an effort to avoid busing.

In many parts of the country desegregation has reduced the amount of busing. For example, in forty-two Georgia districts the number of children bused increased by 14,000 from 1965 to 1969, while at the same time the total number of miles covered by buses decreased by 473,000 miles. Much the same was true in Mississippi during the same period; in twenty-seven districts an increase of 2,500 bused pupils resulted in a decrease of 210,000 miles moved.

The Court's attack on the dual school system set the stage for the busing controversy. These legal rulings did not order busing; in fact, many of the affected districts were already doing that. The elimination of the systems of dual schools could only be achieved by busing. It was not until the 1971 Charlotte-Mecklenberg case that the Supreme Court ruled that busing is a proper means of desegregating the nation's schools. The same court suggested, however, that buses should not be used if the health or the education of the children are endangered.

There are a number of reasons commonly given for opposing busing as a means to integrate schools. The same reason can from one person be a real fear and from another person be a disguised or not-so-disguised statement of racism. One position commonly taken to oppose busing is that one is against "forced" busing. It is important in this regard to note that it is school attendance, not busing, that is compulsory. The bus is one means of getting there. "Forced" is a term reflecting the white perspective of the use of buses to racially integrate schools. Busing is not "forced" when it is used to maintain segregated schools. A corollary to the proposition of "forced" movement is that one has a right to attend a neighborhood school. There is no such right. As we have shown earlier the concept of the neighborhood school is felt to be a right by Whites *only* when such a concept will maintain segregated schools.

Safety is another major concern of those who oppose busing. It is feared that children who are bused are out of reach of their families in case of illness or injury. Two points should be made here. First, safety is taken into account in the planning process, and ways are provided for getting children home in case of illness. In many families both parents work away from home and have managed to compensate for this distance factor. Second, this issue is not raised to such a degree when busing is used to maintain segregation or for other purposes. A similar view is that school buses are not safe. This is simply not true. The National Safety Council regards the school bus as the safest transportation in the United States. Another worry is that fights will occur. No doubt fights will occur in racially tense schools; they also occur in all-black ghetto schools and in all-white suburban schools. In Pontiac, Michigan, student incidents lasted as long as their parents worried about the safety of their children attending black "central area" schools, but it was pointed out by white students that police records showed that white schools were in some cases more dangerous than those about which the white parents were concerned.

It has also been charged that busing increases the time the child is away from play and study. Actually in many cases, as we have shown, the opposite is the case. Longer bus rides to private academies or to all-white public schools to avoid integration have kept white children away from play and study with no argument from white parents. The Center for National Policy Review studied busing in eleven cities, and the length of the average trip increased by as much as 15 minutes in only two of the cities; while in six cities, the length of the average bus ride remained the same after desegregation. Busing need not prevent children from participating in extracurricular activities after school. In Berkeley, California, the use of an activity bus has worked out satisfactorily.

Whites often argue that the black schools should be improved, thus making busing unnecessary. There has been some black agreement on this point, but only if this improvement means black control, which, of course, it does not. In Rochester, New York, for example, there has been black support for both separation and integration of the city schools. The white school board leader has an understanding of the black separatists, "but he is not about to share power with them" (Dworkin, 1968). There are many cities like Rochester in which the black cry for community control is taken by Whites to be identical to their vote against busing. Superficially the two positions may appear to be identical, but there should be no doubt that they are fundamentally different and, in fact, in opposition. Whites oppose busing to maintain their superior position; the black opposition to busing is meant to attack that superior position, believing that community control is a better approach. But black parents are not, or should not be, fooled by proposals, such as that of President Nixon, that more money be spent on black schools, compensatory education, and "culturally deprived" children. It has never worked, for precisely the reason that Whites don't want busing; it would erode the superior position of Whites. The money for the improvement of black schools just never gets there.

A classic case of confusion of black and white attitudes over school integration has been expressed by Senator Robert Byrd of Virginia when he supported the use of buses to maintain school segregation because, "it was the law of the land and generally supported by people—black and white—who were not only satisfied but wanted it that way" (Byrd, 1971). There are a number of questionable assertions in Senator Byrd's statement. First, Blacks have never generally supported segregated schools nor have they been satisfied with the inferior education to which their children have been subject.

Going to school with Whites has often meant an upgrading of black education, not because of anything inherently good in whiteness, but because when black children go to school with white children, the white schools receive one thing that black schools do not—money. As a black parent comments,

> Within one month, the parents of the white children who were bused managed to get the black school painted, repairs made, new electric typewriters and sewing machines, and the shelves filled with books. . . . I contend that busing for one year will upgrade all our schools quicker than anything the President or Congress can do.

In Athens, Georgia, integration meant paved driveways and new paint and blackboards for the formerly all-black schools. Another aspect to this policy of moving only black children to white schools has been brought out by Reverend Albert Cleage, Jr.

> The policy of busing black children to "white schools" . . . expresses the underlying philosophy that quality education cannot be provided in inner city schools because if you mix black with

black you can get only stupidity, whereas if you mix black with white you must get something superior to anything all-black and somewhat inferior to anything all-white (Cleage, 1967).

It is also charged that the education of white children will deteriorate if they are forced to attend classes with black children. There is no study that supports this position. In Berkeley, Louisville, Riverside, Denver, and Evanston, for example, the educational progress of white students either remained the same or improved when they were put into integrated schools.

Finally, the more general charge is made that it is not the job of the schools to cure social ills. Depending on the issue Whites say the same thing about housing, law enforcement, employment, and health care. The result is that there is no section of American society whose job it is to cure social ills. The point is that schools are definitely a force in the creation of these social problems, and insofar as they are involved, they can become a force for social change. It is naïve to suggest that schools have not played a major role in the subjugation of Blacks in America.

The basic issue in the debate over schools is the same as that in housing, access. Busing is a phony issue masking the issue of the right of black people of access to quality education. But people in their daily lives rarely are concerned with such nebulous things as rights per se, but the reflections of these rights or their absence in their daily actions, thus the importance of the big, yellow school bus.

De Facto-De Jure

Because the issue of busing has been aimed at ending segregation in the North as well as in the South it has raised the traditional North-South dichotomy of de facto–de jure segregation. This point has put the southern segregationists in league with northern "liberals" who agree (correctly) in theory that segregated education in the North is as bad as that in the South and there needs to be an attack nationally, not sectionally; but these people are apparently ignorant of the inability and unwillingness on the part of the federal government to attack school segregation nationally. Again a good example of the quicksand upon which racial attitudes of the northern liberal rests: unable to recognize the deceit of the segregationist position, the liberal leaves the black children in the same segregated schools in which they have for so long struggled.

There is another very important point. That is, segregation in the North is not really de facto at all but de jure. Northern segregation has not taken place by accident but by numerous governing procedures, including zoning, site selection, gerrymandering, and by local, state, and federal governments. To raise the issue of differential attacks upon de facto and de jure segregation is but another ruse without centering on the basic issue that whichever method is used it still is racism.

The distinction between de jure school segregation—that imposed by law— and de facto—that which is not the result of state law or purposeful discrimination by school authorities—has been an important one both in and out of the

Malverne, New York in 1963. The "for sale" signs are in protest of a school board plan designed to integrate local schools.
Wide World.

courts. Recently the courts have minimized the difference, making almost all forms of school segregation de jure. It was the Brown case in 1954 on which the argument that only legally based segregation violates the Constitution is based. Although the United States Supreme Court dealt with the explicit issue of de facto segregation for the first time in 1973, the Court failed to make a distinction between de facto and de jure segregation at that time.

Lower courts in the late 1960s have expanded the de jure concept to include many practices that earlier would have been considered de facto. Such practices as gerrymandering of school boundaries, segregated schools based on segregated residential patterns (neighborhood schools), and school site selection have been found by courts to be examples of de jure segregation. A number of courts have seen the distinction between de facto and de jure to be spurious; it is the racial separation that has been considered important.

In recent court decisions in Denver and Washington, D.C., the courts have come close to finding the state responsible for the physical inequality of the schools. Inequalities in school financing generally are to the disadvantage of black children, as less is spent on their education. It should be emphasized here that money is by no means the main determinant of quality education, but it has been a factor in the overall process of unequal education in the country. The race of the children has been a prime factor in the distribution of funds—with black children receiving less—in California, Texas, Minnesota, New Jersey, and Arizona.

White Flight

One of the dominant white reactions to court-ordered school desegregation, especially in northern cities, has been "flight." This takes the form of either residential movement to the suburbs or movement of the children to private schools. The year 1970-1971 saw a rapid increase in the number of private schools and a decline in the number of white children in public schools in desegregation situations. The Southern Regional Council estimated that in 1970-1971, 450,000 to 500,000 students attended private segregated schools in just the eleven southern states. In Alabama, for example, enrollment in these schools doubled from 1964 to 1970. In Arkansas enrollment in segregated academies rose almost six times from 405 in 1969 to 2,348 in 1970. In the 1971-1972 school year the enrollment in the segregated schools in the eleven southern states increased by 35,000. In general there are three types of segregated private schools: established nonsectarian private schools, church-related schools, and academies established to avoid public schools. It was estimated that 50 percent of the drop of 28,000 students in the Georgia public schools in 1970-1971 was a result of "white flight."

In cities such as Gainesville, Tampa, and Pensacola, public schools which lost white students to private schools have been reclaiming them after 1 or 2 years. The reasons are that the private schools are too expensive, they do not receive accreditation, or after watching the change in the public schools, the white parents realize that chaos does not occur. In northern cities such as Evanston and Harrisburg, it was not flight to private schools as much as it has been residential flight to the suburbs that has created a problem. Unlike the situation which arises from parents just moving their children to private schools, when the family moves its residence to flee integration, the schools do not tend to regain white students after a couple of years. In Pontiac those parents who switched their children to private schools are beginning to return them to the public schools, but those families who moved are now sending their children to the white suburban schools. One of the important side effects of the growth of private schools is that Whites, while moving their children to all-white classrooms, still retain control of the black schools.

The federal government has given indirect financial aid in the form of tax-exemption status to these segregated schools. Even though the Internal Revenue Service announced on July 10, 1970, that it would no longer grant tax-exempt status to racially discriminatory private schools, hearings before the Senate Select Committee on Equal Educational Opportunity indicated that the IRS was still subsidizing segregated schools. Except in Mississippi, the IRS grants exemptions based on "good faith" assurances that the schools have open enrollment policies. Mississippi is an exception because of the 1971 *Coit v. Green* suit in which the U.S. Supreme Court upheld the district court ruling that racially discriminatory private schools are not entitled to tax-exempt status. Although the case specifically dealt with Mississippi, the Justices made it clear that their decision was not limited to that state. Despite the fact that the Court laid down its ruling as a broad principle and not a special ruling for

Mississippi, the IRS continued to require racial data as stated by the Green decision from only Mississippi: As a result of the case thirty-three schools lost their tax-exempt status in Mississippi. According to the IRS there were between 14,600 to 16,000 private schools with tax-exempt status in the country in 1972.

As we have indicated throughout the book, it is often very easy to lose sight of the fact that the general social processes discussed in a book of this type happen to real people. The brief description below is not meant to be typical nor is it meant to describe all black children, but only two black children— that is what makes it so important—who find themselves trying to achieve an education in America.

> John and Mary Jane Turner came to Boston from the South. Being the eldest, 15 and 17, of the family's four children, they migrated North with one parent; the other parent followed later with their younger brother and sister. Mr. Turner had a job, earning $62 a week. The children had no winter clothes. Both parents wanted the children to go to school; this was in fact one of their reasons for moving North, where they heard the schools were better.
>
> Mary Jane and John had the equivalent of a second-grade education. Mary Jane was 1 year too old to go to school. There were no classes in the Boston school system for children over 16 who were that far behind. Also, her heavy accent was very hard for school personnel to understand.
>
> John was sent to the School for Immigrants. He wrote at the top of all his papers: 'John Turner, Immigrant.' When he tried to register at his neighborhood school, he was found to be too far behind and was sent home (Task Force, 1970).

SELECTED BIBLIOGRAPHY

1. Anderson, Robert E., Jr.: The Congress, the Courts, and the National Will, in "Lawlessness and Disorder: 14 Years of Failure in Southern School Desegregation," Special Report: Southern Regional Council, 1971.
2. Bardolph, Richard: "The Civil Rights Record: Black America and the Law 1849–1970," New York, Thomas Y. Crowell Company, 1970.
3. Barker, School Report Says Many Southern Cities Are Lagging, *South Today*, vol. 3, June 1972, pp. 1, 3–4.
4. Bennett, Lerone, Jr.: "Confrontation: Black and White," Baltimore, Penguin, 1965.
5. Bowler, Mike: North or South: Who Will Show the Way to School Integration, *South Today*, vol. 2, pp. 5–8, December 1970.

6. Byrd, Robert C.: School Busing and Forced Integration, *Vital Speeches of the Day*, vol. 38, October 15, 1971, pp. 7–10.
7. Clark, Kenneth: Public School Desegregation in the Seventies, *New South*, vol. 27, pp. 21–28, Summer, 1972.
8. Cleage, Albert B., Jr.: Inner City Parents Present Program for Quality Education in Inner City Schools, Paper Presented to Detroit Board of Education, June 13, 1967.
9. Crain, Robert L.: "The Politics of School Desegregation," Garden City, Doubleday, 1969.
10. The Diminishing Barrier: A Report on School Desegregation in Nine Communities, Washington, D.C., U.S. Commission on Civil Rights, 1972.
11. DuBois, W. E. B.: "Black Reconstruction in America," New York, Atheneum, 1969.
12. Duster, Troy: Violence and Civic Responsibility: Combinations of "Fear" and "Right", in Raymond W. Mack, "Our Children's Burden," New York, Vintage, 1968.
13. Dworkin, Rosalind J.: Segregation and Suburbia, in Raymond W. Mack, "Our Children's Burden," New York, Vintage, 1968.
14. Franklin, John Hope and Isadore Starr: "The Negro in Twentieth Century America," New York, Random House, 1967.
15. Hamilton, Alexander: *The Federalist* no. 78 (rev. ed.), New York, The Colonial Press, 1901.
16. Hayes, Edward C.: "Power Structure and Urban Policy: Who Rules in Oakland," New York, McGraw-Hill, 1972.
17. Irwin, Marjorie Felice, "The Negro in Charlottesville and Albermarle County," University of Virginia, Phelps-Stokes Fellowship Papers, no. 9, 1929.
18. Jenkins, Ray: By Way of the Bus, *South Today*, vol. 3, October 1971.
19. Johnson, Charles S.: "Patterns of Negro Segregation," New York, Harper and Brothers, 1934.
20. Katz, William L.: "Eyewitness: The Negro in American History," New York, Pitman Publishing Corp., 1968.
21. Lewis, Hylan: "Blackways of Kent," Chapel Hill, N.C., University of North Carolina Press, 1955.
22. Litwack, Leon F.: "North of Slavery, The Negro in the Free States, 1790–1860," Chicago, University of Chicago Press, 1961.
23. Maniloff, Howard: Busing No Longer Bothers Charlotte, *South Today*, vol. 4, pp. 1–8, January-February 1973.
24. Maxwell, Neil: Busing Perspective, *South Today*, vol. 3, pp. 7–8, October 1971.
25. Meltzer, Milton (ed.): "In Their Own Words, 1619–1865," New York, Thomas T. Crowell, 1964.
26. Nixon, Richard: Education and Busing, "Vital Speeches of the Day," Southold, New York, City News Publishing Company, Inc., 1971.
27. Powdermaker, Hortense: "After Freedom," New York, Atheneum, 1968.

28. Raper, Arthur F.: "Preface to Peasantry," Chapel Hill, University of North Carolina Press, 1936.
29. Rogers, Harrell R., Jr., and Charles S. Bullock: "Law and Social Change," New York, McGraw-Hill, 1972.
30. "The South and Her Children," The Southern Regional Council, Atlanta, 1971.
31. Taper, Bernard: "Gomillion versus Lightfoot," New York, McGraw-Hill, 1962.
32. Task Force on Children out of School: "The Way We Go to School: The Exclusion of Children in Boston," Boston, Beacon Press, 1970.
33. Terjin, Kitty: Close-up on Segregation Academies, *New South*, Southern Regional Council, Atlanta, vol. 27, pp. 50–58, fall 1972.
34. U.S. Commission on Civil Rights: Your Child and Busing, Clearinghouse Pub. no. 36, Washington, D.C.
35. Watters, Pat: That Big Old Yellow Busing Bamboozle, *South Today*, vol. 3, p. 2, April 1972.
36. Weinberg, Meyer: "Race and Place," Washington, D.C., U.S. Government Printing Office, 1967.
37. Wise, Arthur E.: The Constitution and Equal Educational Opportunity, in "The Quality of Inequality: Urban and Suburban Public Schools," Chicago, University of Chicago Center for Policy Study, 1968.
38. Woodson, Carter G.: "The Rural Negro," Washington, D.C., Association for the Study of Negro Life and History, 1930.
39. Zukosky, Jerome: Giving Up on Integration, *The New Republic*, vol. 167, pp. 19–21, October 14, 1972.

E. Landy/Magnum Photos, Inc.

8 Geography as Expressed in the Black Humanities

NOVELS

> "There is no impression of life, no manner of seeing it and feeling it to which the plan of the novelist may not offer a place."

To Henry James's novelists should be added poets and musicians. As human forms of expression, literature and music are evidence and testimony of social and cultural conditions. There is often an intensity of feeling and emotion in the work of a poet, singer, or novelist that escapes the "trained" eye of the social scientist. In fact the latter have been "trained" to exclude this material as nonscientific and subjective, thus not as important as the objective data that he can collect. But as Kenneth Clark has written, "Objectivity that implies detachment or escape from psychological reality decreases understanding and can be used merely to avoid the problem." He adds, "Where human feelings are part of the evidence, they cannot be ignored" (Clark, 1965).

Fiction is not a substitute for nonfiction; they are different modes of acquiring and presenting a point of view which mutually enhance each other if one is to achieve a total impression. By ignoring the evidence provided by the humanities, the social scientist narrows and confines his field of vision.

> Nothing human ought to be alien to the social scientist; if a novel, a play, or a poem is a personal and direct impression of social life . . . [the social scientist] should respond to it with the same openness and willingness to learn that he displays when he interviews a respondent, observes a community or classifies and analyzes survey data (Coser, 1963).

We have said throughout this book that geography is part of a person's as well as of a group's image. Adam David Miller has defined this as aesthetics, "a way of viewing and sensing and the results of what is viewed and sensed" (Miller, 1971). This image and its results are different for Blacks and Whites, with the latter not being able to understand the images of the former. As Lawrence Gellert put it:

>Got one mind for white folks to see
>Nother for what I know is me; . . . (Miller, 1971).

Blacks and Whites, although they have lived in the same political unit, have undergone vastly different life experiences. The process of image formation is central to the self-definition of both the individual and the group. Literature, music, and art become very important in the production of these images because they, rightly or wrongly, are taken to represent windows through which one can view the experiences of others. The poet, artist, musician, and novelist become "the guardian of image" and "the myth-maker of his people" (Gerald, 1971).

For Blacks in the United States, these images have been predominantly controlled by Whites.

>Negroes are the only people in the world who are set apart because of who they are, and at the same time told to forget who they are by the same people who set them apart in the first place (Killens, 1971).

This is based on two somewhat contradictory, yet prevailing, white attitudes. Some Whites know that there has been a drastic difference between their own experiences and those of Blacks, and knowing the reasons for this difference, they are afraid to allow the black view to be expressed. Other Whites, however, simply do not see any difference between their own experiences and the experiences of Blacks. This view suggests that there is a universality in experiences. Killens's response to this view is to suggest that "a story that could have been about nobody is probably precisely nobody at all" (Killens, 1971).

The result of this conflict has been what Fuller has called a "black-white war over the control of image." This is an extremely important conflict, "for to manipulate an image is to control a peoplehood" (Fuller, 1971). As an abstraction this point loses its impact. It is when one remembers that this process occurs to individuals—real people, young and old—that it becomes meaningful. The result of the long domination of the black image by white society has been a "zero image" of the black person. It is essential to re-emphasize the point that this did not just happen, it was made to happen.

MUSIC

If the spatial processes examined in this book have been as important as we allege, one should find evidence of them in the written and oral traditions of black people. These forms of expression, although they seemingly are concerned with a unique set of circumstances, reflect experiences generally familiar to others in the same cultural milieu, which make it easy for them to identify with the situation depicted. "A spiritual may be defined as the utterance of an individual Negro about an experience that had universal application at whatever time that song was popular" (Fisher, 1953). There is perhaps a unique combination of the feelings of the individual and the universality of these feelings among his audience that makes the blues singer, for example, such an important person. On the one hand the blues expresses the personal and immediate experiences of the singer. Jr. Parker adds, "Most of the things we sing about actually have happened to us or to a neighbor, so this is what we go by" (Haralambos, 1970). The same is true for B. B. King. "I've seen many people hurt, homes broken, people killed, people talked about, so today I sing about it" (Haralambos, 1970). Yet these very personal emotions are those intensely felt by a large number of people who live in the same circumstances in which the singer finds himself. Again B. B. King summarizes, "When I sing the blues the whole song may not be about the person, but there are certain things in it they will recognize that have happened to them or some of their friends, and when this happens, then they feel it" (Haralambos, 1970). The implicit importance of the blues lies in their expression of the deep emotions of real men and women, each of whom in their own way could be a blues singer. "Each phase of the Negro's music issued directly from the dictates of his social and psychological environment" (Jones, 1963). Migration, wandering, the importance of place, isolation, and separation are examples of spatial themes found throughout the black experience that are expressed in their music and writing.

There is some debate about whether the early black music in America was just music or was also social comment. Courtlander, for example, does not accept the position that black spirituals were social comment and contained hidden codes and meanings because this would mean that most black songs would be an allusion to freedom. Other scholars, however, disagree.

> Most of the verses of the plantation songs had some references to freedom. True, they had sung those same verses before, but they had been careful to explain that the "freedom" in these songs referred to the next world. Now they gradually threw off the mask, and were not afraid to let it be known that the "freedom" in their songs meant freedom of the body in this world (Katz, 1969).

Songs or spirituals could be used to gather fellow slaves for a secret meeting. Music was used as a means of communication in a society which barred Blacks from participating in all normal flows of communication. Field calls could also hide information from the slaves' masters. Sometimes the call and response among groups of slaves in adjoining fields communicated the escape of a slave. Some verses described the process and hopes of migration to the North. In other spirituals the decision is apparently made to flee to territory in the North. In both cases Heaven and Hell are used metaphorically to mean the North and South, respectively. Frederick Douglass and Harriet Tubman testified that religious songs had social meanings; Canaan, for example, meant Canada and deliverance for the Israelites meant freedom for the slaves. For the early black Christians in America, "freedom" spoken of in the songs could only be achieved through death. It remained for later secular music to speak of freedom here in America.

But, as many Blacks found out, the North was not the "Heaven" that they had hoped for. The following verse from a man who escaped to Ohio from southern slavery describes his dejection in the land of freedom and his further migration plans.

> Ohio's not the place for me:
> For I was much surprised
> So many of her sons to see
> In garments of disguise.
> Her name has gone throughout the world,
> Free labor-Soil-and men
> But slaves had better far be hurled
> Into this lion's den
> Farewell Ohio!
> I cannot stop in thee
> I'll travel on the Canada,
> Where colored men are free (Peskin, 1966).

Or as W. W. Brown put the same sentiments:

> I would think of Victoria's domain,
> And in a moment I seemed to be there!
> But the fear of being taken again
> Soon hurried me back to despair (Gara, 1969).

The North Star was also a common metaphor. As W. W. Brown wrote in his narrative, "We continued to travel by night. Before emerging from our hiding place, we would anxiously look for our friend and leader—the North Star" (Gara, 1969). This was expressed in poetry as follows:

> Star of the North! while blazing day
> Pours round me its full tide of light,
> And hides thy pale but faithful ray,
> I, too, lie hid, and long for night.
> For night; I dare not walk at noon.
> Nor dare I trust the faithless moon
> Nor faithless man, whose burning lust
> For gold hath riveted my chain;
> No other leader can I trust
> But thee, of even the starry train;
> For, all the host around thee burning,
> Like faithless man, keep turning, turning.
> In the dark top of southern pines
> I nestled, when the driver's horn
> Called to the field, in lengthening lines,
> My fellows, at the break of morn.
> And there I lay, till thy sweet face
> Looked in upon my "hiding place,"
> Star of the North!
> Thy light, that no poor slave deceiveth,
> Shall set me free (Gara 1969).

Forced migration along the internal slave trade routes was also evident in song.

> See there poor souls from Africa
> Transported to America;
> We are stolen, and sold to Georgia—
> Will you go along with me?
> We are stolen and sold to Georgia—
> Come sound the jubilee! (Gara, 1969).

Another aspect of the internal slave trade was the splitting up of black families and the forced movement of family members at the whim of white masters. An outcry against this form of separation has been made by Chestnutt in his tale, "Po' Sandy." Like much of black commentary of their condition in America this is a story within the story, one which is not understood by the master white class. In the tale, Sandy is such a good slave that he is wanted by all the master's family. As a result, he is kept moving at the expense of his relationship with Tenie. Tenie, being a conjure woman, and loving her man, decides to turn Sandy into a tree so that he would be in one place. But the master has the tree cut down for a new building and thus destroys the lives of Sandy and Tenie. The implicit cruelty of the slavery system is lost to the white master who sees only a far-fetched and amusing story.

Many of the elements of black music during slavery were carried over and further developed within black life after slavery. The lyrics of the songs which developed with the transformation of the black slave into a serf had the same themes of loneliness, importance of place, wandering, protest, and double meaning which were present in slave music. The texture of the blues is woven with the threads of the insecurity and loneliness of black life, the enforced wandering, a valid protest, and the despair of love.

> The blues does not try to express an attitude toward the separateness of Negro life in America. Protest is only a small thread in the blues. But it is an expression of the separateness of the two racial groups. If the color line was not drawn through the streets and the neighborhoods of American cities the blues would not have been developed (Charters, 1963).

"The blues, as a poetic language, still has the direct relationship to experience that is at the heart of all art" (Charters, 1963). Willie Doss, for example, seemingly used verses in one of his works that could be a survival of a disguised "escape" song from the days of slavery. That should not be surprising as the conditions under which Blacks lived did not change.

Later secular black music clearly had its roots set deeply in the earlier black church traditions. After all, the church was for a long time the only place where Blacks, both slave and free, could carry out any kind of autonomous behavior. Indeed, the church was "the only place the slave had for any kind of vaguely human activity" (Jones, 1963).

> The Negro church, as it was begun, was the only place where the Negro could release emotions that slavery would naturally tend to curtail. The Negro went to church, literally, to be free, and to prepare himself for his freedom in the Promised Land (Jones, 1963).

The period from 1885 to 1930 saw massive change in the South; the proud and rigid kingdom of cotton and slavery crumbled. Cotton and slavery had demanded that the place of the Black be geographically as well as socially fixed. It was a cruel irony that the emancipation of Blacks denied them a place in American society. As bad as it was, it was only as a slave that the Black had a "place" both social and geographic in American society. The social chaos following the emancipation reflected an attempt by white society to redefine the Black's "place" in society. The short-lived freedom of movement that resulted from the disruption of the plantation system was, for many Blacks, not really freedom at all. Now the freed slave could leave the old plantation if he wished, but where would he go and how would he get there? Straying Blacks were already drifting about in thousands. The fall of the plantation and its enforced stability left thousands of Blacks "free" to traipse the countryside, going from mines to sawmills, from railroad crews to turpentine camps, from town to city, from work farm to jail. No matter where or how far the Black wandered he always ended up in the same place.

As one elderly black person put it:

> When Marse he gi' me freedom
> F'om de plantation—f'om slabery
> When Marse he gi' me freedom
> Ah wants to go free
> But ah ain' got no ready-made money
> So ah cain' go free—Lawd ah cain' go free

> Nigger got no place to go where
> Nigger got no shoes to go wit' dere
> Nigger got no corn to eat when he git dere
> Poor Nigger he stay
> Ain' it a shame, shame, shame.
> Nigger slabe fo' forty year—ain' got penny to his
> name (Gilbert, 1969).

In the 1870s there were thousands of black migrant workers moving all through the South. There were also men who just moved around from place to place, not really migratory laborers, just footloose wanderers. The geographic experiences of these individuals were widened, in most cases. The lyrics of their music reflected the fact that this new mobility did not mean a change in social relations with whites.

> Went to Atlanta
> Neber been dere afo'
> White folks eat de apple
> Nigger wait fo' core

> Went to Charleston
> Neber been dere afo'
> White folks sleep on feather bed
> Nigger on de flo'

Went to Raleigh
Neber been dere afo'
White folks were de fancy suit
Nigger de over-o

Went to Heben
Neber been dere afo'
White folks sit in Lawd's place
Chase Nigger down below (Gilbert, 1969).

When asked about the best town for Blacks in the South, a typical reply would be, "Dey ain' none of 'em." Their homeless, roaming, footloose, and lonesome moods became a major theme of the blues.

The hope for an improvement in social position by altering geographic place was expressed after, as well as during, slavery. The early blues singers were drifters, living on society's lowest level—the same level as their audience. The blues are not, nor do they describe, the lives of the settled middle class. The blues singers drifted from small town to small town, from work gang to work gang, ". . . in the poverty and discrimination of the South were strong forces moving them on, forcing them from one poorly paid job to another, forcing them to leave towns where they'd said the wrong thing or gotten into trouble with a boss or a storekeeper. Along the dirt roads and the railroad tracks men moved from the levee camps to the road gangs, from the mills of towns like Birmingham to the docks of ports like Mobile or Savannah" (Charters, 1963).

The mysterious, laughing, antiwhite, travelin' man is a persistent theme in black folklore. Joe Turner who "done been here and gone"; Blue Jim who jeers, "white folks, so long, I'm going up town"; Railroad Bill who shot a sheriff; Long John who whites cannot capture; and the Travelin' Man who,

> They sent down South where his mother had gone . . .
> They opened up the coffin for to see her son.
> And the fool had disappeared!
> He was a travelin' man, he certainly was a travelin' man (Allsop, 1970).

Horace Sprott was also a travelin' man.

> He had been born, no one knew exactly when, to a couple who had been slaves on the Sprott plantation. His mother's name was Bessie Ford, and his father's name was Jim. The only surname his parents had ever claimed for him was that of their owner. He knows very little of his father, except that Jim and one uncle used to get out in the road together and holler songs—songs that were not church songs. When Horace was still a child, Jim left. Forty-two years later, the son heard that his father had died somewhere in Hale County.
>
> At eleven, Horace had run away from home—from his own name, Sprott. The old name still marks a point at an Alabama crossroads

where a general store and post office are operated beneath a sign bearing the master's name. This is all that remains of an establishment that once ruled thousands of acres of Cahaba bottom land and forested hills.

At fourteen, Horace Sprott was working at Heiberger community, for a man named Barwell. And at eighteen, he was sent up to a county farm—Camp 4, at Montgomery. His left wrist was branded and he was committed to hard labor. The sentence was for two years, and it must have been a conviction for assault with intent to kill. He had shot at a girl, but missed. At the end of six months, his sentence was reduced at her request. They were married when he got out, and they stayed married for eight years. Then, because he didn't want to kill her, he left her.

So Sprott became a fugitive, not from prison or sharecropping or the law, but from his own Negro community and its inflexible standards, imposed from above by white owners, of work and subservience and worship.

He took to the road, became a drifter. There he met other drifters who like himself had gotten into trouble and "cut out and banished away." He worked in barrel-stave mills, snuff factories, packing plants, on the docks at Mobile Bay, in the cane fields of Louisiana, in Mississippi pecan groves.

He had begun life with an ear for song. Although he had never been taught to read or write, Horace Sprott had developed the trick of hearing a song through only once and having it right forever after. In this way, he added to the old songs of his slave-family background the songs he heard along the road: blues, reels, songs of bad men and drifters, cotton-picking songs, cotton-chopping songs, good-time songs, bad-time songs, hammer songs, mule skinners' songs, songs going down the road, songs sitting still at home.

Then Horace Sprott returned to the sharecropping community where he had been born. There was no one to welcome him there, but somehow he managed to establish himself as part-time field hand and odd-job man. He married a girl named Annie, a distant Ford cousin who was the daughter of an aging country circuit preacher.

In the more than twenty years that followed, Annie bore Horace two sons—Herbert and Arthur Lee. And for a while an older boy, James Louis King, adopted the Sprotts and lived with them because Horace treated him better than his own father did.

Throughout all his career of wandering and work, Horace Sprott has never stopped making music (Ramsey, 1960).

The problem of vagrancy that had hampered blacks before, during, and after the Civil War remained in the twentieth century. The wandering blues singers had no means of support according to the local law officials, and no place of residence, and were thus subject to be put in jail and forced onto a work gang.

Blues singers that were wanderers included Charley Patton, Son House, Skip James, Robert Johnson, Booker T. Washington "Bukka" White, Willie Brown, Ed Bell, and Blind Lemon Jefferson. As Son House put it, "I was just ramblified, you know. Especially after I started playing music" (Charters, 1967).

Some of their songs describing this process include "Hellbound on My Trail," by Robert Johnson and "Frisco Whistle Blues," by Ed Bell.

Sheriffs, jails, prison farms, and work gangs are a common element in the blues just as they were in the lives of the singers. Charlie Patton sings of the Belzoni, Mississippi, jail:

> When the trail is in Belzoni, ain't no use a
> feeling proud,
> When the trial is in Belzoni, ain't no use a
> feeling proud,
> Mr. Ware will take you by the Belzoni
> jailhouse for life (Charters, 1967).

Willie Newburn, from Shelby County, Tennessee, sang a similar narrative.

> Well, I left Margrit, on the way back to
> Memphis, Tennessee.
> Well, I left Margrit, on the way back to
> Memphis, Tennessee.
> No sooner I got at the bus station, Lord,
> the police he arrest poor me (Charters, 1967).

Robert Johnson in his "Crossroads Blues" desperately cries out for someone to save him, for he knows that "he is in a Mississippi county that jails any Negro found on the roads after dark" (Charters, 1967). Local sheriffs would not hesitate to pick up any unfamiliar Black to work on the roads or on various city projects. In effect the most serious crime for a Black to commit was "to be without a white man willing to talk to the sheriff and the judge" (Charters, 1967). In "Jailhouse Blues" Sleepy John Estes laments:

> You know I could not get a white man in Brownsville, yes, to even
> go my bond (Charters, 1967).

Movement, whether aimless wandering or directed migration, whether by foot, train, or car, was a significant part of the lives of southern Blacks and thus became an important element in the blues.

As during the pre–Civil War days, Blacks felt that they could escape the torment of the South by moving to a northern city. But they found the North to be like the South. Jazz Gillum sang:

> I would stay up North, but nothing here that
> I can do,
> I would stay up North, but nothing here that
> I can do,
> Just stand around the corner and sing my
> lonesome blues (Charters, 1967).

The impetus for much of the movement of black men throughout and out of the South is described in the following verse:

> When a woman takes the blues
> She tucks her head and cries.
> But when a man catches the blues,
> He catches a freight and rides (Charters, 1967).

As with railroads, it is the north-south highways that figure prominently in blues poetry. A survey of blues indicates that it is the odd-numbered highways that are sung about. The odd-numbered highways run north-south while the even-numbered roads run east-west in the United States. Highways 49 and 51 are the best-known ribbons of concrete to southern Blacks. "Highway 49" by Big Joe Williams, "Highway 51" by Tommy McClennan, and "Down the Highway" by Charlie Pickett are blues songs about roads in Mississippi. As Percy Thomas put it: "We played at the juke at Rome down there on the 49 highway" (Allsop, 1970).

The train is perhaps the most persistent image of movement in the blues, for more than any other form of travel the train was used to escape the South or a bad situation whatever it might be. Such was the lament of Charlie McCoy in "That Lonesome Train Took My Baby Away," and of Noah Lewis in "Ticket Agent Blues."

Railroads, both in general and in particular, are on the one hand rebuked for taking one's loved one away, and on the other hand extolled for providing a means of escape. The Cincinnati, Indianapolis, St. Louis, and Chicago takes Leroy Carr's girl from him. Washboard Sam lost his woman to the Flying Crow or the Kansas City, Southern Louisiana, and Arkansas. The Panama Limited, the Sunshine Special, the Shorty George are other trains that steal women from disconsolate black men. The Green Diamond and the Yellow Dog, however, are praised because they offer a way out of the South and its misery. The Illinois Central provided the escape line running from New Orleans to Chicago.

> I got the I.C. Blues and box cars on my mind,
> I got the I.C. Blues and box cars on my mind,
> I'm gonna pack my grip and beat it on down the line.

The Greyhound bus, although not as common as the train, was another means of leaving and as such was included in the blues. As Robert Johnson puts it:

> You can bury my body, down by the highway side.
> Lord, my old evil spirit can catch a Greyhound bus and ride (Charters, 1963).

And Tommy McClennan adds the image of

> Here comes that Greyhound with his tongue
> hangin out on the side (Charters, 1963).

The junctions and termini of the routes of travel of the black migrants and wanderers became subjects of blues: the East St. Louis blues, the Chicago blues, the Dallas blues, the Memphis blues, the Fort Worth blues.

> Used to have a woman that lived up on a hill
> She was crazy 'bout me 'cause I worked at the Chicago mill
> Goin' go Detroit, get myself a real good job
> Tired stayin' round here with the starvation mob (Allsop, 1967).

Of course not everyone could hop a freight or scrape the fare together to ride a bus. For these people trudging the highways was the method of travel. Petie Wheastraw's "Road Tramp Blues" expresses this down, but not out, way of life.

> I have walked a lonesome road till my feet is too sore to walk
> I beg scraps from the people, oh, well, till my tongue is too stiff to talk
> Anybody can tell you people that I ain't no lazy man
> But I guess I'll have to go to the poorhouse and do the best I can
> (Allsop, 1967).

Buster Bennett's "Broken Down Man" relates a similar experience.

> Now I'm roamin' the highways and pickin' up cigarette
> butts and everything I can find
> . . . sure got evil on my mind
> Now I'm eatin' wild berries and I'm sleepin' on the ground
> I'm broken down and disgusted, and I'm tired of
> Trampin' around (Allsop, 1967).

The ultimate destinations for the black migrants and wanderers were north of the Mason-Dixon line. As was the case during slavery, the North meant freedom, at least before the hopeful arrived.

POETRY

Poems such as "Northboun' " by Lucy Ariel Williams and "Bound No'th Blues" by Langston Hughes also express the desire on the part of Blacks to leave the South for the North.

A poem entitled "The Land of Hope" was printed in the Chicago *Defender* and was a rather straightforward poem written as an incentive for Blacks to leave the South in favor of any northern city. It was truly a part of the great exodus because it so aptly expressed the feelings of the Negro. From the Black's point of view the poem essentially says: I've watched other Blacks leave for the northern states and yet I'm still working this same piece of ground. I've worked this piece for years and am no better off financially than when I started. Why shouldn't I also leave this land of hate where the Whites rule supreme and go North where I can surely find happiness.

After the great exodus of Negroes from the South, many of them did not find

Probably the most widely translated of contemporary black American poets, James Mercer Langston Hughes (1902–1967) also received critical acclaim for his novels, short stories, juvenile fiction, and songs. His literary ability was recognized by critics when he was still in his early twenties. Called by many the "poet laureate of Harlem," he termed it the "great dark city," and his works expressed the hopelessness Blacks felt. Hughes was probably the greatest American black lyric poet.

Henri Cartier-Bresson/Magnum Photos, Inc.

immediate happiness as they had hoped. A few contemplated a return to the South. But poems such as "When I Return to the Southland It Will Be" appeared in the Chicago *Defender* and showed the feelings of a majority of Blacks. Essentially, its author said that no matter what happens the only way he would return to the South was in a casket.

One such poem, "Bound For the Promised Land," was published in the Chicago *Defender*. It was read by some young men in Savannah, Georgia, and as a result they were jailed for inciting to riot.

The 1950s and 1960s saw a new destination for black migration, the West Coast. But the problems of the South existed in the West as well as in the North. As expressed in the popular "Dock of the Bay," migration to the urban West from the rural South ends in no job, no love, and a place to sit on the dock. The place changed from Chicago to San Francisco, yet it remained the same, on the bottom, for the black migrant.

The urban North provided new contexts in which the black person had to fight racism. The tenements, the steel mills, the factories, the docks, all these new elements of the black experience made their way into their songs and stories. In the South there is not much need for signs designating White and "Colored" in the small town, since the townspeople know every street and every store front and every foot of pavement, and their own place on it. "If someone stops in town he's expected to look around and find where the color line has been drawn" (Charters, 1963).

OLD JIM CROW

Wherever we live, it's right to forgive,
It's wrong to hold malice, we know,
But there's one thing that's true, from all
All Negroes hate old man Jim Crow.

His home is in hell; he loves here to dwell;
We meet him wherever we go;
In all public places, where live both the races,
You'll always see Mr. Jim Crow.

Be we well educated, even to genius related,
We may have a big pile of dough,
That cuts not a figger, you still are a nigger,
And that is the law with Jim Crow.

But in the North these lines had to be found. Langston Hughes, in his poem "Merry-Go-Round," pictures the confusion of this move on a newly arrived southern child. Accustomed to backseat "Jim Crow" rules on buses and trains back home, she says,

"But there ain't no back
To a merry-go-round
Where's the horse
For a kid that's black?"

Another of Hughes's poems emphasizes this problem as it is experienced by black children.

A little Southern colored child
Comes to a Northern school
And is afraid to play
With the white children

At first they are nice to him,
But finally they taunt him
And call him "nigger."

That colored children
Hate him, too,
After awhile.

He is a little dark boy
With a round black face
And a white embroidered collar.

Concerning this
Little frightened child
One might make a story
Charting tomorrow.

This child bore the mark of the South which the older inhabitants were trying to forget. This child would hear such names as "country boy" and "cornbread." But the North had its racism too. Syl Johnson's "Concrete Reservation" describes the urban tenement living of the Blacks as a type of containment similar to that of the native American. Hughes' "Restrictive Covenants" is the northern counterpart to "Old Jim Crow."

RESTRICTIVE COVENANTS

When I move
Into a neighborhood
Folks fly
Even every foreigner
That can move, moves.
Why?
The moon doesn't run
Neither does the sun
In Chicago they've got covenants
Restricting me—
Hemmed in
On the south side,
Can't breathe free.
But the wind blows there.
I reckon the wind
Must care.

In the northern city, the street corner became the gathering place just as the "juke" had been for the earlier generation of unwanted black males. The earlier black musicians wandered the rural back roads of the South. The more modern black musicians ramble around the urban back streets of the North.

The song "Under the Street Lamp" by Smith Conwell depicts the scene of the "street brothers" in every city of this country, the black males who have nothing to do. They really don't have anything to be happy about except their interpersonal relationships with one another. They all have dreams for themselves, but they also realize that, in order to fulfill their dreams, they are going to have to get out of the ghetto. And to conclude it all, they do not feel bad at all about being in the ghetto, for most black people who have made it big in life started right where they are.

For the black man who was lucky enough to find a job in the steel mills of the North, life was hard and bitter. It has been the factors pointed out in Carole Gregory's poem that drove many men to the street corner groups described above.

GHETTO LOVESONG—MIGRATION

She stood hanging wash before sun
and occasionally watched the kids
gather acorns from the trees,
and when her husband came,
complaining about the tobacco spit on him,
they decided to run North
for a free evening.
She stood hanging wash in the basement
and saw the kids sneak puffs from cigarettes,
fix steel traps with cheese
and when her husband came,
complaining of the mill's drudgery,
she burst—
said he had no hunter's heart
beat him with a broom,
became blinded by the orange sun
racing into steel mill flames
and afterwards,
sat singing
spirituals to sons (Major, 1969).

Though there is some debate about whether early black music and writing expressed revolt against the system in which they were locked, there can be no doubt that more recent black poetry, literature, and music have expressed the black feelings about racial oppression. Black revolt against racism in Chicago, East St. Louis, and Detroit has been the subject of the songs, "East Chicago Blues" by Pinetop and Lindberg and "The Motor City is Burnin' Down" by John Lee Hooker. Marvin E. Jackman's poem "Burn Baby Burn" not only shows the black protest but goes further than the two songs and expresses unqualified support for the burning.

The same sentiments are expressed by Elaine Brown in "A Black Panther Song."

> Have you ever stood
> In the darkness of the night
> screaming silently you're a man
> have you ever hoped
> That a time would come
> When your voice would be heard
> In the noonday sun?
> Have you waited so long
> Till your unheard song
> Has stripped away your very soul
> well then believe it my friends
> that the silence will end
> We'll just have to get guns and be men (Foner, 1970).

In the traditional Br'er Rabbit tales the black rabbit overcomes the superior strength of the white bear and fox through the use of guile and his slyness. But these methods are not seen as appropriate to the Blacks of the modern urban North. Thus, when the Br'er Rabbit tale comes from the urban North his methods are different. He uses power and the threat of violence to get his due as is seen in the following tale.

> Brother Fox had been trying to get Brother Rabbit for a long time. So he told Brother Bear one day, he said, "Brother Bear, now I know how we can trick that old rabbit into giving himself up." Brother Bear said, "How will we do it?" He said, "Now we'll invite all the animals in the forest to a party, all except Brother Rabbit. He'll be so embarrassed and hurt that he won't want to live and he'll give himself up. And we'll have rabbit stew before the week is up."
> So all the invitations were sent around. So that Saturday evening, you know, all the animals were going down to the party. Even the skunk washed up and put the perfume on, went into the party. Brother Rabbit was sitting on the post and all. Said, "Where you all going?" "Down to Brother Buzzard's house." "Brother Buzzard?" "Yeah. Brother Fox is giving a party over there." Rabbit ran to the house and got dressed, and ran down to the house. Brother Buzzard said, "Sorry, Brother Fox and Brother Bear say they don't want you in it. I'm sorry, that's what they told me."
> So that Rabbit turned away with his head turned down. He was feeling sad, downhearted, tears in his eyes. Felt like he was alone in the world. But then he got mad. He said, "I know what I'll do." He went home and shined his shoes, and got his shotgun and went back and kicked the door open. "Don't a motherfucker move." He walked over the table, got all he wanted to eat. Walked over to the bar and got himself all he wanted to drink. He reached over and

An illustration from a contemporary work of Joel Chandler Harris (1848–1908), an American author and journalist. Harris's popular stereotyped folk character, Uncle Remus, was a wise and kindly Black who regaled children with his stories about animals who behaved like humans, of whom Brer Wolf was one.

From: Uncle Remus: His Songs and His Sayings. *Illustration by A. B. Frost, 1880.*

he grabbed the Lion's wife and he danced with her. Grabbed the Ape's wife and did it to her. Then he shit in the middle of the floor and he walked out.

So after he left, you know, the Giraffe jumped up. He said, "Who was that little long-eared, fuzzy-tailed motherfucker just walked in here with all that loud noise?" The Bear looked at him and said, "Now look, no use getting loud. You was here when he was here, why didn't you ask then?" (Like guys, they like that. You always get bad after the other person is gone, but you never say nothing while they is there) (Abrahams, 1970).

SELECTED BIBLIOGRAPHY

1. Abrahams, Roger D.: "Deep Down in the Jungle," Chicago, Aldine Publishing Co., 1970.
2. Allsop, Kenneth: "Hard Travellin': The Hobo and His History," New York, New American Library, 1970.
3. Charters, Samuel B.: "The Poetry of the Blues," New York, Oak Publications, 1963.
4. ————: "The Bluesmen," Oak Publications, New York, 1967.
5. Chestnutt, Charles W.: "The Conjure Woman," Ann Arbor, Michigan, Ann Arbor Paperbacks, 1969.
6. Clark, Kenneth: "Dark Ghetto," New York, Harper and Row, 1965.
7. Coser, Lewis A. (ed.): "Sociology Through Literature," Englewood Cliffs, N.J., Prentice-Hall, 1963.
8. Courtlander, Harold: "Negro Folk Music, U.S.A.," New York, Columbia University Press, 1963.
9. Dorson, Richard M.: "Negro Folktales in Michigan," Harvard University Press, Cambridge, Mass., 1963.
10. Emanuel, James A.: "Dark Symphony: Negro Literature in America," New York, The Free Press, 1967.
11. Fisher, Miles Mark: "Negro Slave Songs in the United States," Ithaca, N.Y.: Cornell University Press, 1953.
12. Foner, Philip S. (ed.): "The Black Panthers Speak," Lippincott, Philadelphia, 1970.
13. Fuller, Hoyt W.: The New Black Literature: Protest in Affirmation, in Gayle Addison (ed.), "The Black Aesthetic," Doubleday, Garden City, New York, 1971.
14. Gara, Larry (ed.): "The Narrative of William W. Brown, a Fugitive Slave," Reading, Mass., Addison-Wesley, 1969.
15. Gerald, Carolyn F.: The Black Writer and His Role, in Gayle Addison (ed.), "The Black Aesthetic," Garden City, Doubleday, 1971.
16. Gilbert, Lawrence: Negro Songs of Protest, in Nancy Cunard (ed.), "Negro Anthology," Westport, Conn., Greenwood Press, 1969.

17. Haralambos, Michael: Soul Music and Blues: Their Meaning and Relevance in Northern United States Black Ghettos, in Norman E. Whitter, Jr., and John F. Szweed (eds.), "Afro-American Anthropology," New York, The Free Press, 1970.

18. Johnson, James Weldon: "The Book of American Negro Poetry," New York, Harcourt, Brace & Co., 1922.

19. Jones, LeRoi: "Blues People," New York, William Morrow and Company, 1963.

20. Katz, Bernard (ed.): "The Social Implications of Early Negro Music in the United States," New York, Arno Press, 1969.

21. Killens, John Oliver: The Black Writer Vis-à-Vis His Country, in Gayle Addison (ed.), "The Black Aesthetic," Doubleday, Garden City, 1971.

22. Major, Clarence: "The New Black Poetry," New York, International Publishing, 1969.

23. Miller, Adam David: Some Observations on a Black Aesthetic, in Gayle Addison (ed.), "The Black Aesthetic," Garden City, New York, Doubleday, 1971.

24. Oliver, Paul: "Blues Fell This Morning: The Meaning of the Blues," New York, Horizon Press, 1960.

25. Peskin, Allan (ed.): "North into Freedom: The Autobiography of John Malvin, Free Negro, 1879–1889," Cleveland, The Press of Case Western Reserve University, 1966.

26. Ramsey, Fredric: "Been Here and Gone," New Brunswick, N.J., Rutgers University, 1969.

27. Scott, Emmett: "Negro Migration during the War," New York, Arno Press, 1969.

Art Shay/Time-Life Picture Agency

9 Black America: Colony or Soulsville?

SOCIOECONOMIC PATTERNS, 1960–1970

Out-migration from the South to the North and West continued during the decade from 1960 to 1970 in about the same numbers as in the previous decade. This was approximately 1.5 million for each 10-year period. But the South still had over 50 percent of the nation's black people. One trend that began prior to 1960 and has continued is that of interurban migration, which is, in a historical-spatial sense, the next stage in the migration hierarchy from rural South, to urban South, to urban North, to urban West.

Black migrants have, of course, moved to the central cities. This has been and continues to be true. Interurban movement of Blacks is from ghetto to ghetto. In 1960, 68 percent of the black population lived in central cities; this increased to 74 percent in 1970. This compares with 32 and 28 percent respectively for Whites. Although the rate of increase of urban population is greater in the South, the proportions of Blacks living in central cities are higher in the North and West than in the South. Blacks tend to move to the larger urban centers. Their percentage in the suburbs (5 percent) remained the same.

It is significant that the economic status of rural, black migrants is no better than that of the native, urban black population. This would seem to substantiate the long-held black view that it does not matter how long Blacks live in American cities; time does not help them climb the economic ladder as it did European immigrants. Table 9.1 indicates that migrants are often slightly better off than native urban Blacks.

Despite the fact that the median income of Blacks has increased, the dollar gap between Blacks and Whites has continued to increase. The percentage gains for Blacks is a result of a lower base figure than for Whites. While the net change in median income from 1947 to 1969 for Blacks was 44.1 percent greater than for Whites, Blacks still remained almost $1,000 behind in dollars, $3,531 to $4,600. In 1960 the dollar gap was $3,251, and in 1969 it had risen to $3,403. Also, the black family with three earners does not make significantly more than the white family with only one earner. The number of Blacks below the poverty level decreased from 1966 to 1969, but increased from 1969 to 1970. Throughout the decade the number of Blacks below the poverty

209

Subject	Rural to urban migrants*	Urban population of urban origin
Population†	2,056	7,040
Median family income, 1966, % population	5,116	5,105
below low-income level, % families	26.6	26.9
receiving public assistance, 1966	17.3	15.6

Table 9.1   Some Poverty Characteristics of Adult Black Population by Migration Status, February, 1967.

° Persons who have lived 50 or more miles from their 1967 address.
† Seventeen years or older, in thousands.
Source: The Social and Economic Status of Negroes in the United States, 1970, p. 21.

line has been over three times the number of Whites. Blacks have made up over 30 percent of the total number of people in poverty, even though they are only 11 percent of the total population.

' In terms of improving one's income, education has not proved to be the benefit to Blacks that it has to Whites. In 1963, for example, the white high school dropout earned $80 more than the nonwhite with more than 1 year of college. Throughout the decade the black unemployment rate was about double that of Whites. The Department of Labor commented in 1966 that the underutilization of black labor was especially severe.

Whether the statistics are for income, employment, health, or education, two points stand out for the period from 1960 to 1970. First, there has been some improvement in the socioeconomic positions of some Blacks; but any large percentage gains are a result of extremely low base figures, not substantial gains. Second, relative to that of Whites the black socioeconomic position has either remained stable or declined. There has been little or no elimination in the inequality in:

1. Median family income
2. Occupational structure
3. Unemployment rates
4. Representation in the system of justice
5. School integration
6. Residential integration

The early 1970s have been called the end of the Second Reconstruction of the 1960s. The first Reconstruction ended in 1877 following a period of relative gain from 1865 to 1876. In both periods the white supporters of black equality tired of the struggle, while white society at large desired to return to a period of quiet stability.

The result has been to "keep the Blacks in their place." Many of the unresolved tensions are, in part, geographic in nature; the transportation link-up between inner-city black neighborhoods and suburban jobs, housing segregation, school busing, health delivery systems. The basic issue has been and continues to be access.

POWER RELATIONSHIPS

In essence the question here is what means are Blacks to use and to which ends are they to aspire. Blacks have been denied access to virtually all forms of power in the United States. White power in America has been confused with virtue and a sign of God's favor. Whether seen as a broad social, economic, and political framework or as the more personalized struggle for identity, the historical geography of America has been one of a struggle between white power and black powerlessness. In the preceding chapters we have seen that power can take many forms and is exercised by many subgroups within a population. Power can be political, social, or economic; it has been exercised by white terrorist groups, white legal systems, white government, as well as white individuals.

Theoretically, a minority group within a country under democratic rule, even if based on the democracy of groups rather than of individuals, has two moral reasons for accepting the rule of the majority. First, it is part of the community and as such acknowledges the unity of the state; and second, it too participates in the running of the state. Morally then Blacks have no reason to accept the rule of the majority, because they have been forced to remain outside of the community, while being forcibly excluded from participating in the affairs of the country.

This relationship is something like the parable of the white and black men crossing the river:

> The white man comes to the wide and roaring river; he jumps on the native's back and shouts to him "swim" and he beats him on through the swirling rapids; the black man finally reaches the opposite bank and reaches up for recompense; but the white man is indignant. "Without me," he says, "you would never have crossed the river" (Caute, 1970).

Kenneth Clark has suggested that the use of ultimate power, that is, force and violence, is no longer appropriate for either the oppressor or the oppressed. This does not seem to acknowledge that there exist different kinds of violence and force. The oppressor, by virtue of his control over the institutions of society, can bring about deaths as a result of the "normal" functioning of the system. The institutionalization of the use of force is often a monopoly of the oppressor and is legitimized and not necessarily exercised openly. In this way the deaths of Blacks through high infant or maternal mortality rates are not defined as violence but as the inevitable faults in the running of a social order. The oppressed, however, do not have the ability to hide their violence in social, economic, and political institutions. Their attacks are overt, and, as such, are seen as unprovoked. Others do not agree with Clark about the use of violence. As colonialism itself is a violent form of human control, only counterviolence operating in the very spheres in which one is oppressed can eradicate it.

Clark has pointed out that there are three levels or stages of power; the first is "pseudopower" or verbal expression; the second is social action, which may or may not lead anywhere; and the third is social change, in which power

The 1963 march on Washington: "a ceremony of democracy in action."
Cecil Layne/NAACP.

is used to bring about meaningful change. Blacks have seen much of the first two stages, but very little of the last stage. Examples of pseudopower have included the innumerable speeches and civil rights acts and laws. Nixon's comment to Agriculture Secretary Hardin with respect to food programs is a classic instance of verbal power. "Use all the rhetoric, so long as it doesn't cost any money" (Kotz, 1971). Social action has, by and large, been a catharsis, that is, a means of letting off steam without affecting change. There is freedom in protest as long as it does not lead anywhere. The 1963 March on Washington and the Poor People's Campaign are good examples of the feeling that the ceremonies of democracy in action are equivalent to progress itself. It is note-worthy that the 1963 March was followed by both pseudopower and real power. The federal government responded with the Civil Rights Act of 1964, and some southern whites responded with bombs and shotguns. Only one of these forms of white power has directly affected the lives of black people. It is the last stage, a demonstrated change in the levels of control over one's life chances, that is significant and therefore more difficult for Blacks to achieve.

Cruse has pointed out that the American ideal of the rights of the individual above all else is a myth. America is dominated by the power of groups. The individual draws his rights from the groups to which he gives his allegiance. For black people, the result has been that their group has had no power, and they have been forced to remain outside of those groups which have power.

Many authors including Kenneth Clark, Stokely Carmichael, Harold Cruse, and Robert Allen have called the relationship we have been describing as colonialism. This is perhaps most dramatically called to mind by the Black Panther phrase "Black Colony and White Mother Country." The colonial relationship has been succinctly and forcefully set forth by Kenneth Clark.

> The dark ghettos are social, political, educational, and—above all —economic colonies. Their inhabitants are subject peoples, victims of the greed, cruelty, insensitivity, guilt, and fear of their masters (Clark, 1965).

Whether in the form of the rural plantation or the urban ghetto, the colonial status of Blacks functions as an integral part of the American institutional framework. To describe the black existence in America as colonial raises the issue of whether or not there has been a conspiracy among the white portion of society to bring about such a situation. That is, has white society deliberately confined and subjugated Blacks and preserved poverty among them. At certain times in American history, there has been definite and deliberate confinement of Blacks by segments of white society. Slavery is an obvious example. Other examples include the tenant-sharecropper form of agriculture that followed the 1860s and residential and school segregation fostered by individuals, private business, and governments.

It is important to recognize, however, that in a complex social structure that has developed with racism as part of its logic of existence, acts by individuals or institutions need not be deliberate to be racist. There does not need to be a conspiracy for racism to occur; it has become an integral part of the fabric of the ongoing social structure. "Every single white American does not need to oppress Black people—it is their indifference coupled with the deliberate racism of the power structure that carries out colonialism" (Carmichael and Hamilton, 1967). "It must be emphasized that our [Black] colonial status, in both its rural plantation and urban ghetto form, does not function separate and apart from the general contours of American life" (O'Dell, 1967).

White Americans generally fail to understand the nature of this charge of colonialism. They, or rather a certain segment of them, express support for various liberal programs such as improved textbooks and integrated housing. But what they fail to understand, and Blacks understand well, is that these are expressions of peripheral beliefs that so often prove inconsequential when it comes to black socioeconomic progress. It is the deep-seated central belief system that determines actual behavior, and for Americans this has been essentially racist. The central part of one's belief-disbelief system is unstated and is formed early in life, and its validity which is not questioned. From these primitive, or basic, beliefs intermediate and peripheral beliefs emerge. These are more easily changed but have less effect on the person's behavior patterns than do alterations in his central beliefs.

The essence of the colonial relationship is the establishment and maintenance of the subordination of one group of people, for an extended period of time, by another group with effective power kept within the control of the dominant group. American colonialism is domestic; it takes place in the homeland

and not in some far-off land. The spatial dimension of colonialism in America is one that seems to be at odds with colonialism in other parts of the world. In the traditional cases the geographic dimension in the colonial relationship has been one of the separation of the colony from the mother country by great distance. Historically the colony has usually meant the establishment of small enclaves of people sent off from the mother country to settle, to explore, or to extract riches. In many of these instances the detached settlement grew to a point that it engulfed, controlled, and destroyed indigenous cultures for the benefit of the home country. This spatial separation between colony and mother country is what distinguished the colonialism of Europe from the fifteenth to the nineteenth centuries from that of the Americans in the United States. "The only factor which differentiates the Negro's status from that of a pure colonial status is that his position is maintained in the 'home' country in close proximity to the dominant racial group" (Allen, 1970). Carmichael agrees. In describing the third world, he said that the difference between Blacks and other third-world peoples was that "Our people are a colony within the U.S.; you are colonies outside the U.S." (Allen, 1970). The important point is that spatial proximity has not been sufficient to produce a single society in America. Indeed, it is the proximity that has heightened the importance of the spatial dimension of colonialism in the case of Blacks in America. But the important characteristic of colonialism is not the distance separating the mother country from the colony, but the fact that the dominant group controls the institutions which in turn control the lives of the colonized people. The key relationships are (1) economic control and exploitation from outside, (2) political dependence and subjugation from outside, (3) personal oppression and dehumanization as a member of a group.

Geography does play a role in the legitimization of majority rule. If a minority group occupies a single piece of territory, it is likely to try to form a separatist form of politics. This may be seen as partly legitimate as it has a land base upon which to form a political group. If the minority is dispersed, however, then the issue is not the integrity of their union, but the legitimacy of the majority rule. By dispersion within the space of the majority group, the minority loses its claim to a piece of land and as such a possible legitimate source of power. This, of course, is an academic argument as far as Blacks in America are concerned. The land on which they reside is not owned or controlled by them.

INTERNAL COLONIALISM

Economic control is a basic tenet of the colonial system. The natural resources —land, capital, labor—of the colony are exploited for the benefit of the outside power. In turn, the colony provides a market for the goods and services of the controlling state. The black ghetto has acted as a source of menial labor and as a market for white production. The black institutions, though ostensibly under local control, are directed from the outside. For example, a significant portion of the urban ghetto savings goes into financial institutions whose investment policies are aimed elsewhere.

Political power has functioned in much the same manner as economic control. Whites have had, until recently, a virtual monopoly in this area. There have been some gains for Blacks in the area of political office holding. But it is important to remember that there may be a significant distinction between Blacks holding political office and having power. In 1970 more than 300 black candidates ran for political office in the South; of these, 114 won their races for offices ranging from U.S. Congressman, state legislator, mayor, and sheriff to county commissioners, school board officials, and city council members. The importance of these gains must be seen in the light of the fact that the inequality of political power remains extreme. In 1970, for example, only thirteen, or 0.03 percent, of the 435 members of Congress were Black although 10 percent of voting-age Americans were Black.

But even with their gains in political positions black leaders still find that they are subject to white power. The result is a kind of "indirect rule" of inner-city ghettos. A black mayor or senator does not indicate the transfer of real power. As Richard Hatcher, Gary's mayor, pointed out, "visible Black leadership by no means implies real Black control" (Allen, 1970). In Chicago, less than 1 percent of the effective power is held by Blacks.

The ultimate impact of these forces is on the black individual; he or she is depersonalized in the process. Oppression is directed at Blacks as a group. The black individual is victimized by it by virtue of being alive.

The violence inherent in the colonial relationship is in part cultural and psychic. The reason for this is that colonial subjugation is not only economic, political, and social, but generic. That is, Blacks are discriminated against and separated not on the basis of their characteristics as individuals but on the basis of their membership in a group. White actions, whether moral, social, or legal, are not aimed at restricting only certain black people, but all black people. "He" becomes "they," an anonymous collectivity. Colonialism also aims at the destruction of the culture of the colonized group and remolds the group and the psychocultural framework within which human contact is maintained. In effect, the colonized people become depersonalized. Bettelheim has pointed out that an essential factor in one's sense of individual freedom is "the problem of how much to let the state modify one's life becomes a very personal one that everyone has to solve for himself" (Bettelheim, 1960). Our question is, for Blacks is there a realistic choice? The evidence seems quite clear that, for a majority of black people, the decision about the influence of the state upon their lives is not left up to them, indeed they have little, if anything, to say about it. "But barring an individual from a part in decision making on matters that deeply concern him tends to create a feeling of impotence which we will call being subject to tyranny" (Bettelheim, 1960). Those areas in one's life in which it is felt to be important to have a say in decisions may change with time. Hegel has called this the "consciousness of freedom." Groups within a society not only have different levels of consciousness, but are concerned about different freedoms at the same time and these, at times, conflict. Such is the case with integration in housing and schools. To Whites the consciousness of freedom to sell to whom they please takes precedence over the freedom of living where one pleases; the scheme is reversed for Blacks.

It is important that, because of different life experiences, groups, in this case Blacks and Whites, will have different levels of consciousness on a particular freedom. What is experienced by Blacks as tyranny, for example, in the administration of "law and order," is seen by Whites as warranted or justifiable law enforcement, or just silly accusations. This is the crux of the difference in the Black and White perceptions of the former's inability to alter ghetto conditions. It is worthwhile to quote Bettelheim again.

> Whether in childhood or adulthood if one finds it impossible, first to influence one's social and physical environment, and later to make decisions on how and when to modify it, this is harmful if not devastating to the human personality (Bettelheim, 1960).

In an oppressive environment these decisions may have no effect on one's life. Thus in such an environment decisions geared toward making practical adjustments in one's life are thwarted and end up as a waste of energy, and henceforth there will be seen little need in making these kinds of decisions. From the white vantage point this inability to effect change in black environments is seen as apathy. To the Blacks it is viewed as tyranny.

Housing: A White Program for Black Containment

Within this colonial framework, the various federal poverty programs become foreign aid. As far as Blacks are concerned, poverty programs are "white colonist imperialism" (Moynihan, 1969). One facet of this colonialist approach has been in the provision of and access to housing for Blacks.

We discussed public housing and urban renewal in Chapter 3 as factors in the maintenance of segregated housing patterns. Here we are interested in them as white programs to keep Blacks in an inferior position. Again, we emphasize that it is not necessary for these programs to be conscious manipulations of Whites to oppress Blacks. Public housing was not designed to reach the truly poor, but the temporary poor, for those segments of the middle class who found themselves temporarily below their "proper" social rank, through no fault of their own, of course. Programs like public housing, urban renewal, and welfare have never been intended to eradicate poverty or the conditions that promote it. The public housing programs of the 1930s were for the unemployed middle class and defense workers. Public housing as a refuge for the poor has been an example of "hand-me-down" schemes with which they are so familiar. They got public housing after it had served its purpose of helping the middle class.

It is a sad irony that the government move to urban renewal in 1949 was a result of a push for a federal subsidy to the city to balance the one that was paid to the middle class which was moving to the suburbs. Again, the program was not to be for the poor or black. Public housing still goes on but makes little impact on the number of new, safe, and adequate residences available for Blacks. This is contrasted with the rapid destruction of low-income housing through urban renewal and the expansion of white business districts and highways. Urban renewal has not been a program to provide housing for the poor, but to physically rebuild the cities. At best the relocation process associated with urban renewal can move the poor to other low-rent structures, thus increasing the crowding of these areas. Relocation does not produce new houses; it only tries to find already existing ones.

Since its inception in 1949, federally supported housing has been segregated as a matter of course. It was not until 1962 that race could no longer be used as a criterion for public housing, but, that was on paper. This is another example of second-stage social action that does not produce change. Public housing projects in Chicago, Detroit, Philadelphia, St. Louis, Tampa, Savannah, New York, Cleveland, and Dallas, for example, were segregated in the 1960s. Under the 1949 act federal money could be spent only if the area to be redeveloped had been a slum; houses for the poor were torn down to be replaced by houses for the rich, to expand university campuses, and to provide public parking and recreation facilities.

Public housing and urban renewal were white middle-class programs for the benefit of that class. As far as the poor and Blacks were concerned, the logic goes that by renewing the blighted space the people were renewed. Even though the Housing Act of 1954 seemed to tighten federal control over some of the problems that had hurt the poor, local governing bodies still retained the important veto power. Urban renewal has been another technique to keep Blacks "in their place" by attacking not Blacks per se, but the conditions under which they are forced to live. Another aspect to this is that the land upon which the urban black population lives is brought by speculators and either not improved, razed and paved for a parking lot, or left vacant until it can be resold to the federal government for public housing or urban renewal. It is sold to the government for "fair market value" when, in fact, there is no market value, because the federal government is the only potential buyer.

Public housing, and its modern counterpart, model cities, is often seen to function as a mechanism for spatial containment. Housing projects for Blacks are kept within the bounds of the black community; such has been the case in Chicago, Dayton, Indianapolis, and St. Louis. The cities allocate space, and the black population gets the less-desirable space. In "Iron City" (a name for Montgomery, Alabama) the implementation of a federal housing program amounted to "apartheid." The racial-residential pattern in "Iron City" was typical of middle-sized southern cities. Blacks were scattered in clusters throughout the city. When social change of the 1950s and 1960s came to the city with its school integration and Blacks "forgetting their place," the city planning commission came up with a containment plan. With federal aid and the approval of local whites, it decided to "plan" the sociospatial development of the city. Through the use of urban renewal and public housing, it was able to gather up the scattered black population and concentrate it into two high-density black areas.

But local and federal governments are not the only supporters of the sociospatial containment policy inherent in the colonial structure of black America.

These governmental policies are supported by the majority of Whites. The result is a cycle in which the individual says that the fault is with the politicians, while the latter say that they are just implementing the desires of those who put them in office.

The social problem of race has developed into a spatial game of "run and hide." As Blacks move into the central cities, Whites run to the suburbs. Then as the inner-cities become "renewed" and developed for Whites, it has been suggested that Blacks could be moved in groups to the suburbs. But Whites have escaped to these areas, and they are not going to let Blacks move into their neighborhoods. The Los Angeles city council, for example, defeated a proposal to rezone the Woodland Hills community to allow multiple-unit, low-income housing. Such political action to keep out Blacks has been accompanied by referendums and rezoning to keep the suburbs white.

These patterns of spatial containment are often ignored or become integral parts of future plans. In the Philadelphia Comprehensive Plan, for example, Blacks are ignored, while in the "Plan for the Year 2,000—The Nation's Capitol" the present pattern of racial segregation is continued.

Housing is not the only aspect of life of the Black that is controlled by forces outside of his community. The whole range of welfare and health programs are further examples of "foreign aid", in some cases to contain, in other instances to pacify, but never to strike at the basic causes of the colonial situation.

The Urban Rip-Off

The Random House Dictionary defines the word "urban" as pertaining to cities and the word "city" as a large or important town. The same reference book tells us that rip means to tear apart in a vigorous manner. The "urban rip-off" then is the tearing apart of large towns in a vigorous or vicious manner. This becomes important and even critical when we consider that these large towns are made up of people and it is they and their communities that are being torn apart. The whys and the hows we intend to supply later. But before we get to that let us review some of the data relevant to the analysis of the urban phenomenon.

To begin with, the number of Blacks, other minorities, and poor Whites inhabiting the cities is increasing significantly while the number of other Whites is decreasing similarly. Black Americans constitute 11 percent of the total population in the United States yet they represent 12 percent of the metropolitan population. Even more striking is the fact that 21 percent of those black people live in the central city. To extend the point a bit further we can examine population data from some of our largest cities. In so doing we discover that Washington, D.C., has 71 percent Blacks; Atlanta, Georgia, 51.3 percent; Baltimore, Maryland, 42.2 percent; according to the 1970 census data, Detroit, 43.7 percent; Cleveland, 38.3 percent; Philadelphia a total of 654,000 black people with 33.6 percent. In Chicago, 1.1 million constituting 32.7 percent; of course New York City has 1.7 million, 21 percent.

By now the message should begin to come through clearly. What types of rip-offs are going down? We have chosen two basic categories: (1) black displacement or the forced migration of Blacks and (2) the undeclared urban war of selected genocide under the code name of law and order. In our society, that which is done in the name of progress is almost always acceptable. Thus urban renewal has continued to be heralded as the answer to the problems of the city. However, there is at least one other important view of this incredible utilization of technology and technocracy; that is, under the guise of progress, again, urban renewal forces black removal. Black removal, à la urban renewal, is a part of the urban rip-off. Our system permits the government to arbitrarily condemn, by right of eminent domain, any and all properties it wishes. The properties most often condemned and least often justly compensated for are those properties owned by Blacks. To add insult to injury, these *confiscated* properties (almost without exception) are sold to private (nonblack) persons who build profitable enterprises thereon.

What happens to the people who previously lived there? As concrete answers, we will cite examples of two urban renewal projects in Columbus, Ohio. One area is now called Thurber Village. In the old days it was called *Fly* Town (perhaps some of you can dig it). Historically, it was inhabited by some poor Italians (who very quickly learned English, then moved out) and Blacks. Then one day the federal government decided, "Let us renew our urban." They asked, "Where shall we start?" Someone said "Let us go to Fly Town." Granted there were some old dilapidated houses there, but it was not what one would call a typical slum, the kind of slum that can be seen in Chicago, New York, and Detroit.

At any rate they decided that they would renew the urban in Fly Town, and proceeded to condemn the property. So the Blacks were given a pittance for the property which they owned.

There was even something greater than economic factors at stake, a sense of belonging. This is where the people lived, this was their home, this was their neighborhood, this is where the happenings were with them, and this was where their church was. Without any concern for the above, in the name of progress, the urban was renewed. The properties were bought, the buildings were demolished, and the properties were sold. And in the place of the single-family dwellings of black people, huge brick buildings were constructed, a tower, townhouses, apartments. For whom? At $200 a month for rent, can you guess for whose benefit the urban was renewed?

The second example is called the Market Mohawk section and is located within the Columbus business district. Historically (from 1827) the area was exclusively residential, but by 1940 the area had been invaded by small businesses, rooming houses, and remade apartment buildings. The buildings were close to each other and most of the lots had permanent buildings in the rear. The few open spaces and yards were cluttered with waste and rubbish. Ragged and dirty little street urchins played on the sidewalks and darted through traffic as if to play tag with the cars. The lots were unfit for play because of the demolished buildings.

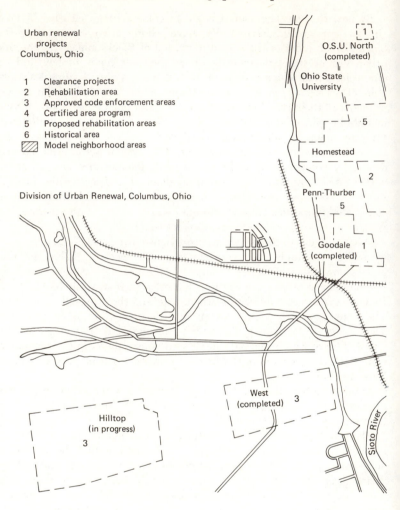

Urban renewal
projects
Columbus, Ohio

1   Clearance projects
2   Rehabilitation area
3   Approved code enforcement areas
4   Certified area program
5   Proposed rehabilitation areas
6   Historical area
▨   Model neighborhood areas

Division of Urban Renewal, Columbus, Ohio

O.S.U. North
(completed)

Ohio State
University

Homestead

Penn-Thurber

Goodale
(completed)

West
(completed)   3

Hilltop
(in progress)
3

Sioto River

Figure 9.1   Map of the Entire Columbus Urban Renewal Project.

In 1940 the area known as Market-Mohawk had a population of 10,000 persons or 3,000 families. A block-by-block survey of the area showed a high rate of crime, prostitution, venereal disease, and juvenile delinquency. The racial composition was 40 percent black and 60 percent white. The Market-Mohawk area had only 2.7 percent of Columbus' population but had:

3.4 percent of all Columbus' dwelling units
4.6 percent of all Columbus' tenant-occupied units
12.6 percent of all Columbus' night clubs
11.9 percent of all Columbus' rooming houses
22.9 percent of all Columbus' dwellings unfit for occupancy

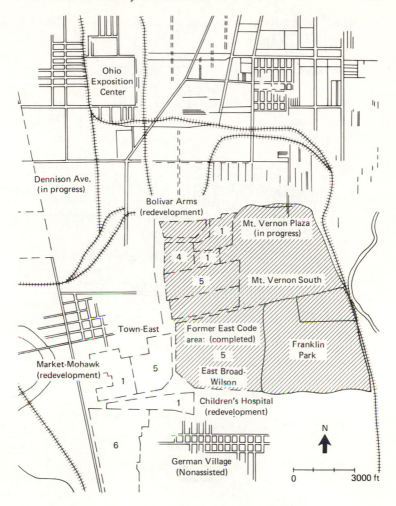

Figure 9.1 Continued

31.2 percent of all Columbus' known prostitutes
11.3 percent of all Columbus' families on relief
 6.7 percent of all Columbus' new cases of tuberculosis
11.4 percent of all Columbus' new cases of syphilis
12.0 percent of all Columbus' new cases of gonorrhea

It is obvious that in all categories the Market-Mohawk section had severe urban problems. Yet it took nearly 20 years for the city of Columbus to even pretend to begin to deal with these problems. On rare occasions the city admitted the problem but did nothing to improve the conditions.

Finally in the late 1950s the city of Columbus initiated the Market-Mohawk Urban Renewal Project for the purpose of clearing the low-taxed slum and

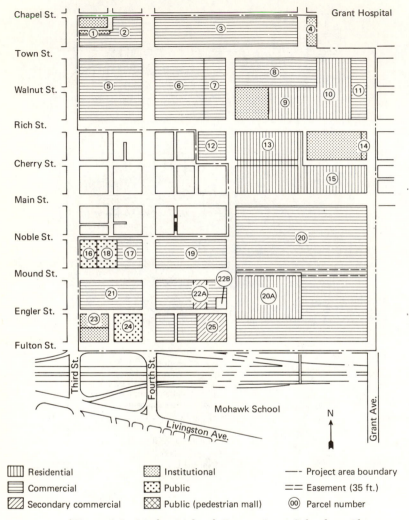

Figure 9.2 Market-Mohawk Project Area, Columbus, Ohio.

renewing it with commercial buildings, which would greatly raise the taxes on the land and buildings. In the long run the city would benefit from these added taxes.

The city presented its plan to the federal government and included the following reasons for a need to redevelop the area:

1. The operation of wholesale produce businesses was objectionable in that the produce was received and shipped from each of those enterprises entirely by trucks which were loaded and unloaded mainly at the Town Street side of each building. This seriously impeded traffic, pedestrian as well as vehicular.

2. Loading space at the wholesale houses was insufficient to accommodate all the trucks loading and unloading. This resulted in the parking of waiting vehicles along the other right of ways in the area, further impeding the orderly flow of the traffic.
3. Sidewalks and curbside stalls seriously impeded pedestrians and also vehicular traffic along the Fourth Street side of the market area, as well as reduced the number of street parking spaces.
4. The policing of the market's Fourth Street frontage after market day left a great deal to be desired and resulted in an unsanitary condition.
5. The area was blighted and could only be redeveloped through clearance.
6. Commercial reuses, parking reuses, industrial reuses, and light manufacturing were all possibilities.

This project was approved on June 11, 1959.

Since not one of the six reasons given deals with human needs, it is unnecessary to mount an argument to convince readers that the city of Columbus was motivated strictly by economics. Nonetheless, urban renewal programs are supposed to benefit people. Granted most of the people lived in dwellings that would not please most people, but it was theirs, and who is to say that they wanted their urban renewed. The question is, were they ripped off? Our limited research indicates that the planners, architects, and the "money men" got together and said, "We will build a very, very important business section here. We will put the open-market out of business." Economics continue to have serious spatial consequences on the free enterprise system.

This is not just an adventure that was injurious to Blacks; it was harmful to poor whites as well. When you get right down to the "nitty gritty," there are the "haves" and the "have nots," and when the rip-off comes, if you are a "have not," you are likely to suffer. Think about it.

At any rate, where these poor people's homes were and where these poor people's open market was are now multistoried business buildings owned by some of the wealthiest people in Columbus. An additional disturbing fact is that federal monies, i.e., some of the tax dollars of the poor people in the Market-Mohawk area, helped to renew the urban that ripped them off. For whose benefit is the urban renewed? If we were to examine St. Louis, Kansas City or any major city in the United States, we would find evidence of the same type of rip-off.

Urban renewal programs were designed to deal only with the symptoms and not the causes of urban blight. The substandard houses were razed and the social ills were reduced and new (private commercial) buildings replaced the old structures. However, nothing was done to improve job opportunities and the economic plight of these slum dwellers. No program was instituted to deal with the problems of health, jobs, education, and social welfare of the residents. No effort was made to force absentee landlords to comply with building codes.

It seems clear that the only significant phenomenon which occurred in reference to Blacks and other urban poor was relocation (see Figure 9.3).

This constituted a relocation of slums. With restrictive covenants and racist lending institutions, Blacks were forced to relocate on the near east side of

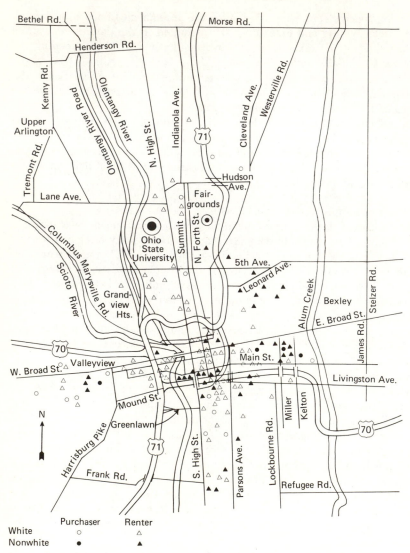

	Purchaser	Renter
White	o	△
Nonwhite	●	▲

Figure 9.3 Relocation of Families from the Market-Mohawk Area by Race and Occupancy.

Columbus. This was an area which was being vacated by a sizable middle-class population. To more graphically understand the problem, let us examine one census tract.

Table 9.2 contains the data which show the tremendous amount of internal mobility that occurred within census tract No. 37 from 1955 to 1964.

Figure 9.4 shows that in only 15 years the nonwhite (black) population changed from 76 to more than 2,800.

Figure 9.5 clearly shows that the population shift caused a significant decrease in the percentage of persons who attend college and a notable increase

			MOVED TO PRESENT RESIDENCE SINCE 1955 FROM:				
	Total popu- lation of tract	Number with stable resi- dence since 1955	A house located in Colum- bus City	Else- where in the SMSA. exclud- ing Colum- bus City	Outside the Columbus SMSA.	Abroad in 1955	Un- known and chil- dren born since 1955
White	5,680	1,726	1,680	146	1,116	86	926
Nonwhite	2,717	119	1,666	21	364	16	531
Total	8,397	1,845	3,346	167	937–543	102	1,457
% of total	100.0	22.0	39.8	2.0	11.2–6.5	1.2	17.4

Table 9.2   Residential Mobility

in the percentage of persons who dropped out of high school and elementary school.

Figure 9.6 shows a marked decrease in professional and skilled jobs and a doubling of the labor force in the areas of service and labor.

The following crimes increased dramatically: burglary, breaking and entering, larceny, theft, prostitution, commercial vice, narcotic, drug laws.

As Figure 9.7 indicates, this tract ranks low on all the socioeconomic and health characteristics. In 1960, 34 percent of its families had incomes of less than $4,000; 56 percent of its residents over 25 years of age had not completed high school, and its male unemployment rate was nearly twice that of the country. The area is rapidly integrating, with approximately two-thirds of the housing units renter-occupied and 25 percent of the units deteriorated or dilapidated. The mobility rate is high, with only 25 percent of the residents having lived here since 1955. Of the children under 18, 26 percent were not living with both parents and 28 percent of the working wives had preschool children. Crime and delinquency rates are high. This is therefore an area which is demonstrating an increasing concentration of socioeconomic and health problems.

These statistics are representative of the entire near east side, and show convincingly that even though the Market-Mohawk area has had its urban renewed, no significant imprint has been made on the urban blight in Columbus, Ohio. Blacks have been forced from familiar slum to unfamiliar slums, and when they owned property, they were forced to sell their property for less than fair market value. Bessie Lou (not her real name), a property owner, received less than 69 percent of the appraised value of her property while "Mr. Big," a major absentee landlord, received more than 94 percent of the appraised value of his property. The economics of the sociospatial manipulation is a modern-day exercise in mechanism: the existence of the colony (and the colonials) for the good of the mother country.

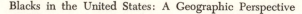
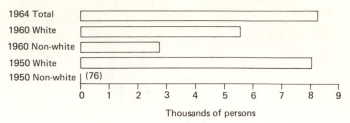

Figure 9.4   Changes in White and Nonwhite Population, 1950–1964.

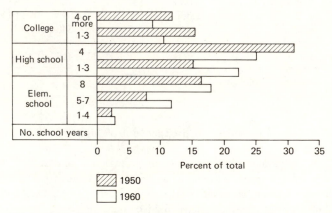

Figure 9.5   Education of Persons 25 Years and Older.

Displacement of Blacks in urban areas frequently results when the government, state or city, decides to construct a noxious facility. A noxious facility is one which is a nuisance because of excessive noise or unpleasant odor. The noise of a freeway and the odoriferousness of a rendering plant or a sewage treatment plant would be good examples. Julian Wolpert, at the University of Pennsylvania, has given a great deal of attention to the location of noxious facilities during the past 4 or 5 years. His research has surprised many. Again, the state has the right to force the sale of any property it wishes and states is needed. A classic example of the location of a noxious facility and its severe consequences to a black community would be the case of the kink in I-40.

The Kink in I-40: A Case Study of an Urban Rip-Off

In the mid-1950s a New York landscape architecture and consulting engineering firm was hired by the state of Tennessee to plan 1,000 miles of interstate highway system to link the major cities of that state. The move was made to prepare for the passage of the federal Interstate Highway Act of 1956. After several months of work, Clark and Rapuano (consulting engineers) submitted a preliminary route plan to the Tennessee State Highway Department.

This preliminary plan was approved by representatives of the Highway De-

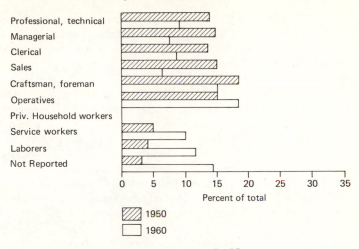

Figure 9.6　Occupation of Males 14 and Older.

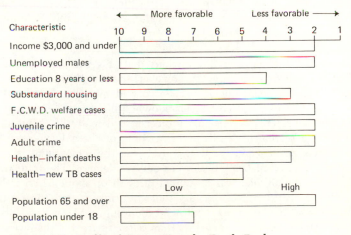

Figure 9.7　Profile of Census Tract by Decile Rank.

partment, the United States Bureau of Public Roads, the city, and the county, at a meeting held in July, 1955. However, despite official sanction, Clark and Rapuano's proposal did not yet include the controversial I-40 connecting link, instead a very curious thing happened. After this initial approval the route underwent a radical change before its final approval in 1957.

No adequate explanation of the reasons for the change were offered, even though the new route caused much more severe damage to the black section of north Nashville than the original route would have. Therefore, a thorough examination of the circumstances surrounding the kink in I-40 seems appropriate.

Yale Rabin, a planning consultant for the NAACP Legal Defense Fund, testified at the 1967 trial that there was no record of any kind in the files of the Planning Commission from the time of the initial approval of the Clark and Rapuano preliminary route in July, 1955, until a memorandum of September, 1956, which referred to the new plan.

From a casual examination of the change in sites, one can quickly surmise that the kink in I-40 guaranteed considerably fewer adverse effects on white holdings in department stores, shopping centers, and railroad property, than on the property of Blacks. In fact it seems quite clear that no concern was given the preservation of the schools, churches, and shops along Jefferson Street in (black) north Nashville. The above charges were made by the black citizens of Nashville and never successfully refuted by the state.

The kink in I-40 had several immediate and disastrous effects on north Nashville, and those who lived there. The effects compile an overwhelming case against the highway. It should be noted that the judge in the 1967 trial stated:

> Plaintiffs have shown that the proposed route will have an adverse effect on the business life and educational institutions of the North Nashville community. The proof shows that consideration given to the total impact of the link of I-40 on the North Nashville community was inadequate (Nashville I-40 Steering Committee, 1967).

By now it should be perfectly obvious that this was just one more spatial rip-off of the black community. If, however, the skeptic needs more proof, let us look further. It could not have been coincidental that "new" I-40 resulted in the elimination of 80 percent of black-owned businesses. A few years earlier an urban renewal (black removal) project forced many black businesses from the downtown section of Nashville. For some of these businesses it was the second forced closing, and the last, considering the sociospatial restrictions regarding the location of black businesses and residences. The total value of the establishment demolished was an annual growth of about $11.5 million.

Equally as disturbing, is the fact that the kink caused the destruction of 650 homes and twenty-seven apartment buildings. Many residents reported that: (1) they received much less than a fair price for their property, and (2) they had been given no assistance in their efforts to relocate.

Another flagrant aspect of this massive rip-off is the fact that it was carefully designed to cut between the campuses of the three major black institutions of higher education. Fisk University, Meharry Medical College, and Tennessee A & I University are all located in the black quadrant of Nashville. Each school has suffered from the limits imposed by the newly-erected concrete barriers. They prevented both physical expansion of the campuses and disrupted the many programs (already underway) to unite students and faculties in productive exchanges. In addition, large numbers (61 percent according to a report for the Center for Community Studies) of the 12,000 to 20,000 people served by a hospital associated with Meharry Medical College had no form of private transportation and therefore were forced to cross the highway on foot to get to the hospital. The highway was a physical as well as a psychological barrier. The fact that all three schools are well-known and respected institutions (Tennessee A & I being a major school in the state university system, Meharry furnishing most of the black doctors and dentists in the United States, and Fisk being one of the oldest black universities and alma mater of some of the great black leaders) also added to the tragedy of the disruption.

Control of Access to Needs = Spatial Containment

Deutscher has described a function performed by certain people in public housing that may be enlarged upon. The "gatekeeper" is the person who makes critical decisions about whether a person is allowed in or out of a given institution. We enlarge the scope of this concept to encompass space as well as institutions. In effect the gatekeeping process and the gatekeepers control the access of people to life goals. For the poor Black this means that decisions about his access to housing, welfare, health care, jobs, and schools are made by other people. It does not make any difference whether the black person is living in Boston, Oakland, or a rural town in Alabama. The following testimony of Mrs. Randale illustrates the role and effects of the "gatekeeper."

> For example, she testifies that the County Health Department made an appointment for her to have an eye examination at the medical center in Tuscaloosa, about 50 miles away. No transportation was provided so she paid a neighbor $10 to take her there. But when she got to Tuscaloosa, the physician's office at the medical center decided there had been some mistake.
>
> "Well, I can't hear so good," Mrs. Randale relates, "I thought the lady told me—I wanted to sit down and she told me to go outside. But I thought she was going to wait on me. So, I had to go back home."
>
> Mr. Glickstein: You paid $10 to go up there and you thought you had an appointment, and you had to go back home?
>
> Mrs. Randale: I had to go back home.
>
> Mr. Glickstein: Have you gone back since then?
>
> Mrs. Randale: No sir, I haven't. She treated me so cold I did never go back (Good, 1968).

One of the principles of American law is that in a crime the burden of proof rests with the state, not the suspected wrongdoer. This system of law does not apply to the colonized. They are under not the system of "law" but that of "justice." When they receive welfare and are accused of some wrongdoing, they must prove their innocence to their accuser with no impartial intermediary.

Welfare provides just enough money so that the middle class is proud of itself, but it is done in such a complicated way that neither the recipients nor the middle class understand the rules. And the Black remain poor. In some cases the state government lies about welfare so that the public vendetta of less money and more "law and justice" is kept at a high pitch while keeping the Blacks poor and contained. Connecticut officials, for example, report that welfare accounts for one-third of the state budget, when in fact the figure is 17 per-

Types of public assistance	1967	1969
Children	3,500,000	4,815,000
Over 65	2,100,000	2,000,000
Mothers	900,000	1,900,000
Blind, severely handicapped	700,000	808,000
Disabled fathers	100,000	No data
Total employable	50,000	80,700
	7,300,000	9,503,700

Table 9.3   Number of People in Various Types of Public Assistance, 1967, 1969.

Source: *1967 data from Urban League, 1967, p. 6; 1969 data from Christian Science Monitor, Aug. 14, 1969.*

cent; they accuse clients of cheating when only 2 percent have been certified as frauds; they say recipients come to Connecticut because of high payments, when in fact all the surrounding states offer higher payments. In 1967 the Southern Regional Council studied the 100 poorest counties in the United States and found that, rather than reaching those in need, public assistance was inadequate while the needs were extreme. Public assistance laws in many states assure that recipients can have only homes of low value and deter any improvements that would increase the value of the home.

Bridgeport, Connecticut, has become a "dumping ground" for poor Blacks in the state's program to contain and isolate them. The city has lost 10,000 Whites replaced by an equal number of Blacks. The welfare offices in surrounding communities are closed in the hopes that the people on assistance will then move to the remaining office in Bridgeport. The state office in Norwalk has been closed, so 2,200 recipients must go 25 miles to Bridgeport for aid; few families have cars, the state cancelled the "transportation allowance" and the round-trip fare is $3.10 by bus. The "flat grant" system was instituted by the state in August, 1972, with the result that segregation was increased. The new policy in practice eliminated rental allowances, consequently poor black people were evicted and forced into the designated black areas.

It is often argued that welfare is used by people who just do not want to work, when in fact less than 0.007 percent of the total number of people on public welfare in 1967 were employable. In 1969 the figure was 0.008 percent employable. It is noteworthy that the 7.3 million accounted for only 21 percent of the total number of people in poverty in 1967 (Table 9.3).

The provision of health care is similar to welfare practices; that is, it is designed to meet the needs of the white middle and upper classes. The health care systems continue to be racist. Statistics comparing the health of Blacks and Whites consistently show the effects of racism.

As is the case with housing and jobs, geography is an important factor in the lack of health care for black people. One of the major causes of poor health care for Blacks is the spatial distribution of health care facilities and practitioners. Services are both geographically and socially distant from the poor and

Infant Mortality°		Maternal Mortality†		Death Rate‡ (age adjusted)		
					Male	Female
White	21.5	White	21.0	White	9.1	5.3
Nonwhite	40.3	Nonwhite	83.7	Nonwhite	12.4	8.5

Table 9.4 Comparison of Black and White Death Rates, 1965.

° Per 1,000 live births.
† Per 100,000 live births.
‡ Per 1,000 population.

black. Who gets health care, when, and where are almost exclusively in the hands of Whites. The result is that white physicians do not practice in black areas. Blacks are commonly restricted to county hospitals, like Cook County in Chicago and Los Angeles General. In fact, "the best single criterion of the status of medical care for Negroes in a community is the presence and character of the Negro Hospital" (Reitzes, 1958). As we have pointed out before, access to basic services is withheld in the colonial situation. Working in the black community in Detroit, Nancy Milio found that decentralization of health care services was among the most often mentioned problems of Blacks.

If the health care services are geographically available to the black population, they are often then socially distant. Any person in the role of patient is apt to feel insecure in the health professional–patient context, and racial barriers compound this problem. Nurses, among others, have suggested that services need to be brought not only spatially but socially nearer the patient. Blacks should be involved in the planning and structuring of the services that are in their communities. The "Mom and Tots" center in Detroit is an example of community people and health professionals working together to solve the community's problems. The dental clinic of the Boston City Hospital is an example of the opposite approach. It provides only extraction services, no other treatment. This is perceived by dental students as Blacks do not care about their teeth and only want them pulled.

There are three basic determinants of illness behavior: (1) situational factors, (2) recognition of and significance attached to symptoms, and (3) faith in the delivery system. Research has shown that poor health care among Blacks is a result of factors 1 and 3. "A person who believes himself vulnerable to illness can act only if he has a cognitive map of routes to avoid or reduce the feeling of vulnerability. If no paths are evident or seen as not appropriate, it is likely that further denial will occur" (Kegels, 1969). Health care is like public housing, urban renewal, and welfare in that it is not designed to reach Blacks.

Black Americans, urban and rural, have served as sources of manual labor and exploited consumers. The control of financial resources has been systematically denied to Blacks. The inability to get credit and insurance are two of the pressures that curtail the expansion of black business. Many insurance companies will not insure businesses in black ghetto areas. Other factors impeding the development of black enterprise include lack of capital and ex-

Place	Industrial %	Commercial %
United States	62	52
Los Angeles	85	63
Washington, D.C.	96	91
San Francisco	84	72
Boston	81	74
Chicago	77	67
Philadelphia	75	75
Atlanta	71	44
Detroit	70	80
St. Louis	67	75
Cleveland	61	74
New York	61	64
New Orleans	58	66
Dayton	56	78
Indianapolis	52	55

Table 9.5 Percentage in Suburbs of All New Private Nonresidential Building Construction in Metropolitan Areas, 1960 to 1965, Percentage of Valuation of Permits Authorized.

Source: *The Racial Gap; 1955–1965, 1965–1975, National Urban League, 1967, p. 21.*

perience. In addition, as Dr. Goodlet, owner of a black newspaper in San Francisco, pointed out, "If you cater to a poor clientele, you in the main will conduct a very poor and insecure business" (U.S. Commission on Civil Rights, 1967). The location of black business along a black main street functions as a cultural and social center; but is also a result of white discrimination. Such streets include Auburn Avenue in Atlanta, Basin Street in New Orleans, Beale Street in Memphis, 47th Street in Chicago.

What happens to black business also happens to black individuals. As they commonly do not have the ready cash, black ghetto residents must rely on credit at exorbitant rates. They also find higher prices, and prices raised at the time they receive their welfare checks. They form a captive market.

Another aspect of this economic exploitation is spatial in nature. Jobs are following whites to the suburbs. Again the problem for the black person is access. Both the Kerner Commission, for the country as a whole, and the McCone Commission, for Los Angeles in particular, found access to employment opportunities that had fled to the suburbs to be a major issue for Blacks in the inner-city. Table 9.5 illustrates the trend toward new industry being built in the suburbs.

This trend toward urban relocation has "improved the options for the affluent suburbanite while reducing the opportunities for the black inner-city resident. The organization of urban bus and mass-transport systems has been and appears to be regressive in its effects on income, penalizing the inner-city poor, and subsidizing the affluent suburbanite."

The type of urban transportation system that Meyer calls the "inside-out system" has not been adequately developed. This system links the inner-city residents with suburban jobs. Where these types of networks have been tried, in Boston, Baltimore, and New York, they have not proved effective. One reason is that inner-city residents do not have the extra time and money for transportation. This is compounded by the fact that years of racism in education, job training, and discriminatory hiring practices have left the bulk of the black potential work force behind in the level of skills needed for the new suburban jobs.

This transportation problem is compounded by surburban housing restrictions. Suburbs zone land for industrial parks but not for housing needed by the workers. Ford Motor Company found this problem when it built an assembly plant in Mahwah, New Jersey. As one company official put it, "town officials want the plant but they don't want the hourly worker. They want the executive who will live on 2 acres of land in an $80,000 home" (*Wall Street Journal*, November 27, 1970).

The suburbs hold the balance of political power and, through restrictive zoning, are able to keep out Blacks. A public referendum in San Jose, California, defeated the city council's decision to accept a public housing project. The eventual result was a Supreme Court decision (5 to 3) upholding the referendum to be not racially discriminatory. Justice Black made the point that, "provision for referendums demonstrate devotion to democracy, not to bias, discrimination, or prejudice." President Nixon followed the same line of thought in a policy statement on June 11, 1971, in which the following four points were made:

1. Denial of equal housing opportunity to a person because of race is wrong, and will not be tolerated.
2. Such denial will not be tolerated whether practiced directly and overtly, or under the cover of subterfuges, or indirectly through such practice as price and credit discrimination.
3. In terms of site selection for a housing development, the federal role is one of agreeing or not agreeing to provide federal subsidies for projects proposed by local authorities or other developers.
4. A municipality that does not want federally assisted housing should not have it imposed from Washington by bureaucratic fiat; that is not a proper federal role.

In these two policy statements we again see the extent to which racism is worked into American governmental practice. Justice Black simply does not seem to realize that voting and spatial allocation have frequently been used to discriminate against Blacks. Whites vote democratically to keep out Blacks. Nixon gives "paper" recognition and compliance to civil rights laws in points 1 and 2; then in the same policy statement leaves the way open in points 3 and 4 for "local control," which is decidedly racist. Denial of access to needs, services, and opportunities produces the kind of spatial containment which leaves a people increasingly easier to control. A well-contained people are ready for genocide.

Genocide: One Step Beyond Spatial Containment

The continuation of these colonial-racist practices has resulted in a group of black Americans charging the United States with genocide as defined by the Genocide Convention of the United Nations in 1948; which was, incidently, signed but not ratified by the United States. Genocide is defined to be "any intent to destroy, in whole or in part, a national, racial, ethnic, or religious group." This includes:

a. Killing members of the group
b. Causing serious bodily or mental harm to members of the group
c. Deliberately inflicting on the group conditions of life calculated to bring about its physical destruction in whole or in part
d. Imposing measures intended to prevent births within the group
e. Forcibly transferring children of the group to another group (Patterson, 1970).

As with the term "colony," "genocide" is a sensitive word, one that draws primarily emotional responses. Our purpose is not to be involved in a debate over terminology, but rather to point out that from the perspective of certain black people "genocide" is an accurate description of their condition in America. Dr. Sinnette has written, for example, that the 1948 genocide statement remains valid in 1972. Blacks have been subjected to all the conditions set forth in the five points above. Obviously, these conditions are not all inflicted deliberately. But we have argued throughout the book that measures which are racist do not have to be deliberate to be effective.

Much of the data in this book supports points a, b, and c above. The evidence to support points d and e is not as widespread. There is, however, sadly, some evidence to support these two points.

Domestic pacification programs may be seen as examples of point e. That force does not need to be used in the United States is perhaps more a sign of the subtlety and sophistication of group control rather than of the absence of such a policy. Since 1968 the Department of Defense (DOD) has run Domestic Action Programs (DAP) which appear "to translate into control or pacification of ghetto populations" (Corey and Cohen, 1972). The DAP runs summer camps for the "disadvantaged" which include the typical camp activities as well as lectures, demonstrations, and training in police, military, and patriotic subjects. Superficially, this appears to be an altruistic concept, but in reality it can function quite differently. "The key idea that recurs in a majority of the reports, pamphlets and brochures is that the program will enhance [DOD's] ability to provide total national security" (Corey and Cohen, 1972). These programs take potential rioters, aged 10 to 21, out of the cities for a period during the summer; but it does nothing about the conditions to which they must return. Positively, the programs do provide an opportunity for youths to enjoy an environment that they otherwise are kept out of. The negative aspect of the camps is that "such a mechanism is tantamount to establishing preventive detention centers for children" (Corey and Cohen, 1972).

Point d, "imposing measures intended to prevent births within the group,"

Benedict J. Fernandez.

is evident in Mississippi House Bill 180, commonly known by civil rights workers as the "Genocide Bill." It was passed by the Mississippi Senate in May, 1964. It provides the choice of a steep fine or a prison term for any woman giving birth to a second illegitimate baby. The penalties increased for a third illegitimate baby. The original House version was even stronger, proposing a prison sentence of from 1 to 3 years or sterilization for a second illegitimate baby. "The intent of this was to get rid of excess Negroes, no longer needed because of automation, and a new threat because of the possibility that they might vote" (Greenberg, 1969). This is in sharp contrast to the practice of breeding Blacks that took place a century earlier.

Genocide is by no means a simple phenomenon. It does not occur automatically. One group of people cannot just go ahead and wipe out another group of people. It is necessary to pass through several stages—the group must live out a peculiar and deadly pattern.

The most important prerequisite for a group to perpetuate genocide is to create and perpetuate the belief that they are superior to their victims. They must believe that they are entitled to the control of the life and death of their victims.

In Hitler's Germany, the Germans were supplied with elaborate charts and complicated theses, to prove the superiority of the Aryans. Of course, at the top of these charts were Nordic peoples and at the bottom of these charts were the colored peoples of the world, with black people holding down the very last rung on this ladder. Similar kinds of programs and practices have surfaced in recent years. One notable example was the study which the Department of the Navy did to determine what groups had the greatest right to live.

Recently, during a lecture at Lincoln University in Jefferson City, Missouri, a radical geographer coined the term "The Undeclared War of Urban Genocide." The Nixon administration sounded the death knell to any plans of Blacks to leave the central city by vigorously opposing the construction of low-cost housing in the suburbs. This served to contain the black community for easy isolation and occupation by military forces. At the same time, under the code name of "law and order," old laws were redefined and new laws were passed to ensure the spatial containment of urban Blacks.

First, Public Law 831 was dusted off for use against (so-called) rioting Blacks instead of communists. Originally, the McCarran bill was known as the Internal Security Act of 1950 and Subversive Activities Control Act of 1950. It was designed to protect the United States against certain un-American and subversive activities by requiring registration of communist organizations, and for other purposes. Title II of the Act authorizes the Attorney General, in times of emergency as declared by the President, to hold in detention centers persons *he believes* "probably will engage in . . . acts of espionage or sabotage." It is important to note that these are persons who have not yet committed an act, but who *might* do so. In the aftermath of the rebellions of the late 1960s the detention camps were again in the minds of some Americans, black and white. Some Blacks feared that the camps would be used against them, and some Whites discussed this possibility. In its 1968 report, "Guerilla Warfare Advocates in the U.S.," the House Un-American Activities Committee recommended a plan by which black citizens, like those who participated in the rebellions of the 1960s, could be "isolated and destroyed in a short period of time." The HUAC plan is set forth as follows:

GUERRILLA WARFARE IN THE UNITED STATES

Report by the Committee on
Un-American Activities, Ninetieth
Congress, May 6, 1968, p. 59.

. . . Once the ghetto is sealed off, and depending upon the violence being perpetrated by the guerrillas, the following actions could be taken by the authorities:

(1) A curfew would be imposed in the enclosed isolated area. No one would be allowed out of or into the area after sundown.

(2) During the night the authorities would not only patrol the boundary lines, but would also attempt to control the streets and, if necessary, send out foot patrols through the entire area. If the guerrillas attempted to either break out of the area or to engage the authorities in open combat they would be readily suppressed.

(3) During a guerrilla uprising most civil liberties would have to be suspended, search and seizure operations would be instituted during the daylight hours, and anyone found armed or without proper identification would immediately be arrested. Most of the people in the ghetto would not be involved in the guerrilla operation and, under the conditions of police and military control, some would help in ferreting out the guerrillas. Their help would be invaluable.

(4) If the guerrillas were able to hold out for a period of time then the population of the ghetto would be classified through an office for the "control and organization of the inhabitants." This office would distribute "census cards" which would bear a photograph of the individual, the letter of the district in which he lives, his house and street number. This classification would aid the authorities in knowing the exact location of any suspect and who is in control of any given district. Under such a system, movement would be proscribed and the ability of the guerrilla to move freely from place to place seriously curtailed.

(5) The population within the ghetto would be exhorted to work with the authorities and to report both on guerrillas and any suspicious activity they might note. The police agencies would be in a position to make immediate arrests, without warrants, under suspension of guarantees usually provided by the Constitution.

(6) Acts of overt violence by the guerrillas would mean that they had declared a "state of war" within the country and, therefore, would forfeit their rights as in wartime. The McCarran Act provides for various detention centers to be operated throughout the country and these might well be utilized for the temporary imprisonment of warring guerrillas.

(7) The very nature of the guerrilla operation as presently envisioned by certain Communists and black nationalists would be impossible to sustain. According to the most knowledgeable guerrilla war experts in this country the revolutionaries could be isolated and destroyed in a short period of time.

In 1968 Public Law 90-351 was passed. It is known as the Omnibus Crime Control and Safe Streets Act of 1968, to assist state and local governments in reducing the incidence of crime, to increase the effectiveness, fairness, and coordination of law enforcement and criminal justice systems at all levels of government and for other purposes.

Wiretapping, firearms control, riots, and civil disorders all came under the aegis of the safe streets acts and omnibus crime bills of 1970 and 1971. These acts served as the logical extension of the earlier Subversive Activities Control Act, except that they were intended to function more against Blacks than against Communists.

TITLE II: CRIMINAL PROCEDURES

Allowed the Government of the District of Columbia to appeal an order suppressing evidence against a defendant.

Provided for a nighttime search warrant when there was "probable cause to believe" that: it could not be executed in daylight; the property sought was likely to be removed or destroyed if not seized immediately; or the property was not likely to be found except at certain times and in certain circumstances.

Provided for "no-knock" search and arrest warrants (allowing policemen to enter premises without notice) if the officer had "probable cause to believe" that notice was likely to result in destruction of evidence sought, danger to the life or safety of the policeman or another person, escape of the party to be arrested or where such notice would be a useless gesture.

Provided for "no-knock" entries by officers without such authorization in the warrant if they found the specified circumstances after obtaining the warrant. If the circumstances were known at the time of the application for warrant, the "no-knock" provision must be included in it.

Authorized pretrial detention for up to 60 days of a person charged with a dangerous crime (forcible taking of property, unlawful entry, arson, forcible rape, or unlawful sale or distribution of drugs) when a court found that there was no combination of release conditions which would assure the community's safety from him.

They have renovated the internment camps (concentration camps). Job Corps centers (to have been used to provide vocational education for Blacks and other economically disadvantaged youngsters) have been put in order so that they too might serve as internment camps. And so you say it can never happen. Obviously it did happen in the United States of America. It happened to the Japanese-Americans and it happened because they were not white. It did not happen to the German- and Italian-Americans because they were white. We were at war with Japan, Germany, and Italy, yet the treatment varied according to ancestral origin (race).

So frightening were the thoughts of the District of Columbia Court Reform and Criminal Procedure Bill, that Senator Sam Ervin said:

> I am personally satisfied that preventive detention prostitutes the purpose of bail and runs afoul of the Eighth Amendment. Funda-

mental to due process of law is the tenet that a man is presumed innocent until proven guilty beyond a reasonable doubt. Under our system of justice the Government cannot deprive a man of his liberty on the basis of a mere accusation or assumption that he has committed a crime or is likely to do so. In practical effect, preventive detention legislation convicts individuals of "probable" guilt and "dangerousness" and sentences them to 60 days' imprisonment without trial and conviction of a crime. Such flagrant violation of due process smacks of a police state rather than a democracy under law. It is reminiscent of similar devices in other countries which have proved all too useful as tools of political repression (Ervin, 1969).

The failure of the United States to ratify the Genocide Convention has once again left bare the rampant racist face of this country for all to see. Instead of a leader in the quest for law and justice, the United States continues to suffer from its seemingly incurable schizophrenia. Seventy-five nations ratified it in record time, but the United States Senate withheld this country's ratification. At best there was a token gesture of support from President Nixon.

Sam Yette says:

> This is the "benign neglect" on which Black survival largely depends in the new decade. If it is the choice of the new decade—and it appears to be—then the inevitable second choice belongs to Black people in America. The choice is the style in which they— and America—will die (Yette, 1971).

BLACK ALTERNATIVES: SOULSVILLE

The first half of this chapter discussed the colonialism inherent in American race relations. There have been many proposals to alleviate the present status of black Americans. Many of these have been directed at the simple fact that the poor black person lacks money. A multitude of programs supposedly have been aimed at solving this problem. But most of these programs—welfare, guaranteed annual income, negative income tax—either have been designed to keep people poor or have remained at the "pilot program" stage. Other proposals have been directed at enriching the ghetto, more often known as "gilding the ghetto", and "black capitalism." These have been both unsuccessful and unrealistic. Another choice has been the dispersal plan, in which Blacks are removed from the inner-city to other segregated areas, primarily because Whites want the valuable urban land.

Many of the black proposals, past and present, whether basically economic or political, are based on the acquisition of a land base. Modern black movements have been preceded by black attempts to establish separate communities in the United States. The communities, although they were a response to white racism, reflected the dominant social, political, and economic ideals of the white middle-class. Most of these attempts at economic self-sufficiency eventually failed.

> "I am the whole cause of the migration. Nobody but me," Benjamin Singleton repeated time and again, jutting his square jowl till its sparse whiskers bristled. "I am the Moses of the colored exodus!" (Bontemps and Conroy, 1966).

Singleton believed that because of continued white racism, Blacks should move to new areas and settle separate from Whites. His was the first black separatist movement. At first he formed the Tennessee Real Estate and Homestead Association whose purpose was to settle ex-slaves on farms in Tennessee. But he had to reject that state as a location and he substituted Kansas.

Singleton and Henry Adams of Louisiana caused about 40,000 Blacks to leave the South for Kansas and its neighboring states. Black towns were established in Kansas in 1879 and 1880; four were Baxter Springs, Nicodemus, Morton City, and Singleton. But Kansas could not hold all the Blacks who wanted to leave the South. Singleton joined others, including W. E. B. DuBois, in advising Blacks to remain in the South or to seek new asylums. Not only had Kansas reached its saturation point but the severe winter of 1879 to 1880 proved to be a tragedy for the ill-prepared and poverty-stricken black immigrants. There was a shift in destinations. Now, Oklahoma became the major destination. At first Blacks fought for a black state in what was then the Twin Territories but this failed. As a result all-black towns were created in Oklahoma. Four of the towns were in the Indian Territory. There were three basic, general causes for the existence for these towns. Some were boom towns, others were organized as utopian escapes, and still others were promotional schemes.

These communities steadily declined. In 1952 there were fifteen remaining; in the 10 years from 1952 to 1962, they declined further from 4,956 total population to 3,335. They were doomed to failure, because they functioned as temporary escapes from white racism and remained rural communities without strong economic foundations.

DuBois sought economic self-sufficiency but not one based on a separate geographic state. One of the points in his economic program was that a cooperative Negro industrial system could be established in the midst of and in conjunction with the national industrial organization. Garvey went further than DuBois; his program included geographic separation as well as economic self-sufficiency. This separate state was to be in Africa, not in the United States.

Modern black authors also assert that land is essential to the black struggle in America. Racial revolts of the 1960s are viewed by some as an attempt to gain control over a given territory. Community control of schools, poverty programs, and businesses is a fight for "home rule."

There are at least five modern black proposals based on the control and acquisition of land. These are Floyd McKissick's "Soul City," CORE's program, the "Black Manifesto," the program of the Republic of New Africa, and the program of the Nation of Islam.

One of the essential elements of the Muslim plan for economic development

Chicago, 1973: Women of the nation of Islam.

George L. Walker/Black Star.

is spatial separation, especially developing an agricultural land base. Land is by no means the only economic enterprise in which the Black Muslims are engaged; other activities include a printing and a meat-packing plant, office buildings, restaurants, bakeries, grocery stores, a small clothing factory, clothing stores, service stores, and a college and hospital are in the planning stages. The success of much of the Muslim economic activity seems closely tied to the acceptance of Elijah Muhammad. Although his leadership is far from universally accepted, "his influence in changing Black self-concepts and fostering

Black pride has been unmatched by an individual since Marcus Garvey" (Lincoln and Lincoln, 1972). It is, from outside, impossible to know how much it is his charisma that keeps the economic activities together and on his passing whether the unity of the Muslims can be maintained or whether the internal differences that seem to be present will factionalize the group to the point where its economic programs will suffer or be destroyed.

CORE's economic program is also built on the principle that ownership of property is imperative. CORE's proposals are set forth in the Community Self-Development Act and the Rural Development Incentive Act of 1968. The National Black Economic Conference put out a "Manifesto" in 1969 in which:

> We call for the establishment of a Southern land bank to help our brothers and sisters who have to leave their land because of racist pressure for people who want to establish cooperative farms, but who have no funds. . . . We call for $200,000,000 to implement this program.

The program of the RNA (Republic of New Africa) is explicitly one of separation. At first, however, its founders were not ready to agree with the Muslim concept of a separate territory within America. Their ideas changed by 1967 as they founded the Malcolm X Society in Detroit and a year later began the RNA with a "Declaration of Independence." This program, in part, claims the states of Louisiana, Alabama, Mississippi, Georgia, and South Carolina as the National Territory of the Black Nation that they propose. Following the "Declaration" the RNA obtained 165 acres from a black farmer in Hinds County, Mississippi, 25 miles from Jackson. The agreement was verbal; this was to cause trouble later. The black farmer was under pressure from local whites and FBI agents not to sell to the RNA. As of January, 1972, the RNA had not yet come up with the money for the land.

Other programs include the call for a "Homestead Act" in 1971, or land reclamation in the inner-core areas of every major American city. A somewhat different proposal involves the relocation of industry coupled with black migration. The basis of this program seems to rest on the out-migration of Blacks from those areas of high unemployment to new areas, based on information available so that the migrants could make optimal rather than haphazard decisions about where to relocate; this relocation would be coordinated with industrial relocation.

The black man in America has faced a serious spatial crisis since his manu-mission. In an effort to solve his problems he has experimented with the following:

1. Development of nation-state abroad
2. Development of "nation" at home
3. Integration
4. Nation within a nation
5. Various types of economic self-determination programs

Even before the institution of slavery was officially ended within the United States, a number of significant programs had been developed to secure permanent sites for freed black men. The most successful of these programs was responsible for the establishment of the country of Liberia. In the late 1800s thousands of former American slaves made their way across the Atlantic to stake their claims in this new land as a solution to their sociospatial problems.

This, at best, was a limited success. First, it is absolutely impossible to consider the mass migration of all black people in America—past, present, and future—to any area in the black world. There have been and there will always be too many people for this to become a functional hypothesis. Second, even if numbers were not a problem, there still exists the issue of self-sufficiency. The problem of inadequate economic security breeds the kind of dependency which left Liberia vulnerable to the capitalistic and imperialistic whims of the United States. Then it must be clear that to solve one's spatial problems, one needs more than separation and increased square acres per capita; one must possess a viable economic program which guarantees control of that space.

One of the major problems with the "back-to-Africa" movement was that it lacked sincere commitment. In spite of the enthusiasm of the many Blacks who participated or desired to participate, the unfortunate reality was that it was controlled by white racists whose major objective was not to aid and assist Blacks but to get rid of them. While the prospect of an eventual return to Africa remained a dream for most slaves, the ante-bellum free black community especially in the North had a practical means of returning to Africa through the Program of the American Colonializational Society founded in 1817.

It seems obvious that in a country whose legislative body had not seen fit to terminate slavery, the same body could objectively decide on where Blacks should migrate. It was certainly a questionable venture, to say the least, i.e., to send a group of people into an area with which they were not familiar. It was unlikely that they would quickly adjust to the life styles of the indigenous persons and it was impossible for them to develop the technology which they were leaving behind in the United States. This is not only hindsight, because in Philadelphia a group of Blacks began an organization and addressed themselves to their concerns for the above problems, but to no avail.

Finally, the Liberian experiment was doomed to failure because of the domination of the white governors and other white officials. Ultimately, white rule existed for white benefit which is always translated into dollars. They exploited native labor, the plantations and attempted a massive agriculturation that left the Blacks little better off than before their immigration.

Oklahoma was the site of the black man's effort to develop a "nation" at home. Oklahoma was the beneficiary of the failure of the 1879 "Exoduster" movement to Kansas. According to Bittle and Geis ". . . Negro communities flourished and gained notably in size. Five years after the founding of Boley [Oklahoma], the vicinity immediately surrounding the town had nearly five thousand Negroes in residence. The same phenomenal growth, but to a proportionately smaller degree was experienced by other Negro towns" (Uya, 1971).

This effort at nation building failed for several reasons, most important among them being the total inability to control their economic, social, and political institutions. This is clearly pointed out as people tried to work within the system; they were confronted with the grandfather clause, gerrymandering, and lynching.

Integration failed to solve black America's spatial problems for a number of reasons. First of all, integration as a concept for homogenizing independent cultures is not functional. Two cultures cannot come together to form one except when one overwhelms and dominates the other. If Black people permit their ideologies and culture to become co-opted, they become psychologically absorbed, and hence can be convinced they have no spatial problems.

If history has value, then it teaches us to avoid mistakes of the past. It seems clear that the Nation of Islam learned well the need to develop a strong economic base before the acquisition of territory. Not only is the Nation of Islam developing an economic base, but it is also developing and controlling institutions, such as education and health. Earlier in the book you have read of the problems that the Blacks face, particularly in these institutions, so two major steps in the solutions of the major problems facing black America are economic independence and control of the vital institutions that serve black people.

Some believe the kind of program offered in the concept of Soul City to be a viable alternative. Soul City is an urban complex, presently under construction in North Carolina, with Floyd McKissick as its principal architect. Black persons are to have the leadership in the organization and administration of Soul City once it is established. But disturbingly, the funds for Soul City are to come from the federal government, which means that these black people even prior to construction are totally dependent upon Whites. It seems a questionable alternative, with so much dependence on people from the outside whose interests are at best cursory. There is little real opportunity for independence in this kind of an arrangement; therefore it is essentially a nonsolution to the real spatial problems of black Americans.

The ultimate success of the black man's efforts to control his institutions is to be found in a larger structure that brings unity. The structure cannot simply be one that has nationalism at its core, but something stronger and more basic. There must be a religious fanaticism which forces total commitment of all black people in order to gain that sort of unity; hence, that precious control of space. If an oppressed minority is to exist with any dignity, independence, and control of its own turf, it must have a zealousness such as the Jews possessed which allowed them to build Israel, their own nation-state.

The foundation for developing the kinds of attitudes and structures mentioned above has existed for a long time in the black community. In fact, many of the functions have historically been performed by the black churches, except on a small isolated scale and without the revolutionary fervor required to effect permanent change.

Already there exist within the black community nuclei for the type of religious organization which we have advocated. One, the Nation of Islam, has already been discussed. The Nation of Islam has clearly shown through its dedicated believers that it can control its health institutions, educational institutions, and most of its economic institutions. Further, since the days of Malcolm X, the

Honorable Elijah Muhammed has encouraged increasing interaction between Muslims and non-Muslims.

The second nucleus has taken the form of black Christian Nationalism, the most successful example of which would be the Reverend Albert B. Cleage, Jr.'s, The Church of the Black Madonna. The theology, philosophy, and program of black Christian Nationalism have been developed at the Shrine of the Black Madonna in Detroit. "We realize that everything we are trying to do requires the coming together of Black people everywhere" (Cleage, 1972).

This church began with the basic premise that the black church is essential to the liberation struggle, because it is the only institution controlled by black people and is capable of being restructured to serve a total revolution. A black revolution is impossible unless black people are able to build an entire system of institutions, designed to serve the interests of black people as all American institutions now serve the interests of white people. To build such a system of institutions, it is imperative that black people first develop one basic black institution which has the allegiance of the masses.

Step by step the present self-image which the white man has ruined must be replaced by a new self-image capable of absorbing new information, building a new value system, and rejecting individualism and materialism. The negative self-image cannot accept new information because whatever is taught becomes a part of an antiquated philosophy involving the acceptance of black inferiority and a sense of self-hatred.

Black Christian Nationalism calls black people to commit themselves to the building of a black communal society by accepting the black Christian Nationalism training and discipline. To free the mind from individualism and materialism, it is necessary to participate in vigorous educational programs, to develop necessary skills by attendance at workshops, classes, and cultural activities. The above agendum will lead to restructuring the black church and to developing a power base for the systematic building of the black nation.

Blacks will be linked through one cooperative economic movement which will enable goods raised in the rural counties of the South on black farms to be distributed in northern urban centers where black people are now dependent on white merchants for their produce; Blacks will establish regional canneries and wholesalers to distribute the food that black people grow.

There is nothing new in what we suggest here, for these concepts are reverberating throughout the black community in all the fifty states. In fact, some of these programs were advocated by Singleton, Washington, DuBois, and Garvey. The question then is not how but when?

SELECTED BIBLIOGRAPHY

1. Allen, Robert L.: "Black Awakening in Capitalist America," Garden City, N.Y., Doubleday and Company, Inc., 1970.
2. Baron, Harold M.: Black Powerlessness in Chicago, Trans-action, vol. 6, November 1968, pp. 25–33.

3. Bettelheim, Bruno: "The Informed Heart," New York, Avon Books, 1960.
4. Bontemps, Arna, and Jack Conroy: "Any Place But Here," New York, Hill and Wang, 1966.
5. Carmichael, Stokely, and Charles Hamilton: "Black Power," New York, Random House, 1967.
6. Caute, David: "Fanon," London, Fontana, 1970.
7. Clark, Kenneth B.: "Dark Ghetto," New York, Harper, 1965.
8. Cleage, Albert B.: "Black Christian Nationalism," New York, William Morrow and Company, Inc., 1972.
9. Corey, George D., and Richard A. Cohen: Domestic Pacification, *Society*, vol. 9, July-August 1972, pp. 16–23.
10. Cruse, Harold: "The Crisis of the Negro Intellectual," New York, William Morrow and Company, Inc., 1967.
11. Dunbar, Ernest: The Making of a Militant, *Saturday Review of Society*, vol. 55, January 1972, pp. 25–32.
12. Ervin, Sam D., Jr.: Bail Reform: Two Law-and-Order Views, *Wall Street Journal*, October 30, 1969, p. 19.
13. Foner, Philip S. (ed.): "The Black Panthers Speak," Philadelphia, Lippincott, 1970.
14. Good, Paul: "The American Serfs," New York, Ballantine, 1968.
15. Goodrich, Jim: Black Office Holders Increase Power, *The Black Politician*, vol. 2, January 1971, pp. 40–41.
16. Greenberg, Polly: "The Devil Has Slippery Shoes," New York, Macmillan, 1969.
17. Henderson, William L., and Larry C. Ledebur: "Economic Disparity," New York, The Free Press, 1970.
18. Hersch, Charles: Mental Health Services and the Poor, *Psychiatry*, vol. 29, August 1966, pp. 236–245.
19. Kegels, S. Stephan: A Field Experimental Attempt to Change Beliefs and Behavior of Women in an Urban Ghetto, *Journal of Health and Social Behavior*, vol. 10, June 1969, pp. 115–124.
20. Knowles, Louis L., and Kenneth Prewitt: "Institutional Racism in America," Englewood Cliffs, N.J., Prentice-Hall, 1969.
21. Kotz, Nick: "Let Them Eat Promises: The Politics of Hunger in America," Englewood Cliffs, N.J., Prentice-Hall, 1971.
22. Lincoln, C. Eric, and C. Eric Lincoln II: The Black Muslims Revisited or The State of the Black Nation of Islam, *Afro-American Studies*, vol. 3, 1972, pp. 175–186.
23. Lowi, Theodore J.: Apartheid U.S.A., *Trans-action*, vol. 7, pp. 32–39.
24. Milio, Nancy: "9226 Kercheval.: The Storefront That Didn't Burn," Ann Arbor, Mich., The University of Michigan Press, 1970.
25. Minckley, Barbara Blake: Space and Place in Patient Care, *American Journal of Nursing*, vol. 68, March 1968, pp. 510–516.
26. Moosebruker, Jane, and Anthony Jong: Racial Similarities and Differences in Family Dental Care Patterns, *Public Health Reports*, vol. 84, August 1969, pp. 721–727.

27. Moynihan, Daniel P.: "Maximum Feasible Misunderstanding," New York, The Free Press, 1969.

28. O'Dell, J. H.: A Special Variety of Colonialism, *Freedomways*, vol. 7, Winter 1967, pp. 7–15.

29. Patterson, William L. (ed.): "We Charge Genocide," New York, International, 1970.

30. "The Racial Gap: 1955–1965, 1965–1975," National Urban League, 1967.

31. Reitzes, Dietrich C.: "Negroes and Medicine," Cambridge, Mass., Harvard University Press, 1958.

32. Rokeach, Milton: "The Open and Closed Mind," New York, Basic Books, 1960.

33. Sinnette, Calvin H.: "Genocide and Black Ecology," *Freedomways*, vol. 12, 1972, pp. 34–46.

34. "The Social and Economic Status of Negroes in the United States, 1970," U.S. Department of Commerce, Washington, D.C., 1970.

35. Strauss, Anselm L.: Medical Ghettos, *Trans-action*, vol. 4, May 1967, pp. 7–15.

36. Tolson, Arthur L.: Black Towns of Oklahoma, *The Black Scholar*, vol. 1, April 1970, pp. 18–22.

37. "A Time to Burn . . . A Time to Listen," U.S. Commission on Civil Rights, Washington, D.C., 1967.

38. Uya, Okon Edet: "Black Brotherhood," Lexington, Mass.: D.C. Heath, 1971.

39. *Wall Street Journal*, November 27, 1970.

40. Walzer, Michael: The Obligations of Oppressed Minorities, *Commentary*, vol. 49, May 1970, pp. 71–80.

41. Yette, Samuel: "The Choice: The Issue of Black Survival in America," New York, G. P. Putnam's Sons, 1971.

Joan Larson/Office of Economic Opportunity.

10 Summary

We do not foresee in the near future revolutionary confrontation or the establishment of a separate black nation-state, nor do we see the American people solving the basic problem of racism. There is likely to continue a haphazard movement of alternating periods of crisis and quiescence.

Traditional reform methods have not solved and are not likely to solve the problems faced by black people. The black capitalists, politicians, and intellectuals of 1970 are tokens, the "house niggers" of the 1860s brought up to date. No matter how autonomous the economic and political programs of Blacks, they have remained a dependent subsystem of the dominant white economic and political systems. And, the fact is that white Americans have never had, nor do they now have, a commitment to the elimination of inequality; and as a consequence the resources needed are never made available.

Whether it has been the establishment of a separate black state or community control of local institutions, black alternatives have sought to gain access to the power that white America has withheld. In general Blacks have had very little intended influence on economic, political, and social policy. They have, on the other hand, exerted a great deal of unintended influence on these policies. In other words, their presence affects the decisions of others. Public housing projects are put where they live; jobs and hospitals are planned for other neighborhoods. But their needs and behaviors are not taken into account.

The strategies for gaining real power are either political, economic, or violent in nature. There have been and there will continue to be times when violence will be seen as an effective tactic or as the only possible alternative in a desperate situation. We do not see violent confrontation or guerilla warfare as major tactics of social change.

We see the other alternatives, economical and political, as the more effective large-scale strategies for improving life for Blacks in America. In order for Blacks to obtain access to power, their pressure must be applied as a group at the appropriate levels. Many have pointed out that the poor or oppressed are without power as a group and as such must achieve power as a group. It is obvious that pressure must be exerted at all levels, local and national.

It is at the local level, however, that we see not only the possibilities for significant change but also for major involvement of geographers. It is the local government that makes the decisions that affect the day-to-day lives of poor

1. Access to transportation systems
2. Access to day-care facilities
3. Access to comprehensive water, sewerage, and garbage service
4. Access to housing sites and buildings
5. Access to medical-dental clinics
6. Access to hospitals
7. Access to vocational training and job placement centers
8. Access to traffic safety measures
9. Access to recreation facilities
10. Access to voter registration
11. Access to schools

Table 10.1   Sociospatial Rights and Opportunities

Blacks; this is true even if it is the federal government and its various agencies that make the general policy decisions. It is local government officials who appoint the welfare board, accept or reject food programs, build roads, check buildings for health and building code violations. Local people act as the "gate-keepers" to schools, suburban neighborhoods, hospitals, and public housing.

The following list of sociospatial rights and opportunities when demanded by the black poor are seen as unreasonable, yet they are not luxuries; indeed, they are considered by the white middle class as necessities. And that is what they are. We want to emphasize that access has two equally important components, geographic and psychosocial. Geographic access is the ability to overcome the distance, actual and perceived, between oneself and an opportunity (job) or service (clinic). Psychosocial access is the ability to receive the benefits of the opportunity or service once one has arrived at its location.

There are two equal dangers in writing a final chapter to a book of this type which discusses complex social processes that have continued over a long period of time and have involved a great many people. First, one can end the book with an optimistic forecast that is built largely upon the quicksand of future hopes. Or one can finish by pessimistically predicting the catastrophe built of the dissolution of past hopes. We will do neither. Lillian Smith has put the issue in a perspective that remains as true today as it was when she made it.

> The so-called "racial problem" is not a problem amenable to solution; it is not a problem at all: it is a cruel way of life for which, if we wish to survive as a free nation, a new way of life must be substituted (Smith, 1961).

We will end with the reminder that, in the final analysis, we must not forget that we are talking about and planning with real human beings. For whether it is a young child crying in an urban ghetto tenement or a congregation singing in a rural church, we must not mistake geography for a compilation of statistics, distributions, or locations. Geography is about people.

SELECTED BIBLIOGRAPHY

1. Kahn, Si: "How People Get Power," McGraw-Hill, New York, 1970.
2. Mendoza, George (ed.): "The World from My Window," Hawthorn Books, New York, 1969.
3. Smith, Lillian: "Killers of the Dream," Doubleday, New York, 1961.

Appendix I:
Poverty Exercise

You are a member of a Federal Task Force on Race and Poverty and have been asked to analyze a state in the United States. On the basis of your analysis you are to make recommendations for the allocation of federal money for counties within the state of your choice. Policy makers in the government have made some initial decisions for you regarding the counties that can qualify for aid.

1. They must be counties in which the median family income is either below $3,500 per year or in the fifth (lowest) quintile based on median family income.
2. They must be counties in which over 25 percent of the housing is classed as unsound, deteriorating, or dilapidated, or in the fifth (lowest) quintile based on sound housing.
3. Because of limited funds only six counties may be chosen from each state. As there will probably be more than six counties which meet the above criteria, you will need to make decisions to include some areas while excluding others.

The government agency, in order to correlate your findings with those of other workers, needs the following data:

1. Income, housing quality, race, and urban-suburban-rural characteristics
2. Age-sex pyramid for the "poverty area" that you define
3. Map of the "poverty area" that you define

The government agency also needs answers to the following questions:

1. If there were more than six counties that fit the above criteria, how did you decide which of those was to receive aid?
2. Does the age-sex or racial composition of the "poverty area" indicate any potential problems?
3. How best could the money be used in this area?
4. Is there other relevant data information that should be known?

After your research has been completed, you are to present your recommendations to the agency (the rest of the class) for discussion.

OBJECTIVES

Given a certain problem for which a policy decision must be made that will affect people's lives, the student should be able to do the following:

1. Define relevant criteria
2. Obtain information from available sources
3. Know limitations of data sources
4. Classify areas based on several criteria
5. Make recommendations on the basis of research
6. Realize that decisions made from impersonal statistics affect real people.

Appendix II:
Geography of
Race and Schools

To study the problem of school integration-segregation the class is divided into "citizen" committees. This project can be done with grade, junior high, or high schools. The maps and data included here are from Seattle, but the project is more useful if data from the local area are used.

There are four "citizen" committees:

1. Black Education Committee—four members
2. Citizens for Quality Education—four members
3. Citizens for Integrated Education—four members
4. Four-member committee appointed by school board to make recommendations to the board.

In addition there is a five-member school board.

The number of people in these committees can vary with the size of the class, but should be kept small. If needed other roles and committees can be added.

Each of the four committees will make a recommendation to the school board, which will then make a decision about a plan for the integration of the schools.

PROCEDURE

Students first are given their committee assignments, role descriptions, and a data packet.

Then, they do background reading and exchange ideas and opinions within their committees and with those people of similar beliefs on other committees. They begin gathering data to support their positions and trying to persuade others to accept their positions.

In the third stage each of the four "citizen" committees prepares a plan (written, verbal, and cartographic) which is submitted to the school board. Possible plans include busing, educational parks, and redrawing of school boundaries.

Finally, the four proposals are presented to the school board. Each group presents their plan followed by a brief question-and-answer period. Then the school board deliberates and votes on which plan to institute. The board must present its reasons for acceptance or rejection of each plan. If it finds none of the plans acceptable, the board must substitute a plan of its own.

BASIC RESOURCES NEEDED

1. Maps of school attendance areas (see Figure A2.1)
2. Data on number and percentage of black students in school population and in each school (see Figures A2.1 and A2.2 and Table A2.1)
3. Map showing location of schools and major city streets
4. Map showing city bus routes
5. Other data on student achievement by school and race, incidents of violence, traffic accidents involving children going to and from school will be useful

RESOURCES IN THE COMMUNITY

1. Planning and Research Department of local schools
2. Local social groups—NAACP, Urban League, Model Cities
3. City planning agencies
4. Special interest groups that arise to bring forth a point of view on the issue of school integration-segregation

STUDENT ROLES

School Board

1. President—white university trustee and businessman—approves of reasonable proposals for racial balance as long as "quality" education is maintained, worried about financing large-scale plans such as educational parks and busing.
2. Black university professor—will accept any reasonable plan, not as worried about finances as he is about improving the education of black children so that they can get into the American mainstream.
3. White university professor—believes in integrated education, has always supported nonviolent programs for the improvement of conditions for Blacks.
4. White middle-class businesswoman—does not believe in busing because of danger to children and extra time spent traveling to and from school, believes in "quality" education.
5. White educator—former school teacher and principal, doesn't commit himself, waits to see all the data.

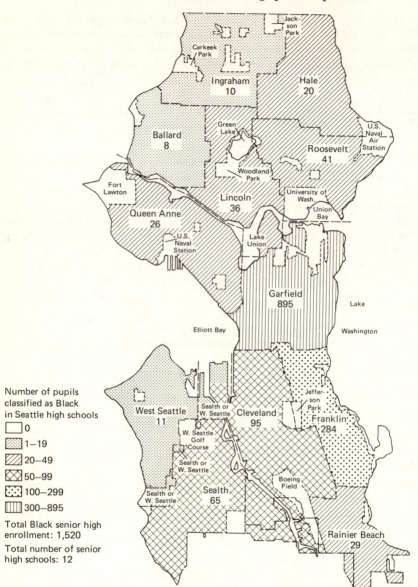

Number of pupils
classified as Black
in Seattle high schools

☐ 0
▨ 1–19
▨ 20–49
▨ 50–99
⬚ 100–299
▥ 300–895

Total Black senior high
enrollment: 1,520

Total number of senior
high schools: 12

Figure A2.1 Enrollment of Negro Pupils in Senior High Schools in Seattle, Washington, December 1966.

(From Research Office, Planning and Research Department, Seattle Public Schools.)

Black Education Committee (all-black)

1. High school principal—favors busing if arrangements are made to help white and black students adjust to their new environments, wants to improve educational opportunities for black children.

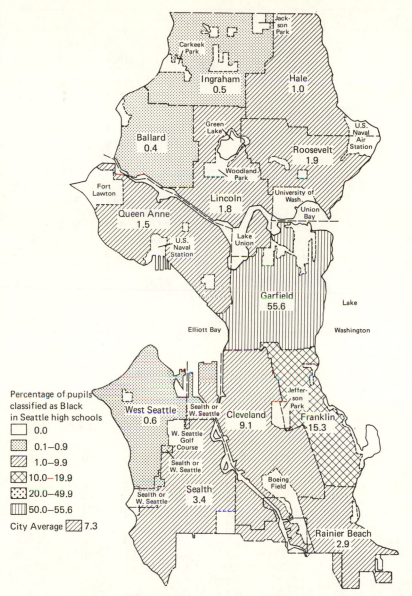

Figure A2.2 Percentage of Negro Pupils in Senior High Schools in Seattle, Washington, December 1966.

(From Research Office, Planning and Research Department, Seattle Public Schools.)

2. Mother—on welfare, involved in welfare rights, worried about safety of black children in white schools, opposed to forced busing.
3. High school student—president of Black Student Union, believes in black control of education, teachers, and curriculum that affects blacks.

WHITE AND NONWHITE

School	1967 ENROLLMENT % rank	White	Non-white	% White	1966 % White	1964 % White	1962 % White	1957 % White
West Seattle	1	1,831	17	99.1	98.8	98.8	99.4	99.4
Ingraham	2	1,812	20	98.9	98.8	99.7	99.2	...
Ballard	3	1,848	31	98.4	98.7	98.9	99.5	99.8
Hale	4	2,082	39	98.2	97.9	97.9	...	...
Roosevelt	5	2,061	81	96.2	96.9	98.0	99.5	99.6
Queen Anne	6	1,715	82	95.4	97.5	97.2	98.6	98.1
Lincoln	7	1,830	123	93.7	95.2	97.4	98.6	99.3
Sealth	8	1,870	135	93.3	94.8	95.2	96.8	97.6
Rainier Beach	9	935	139	87.0	89.8	92.1	96.4	...
Cleveland	10	674	343	66.3	66.4	70.8	83.2	92.0
Franklin	11	1,178	712	62.3	64.6	71.8	81.8	90.1
Garfield	12	520	1,120	31.7	31.1	33.7	35.8	48.1
Total		18,356	2,842	86.6	87.3	89.0	91.6	93.1

BLACK

School	1967 % rank	Number	%	1966 %	1964 %	1962 %	1957 %
Garfield	1	899	54.8	55.6	52.1	51.4	33.9
Franklin	2	313	16.6	15.3	12.4	9.2	3.2
Cleveland	3	93	9.1	9.1	10.3	4.4	2.3
Sealth	4	89	4.4	3.4	3.3	2.2	2.1
Rainier Beach	5	41	3.8	2.9	3.1	1.4	—
Lincoln	6	43	2.2	1.8	1.1	0.1	0.1
Queen Anne	7	40	2.2	1.5	1.4	0.3	0.3
Roosevelt	8	33	1.5	1.9	1.0	0.04	0.04
Hale	9	22	1.0	1.0	1.1	—	—
Ingraham	10	8	0.4	0.5	0.1	0.1	—
Ballard	11	7	0.4	0.4	0.4	0.1	0.0
West Seattle	12	2	0.1	0.6	0.4	0.1	0.4
Total		1,590	7.5	7.3	6.6	5.3	3.8

Table A2.1 Distribution of the Races with Rankings by Percent for 1967 and Trends Since 1962, Senior High Schools (Includes Special and Adjustment Pupils Enrolled in Regular Schools)

Source: *1967 Racial Distribution, Seattle Public Schools, Planning and Research Department, January 1968, p. 18.*

4. Businessman—middle-class family man, lives in black area, likes the idea of educational parks.

Citizens for Quality Education (all-white)

1. Housewife—doesn't believe in busing, worries about safety of children, believes that "they" have "their" schools and "we" have "ours" and that it is natural that way.
2. Lawyer—will defy courts if necessary to keep his kids in "quality" (white) schools, believes black children are not as smart as whites.
3. School teacher—teaches in white school, believes black children need more help and are more rowdy than whites.
4. Housewife—opposes any forced plan, moved to suburb to get away.

Citizens for Integrated Education

1. White housewife—sends children to black school by bus, believes in learning from other types of people.
2. White university student—member of activist group, believes in black control of black schools, but also works to tear down segregation.
3. Black housewife—middle class, believes in integrated education which is synonymous with good education, moved from ghetto to get better education for her kids.
4. White lawyer—works with ACLU, works for legal rights of the poor.

Appendix III:
The Crosstown
Expressway

TO BUILD OR NOT TO BUILD

The original plan for the city of Soulsville, an important historical city, called for streets 50 feet wide. In the early days these streets were adequate, but for today's cars, trucks, and buses, the streets are considerably congested. Like most other cities, Soulsville (population about 4 million) has had to build newer highways to carry its traffic. The map on the next page shows two of the highways that carry traffic in a north-south direction. Another expressway, north of the center of the city, carries traffic in an east-west direction.

For many years, some people have said that another east-west expressway is needed. They thought this one should be built south of the center of the city, where traffic becomes clogged on the narrow streets, especially during rush hours. After many studies, engineers and city planners agreed that the city should build such an expressway. Because this highway would run across the city, it was to be called the Crosstown Expressway. The road would carry eight lanes of traffic.

The planners recommend that all the buildings and stores between South Street and Bainbridge Street be torn down in order to make a path straight across the city for the Crosstown Expressway. One reason is that many of the buildings are already old and decaying. As long as buildings are to come down, the planners felt it made more sense to knock down these decaying buildings than to tear down those in better condition in other areas.

Opponents point out that new expressways had not always solved the traffic problems of cities. These roads have only attracted more cars into the cities, they said, and soon traffic jams had begun all over again. In fact, they say that such roads had often made traffic problems worse, for there are no places to park all the additional cars. These people say that the city should not encourage the use of cars in downtown areas. Instead of building more highways, the city should improve the subway, bus, and commuter railroad services.

Another group of citizens who are unhappy about the Crosstown Expressway live in an old area of Soulsville known as Knob Hill. Knob Hill was right next

Figure A3.1   Map of Downtown Soulsville.

to the proposed path of the expressway. Many of the residents had bought homes built 150 years ago and had spent thousands of dollars fixing them up. Others lived in new apartment buildings. These residents all complained that the road would bring into their neighborhood the pollution and traffic noise of thousands of cars and trucks.

Most of the people who would lose their homes, however, lived in rundown apartments between South Street and Bainbridge Street. Many of them were quite poor and elderly. The majority were black, but many were white. They had lived in this section for many years. This was their neighborhood, and now it was to be destroyed to make room for a highway.

Worst of all, they feared they would not be able to find other housing in Soulsville for the same rent, and they could not afford to pay more. The owners of the buildings would be paid by the government for their property. They could buy other buildings elsewhere. But those who rented the apartments would not be so lucky. They would have to move out but they would get nothing. City governments do try to help people find housing they can afford when they must be relocated, but often the governments are not too successful.

Many people opposed the Crosstown because it would separate white people, who would be living on streets north of the expressway, from black people, who would be living south of it. Many people in both neighborhoods believed it was good for Blacks and Whites to be together as part of the same community. Many people of both races were working hard to encourage this. If the Crosstown were built, it would be a 300-foot-wide barrier of speeding cars and trucks, which no one could cross. It would separate the black and white neighborhoods as completely as would a stone wall 100 feet high.

Even though many people opposed the expressway plan, it did not seem that they could do anything about it. After all, the engineers and city planners said a highway was needed. The federal and state governments were ready to pay for building it.

"The Crosstown Expressway: To Build or Not To Build" is a role-playing simulation concerned with the location of an expressway. Specifically, the objective is to solve the problem of an overburdened traffic system in a hypothetical (East Coast) urban area. Play involves government decisions, citizen reaction, and coalition politics. Some players have both public and private objectives which may be in conflict with one another. Designed as a heuristic device, the game focuses upon a number of issues: (1) inequities in the spatial allocation and distribution of public facilities, (2) the effect of citizen organization on governmental decision-making processes, (3) the potential influence of money power upon politics, (4) civil disobedience as an instrument of power, (5) the pressure that time imposes upon decision makers, (6) the overall nature of group interaction with regard to locational decisions, (7) the increasing displacement of Blacks, and (8) the subtleties of racism.

There are eight major game participants in the "Crosstown Expressway." Their roles include a government official and representatives of citizens from a lower-income inner-city neighborhood of Crosstown. The major roles follow:

You are Emmanuel Boselli Browning III, a resident of an exclusive area in the northeast section of Soulsville. You are a highly successful land developer (in suburban Soulsville) and president of the Soulsville Chamber of Commerce.

The Soulsville Chamber of Commerce has urged the mayor to support the Crosstown Expressway. You say you can show that there really is enough good housing for relocating the residents who will have to move. You suggest that the expressway will not constitute a wall between Whites and Blacks if it is built differently. Perhaps the expressway could be built below ground level, with a special cover over it. This would allow pedestrians and automobile traffic to travel over it.

You, George Dukes, a school teacher, are one of the opponents of the Crosstown Expressway. You have lived in the neighborhood all your life, just a few blocks from where the expressway would be built. You believe the mayor has heard only one side of the story. If all the people who oppose the expressway join together, you surmise, they could have one strong voice instead of many weak ones. Then the mayor would hear the other side and might change his mind. If the mayor does not give his approval, the Crosstown could not be built.

You are Mrs. Alice Lipscomb, a lifetime resident of the area that is in the path of the proposed expressway. You have been a strong influence in your neighborhood already, and you are president of an organization called Citizens to Preserve and Develop the Crosstown Community (CPDCC) which is attempting to stop the building of the highway. The CPDCC wants to show that the highway is not as necessary to Soulsville as some people believe.

A nonprofit housing association has made a special study to find out exactly how many people lived between South and Bainbridge Streets and how many would need inexpensive housing. You have heard that *6,500 people would have to move to make room for the Crosstown.* You have also discovered that there is not enough good low-cost housing available in the city to take care of all these people.

You are Richard Knight, elected to the office of mayor in the last election. Many of the people who opposed the Crosstown had voted for you; therefore, you have a political debt, in addition you are seeking reelection. Of course you would like to make a decision that will please your supporters. But you also have to be sure your decision is the best one for the whole city. You are also keenly aware that the money required to finance your next campaign is on the side of the pro-Crosstown Expressway. You must carefully study the facts and the arguments that are presented to you.

You are E. John Van Dyke, spokesman for the Knob Hill Community Action Committee. You are a relatively new arrival in Soulsville, but live in Knob Hill, one of the exclusive areas. You are a wealthy businessman, and within a short period of time have become a prominent local citizen taking an active role in the Community Action group. The organization meets to discuss issues that affect Knob Hill, and to decide what action, if any, should be taken to better the community you live in. You have accumulated a considerable sum of money in the local community chest, which you use to protect their interests (i.e., to buy property which may otherwise be sold to undesirables).

You are Reverend James Shaw, founder and spokesman for the Inter-denominational Community Council in Crosstown. You are a well-known civil rights leader in Soulsville, a resident of the Crosstown area, and a spokesman for the religious groups of that area. Respected by your followers, you were recently appointed to the mayor's advisory board, and for some time have been actively fighting social ills through the regular governmental channels. You are sincerely trying to improve the living conditions in the Crosstown area.

You are George W. Shipley, a representative on City Council from the Crosstown area. You are the token Black on City Council who has been a vocal dissenter on many issues that have passed through the council chamber. You are generally considered to be a militant and a troublemaker by the more conservative elements of Soulsville. What disturbs the Whites most is your close association with the Black Panthers since your election.

You are Priscilla Wellington, president of the local chapter of the Daughters of the American Revolution (D.A.R.). You belong to one of the best-known families in Soulsville, and your name appears frequently in the society column of the *Soulsville Chronicle.* You devote much of your time to charitable activities as well as fund raising for your favorite political causes. Your family is reputed to have controlled local politics for more than 100 years. You, like most of your friends, live outside the central city in what might be called the suburbs. You are interested in the Crosstown Expressway because it would make the old mansions and other historical sites more accessible.

Index